News After Trump

JOURNALISM AND POLITICAL COMMUNICATION UNBOUND

Series editors: Daniel Kreiss, University of North Carolina at Chapel Hill, and Nikki Usher, University of Illinois at Urbana-Champaign

Journalism and Political Communication Unbound seeks to be a high-profile book series that reaches far beyond the academy to an interested public of policymakers, journalists, public intellectuals, and citizens eager to make sense of contemporary politics and media. "Unbound" in the series title has multiple meanings: It refers to the unbinding of borders between the fields of communication, political communication, and journalism, as well as related disciplines such as political science, sociology, and science and technology studies; it highlights the ways traditional frameworks for scholarship have disintegrated in the wake of changing digital technologies and new social, political, economic, and cultural dynamics; and it reflects the unbinding of media in a hybrid world of flows across mediums.

News After Trump

*Journalism's Crisis of Relevance
in a Changed Media Culture*

MATT CARLSON, SUE ROBINSON, AND
SETH C. LEWIS

OXFORD
UNIVERSITY PRESS

OXFORD
UNIVERSITY PRESS

Oxford University Press is a department of the University of Oxford. It furthers
the University's objective of excellence in research, scholarship, and education
by publishing worldwide. Oxford is a registered trade mark of Oxford University
Press in the UK and certain other countries.

Published in the United States of America by Oxford University Press
198 Madison Avenue, New York, NY 10016, United States of America.

© Oxford University Press 2021

Library of Congress Cataloging-in-Publication Data
Names: Carlson, Matt, 1977- author. | Robinson, Sue
(Professor of journalism), author. | Lewis, Seth C., author.
Title: News after Trump : journalism's crisis of relevance in a changed
media culture / by Matt Carlson, Sue Robinson, Seth C. Lewis.
Description: New York : Oxford University Press, 2021. |
Series: Journalism and politcal communication unbound |
Includes bibliographical references and index.
Identifiers: LCCN 2021031104 (print) | LCCN 2021031105 (ebook) |
ISBN 9780197550342 (hardback) | ISBN 9780197550359 (paperback) |
ISBN 9780197550373 (epub)
Subjects: LCSH: Press and politics—United States—History—21st century. |
Journalism—Political aspects—United States—History—21st century. |
Political culture—United States—History—21st century. |
Trump, Donald, 1946—Influence.
Classification: LCC PN4888.P6 C37 2021 (print) |
LCC PN4888.P6 (ebook) | DDC 071/.3090512—dc23
LC record available at https://lccn.loc.gov/2021031104
LC ebook record available at https://lccn.loc.gov/2021031105

DOI: 10.1093/oso/9780197550342.001.0001

3 5 7 9 8 6 4 2

Paperback printed by Marquis, Canada
Hardback printed by Bridgeport National Bindery, Inc., United States of America

To our families, for all their love and support

Contents

Acknowledgments

This book began as a conversation that Matt had with his wife while unloading the dishwasher: the problem with trying to write about Donald Trump and the US news media is that there is just too much to write about. Any one incident cannot capture enough of the overall picture; it would take a book to do it all justice. Matt reached out to Sue for advice about whether such a book project was a good idea, and instead of talking him out of it, she joined in. Seth, not to be left out, soon joined this book as well. The idea began to take shape at a conference being held, appropriately enough, in Washington, DC, in May 2019; in the months and years since, the three of us enjoyed many conversations over Zoom as we thought through and rethought our approach. This book is a product of our shared academic interests and our decade-long friendship.

But the book also is a product that has relied on many others. Chief among them are Nikki Usher and Daniel Kreiss, the editors of the series in which this book appears, who patiently pushed and prodded us to refine what this book could be, along with an anonymous reviewer who provided particularly incisive feedback. At Oxford University Press, Angela Chnapko kept up her early enthusiasm for the book all the way through to the end.

We wish to thank Ben Toff for allowing us to workshop an early draft of the introduction and proposal with the Media and Politics Research Group at the University of Minnesota. Sid Bedingfield and Ashley Sorensen offered useful feedback that helped set the book on the right track. We also presented ideas from the book at the 2019 Future of Journalism Conference at Cardiff University and at the 2020 annual conference of the International Communication Association. This work informed a number of other presentations and talks that the three authors gave during the Trump era, including a November 2020 panel on race, media, and politics for the Institute for Legal Studies at the University of Wisconsin Law School, a November 2020 postelection symposium at the University of Wisconsin–Madison's School of Journalism & Mass Communication, and a March 2021 Madison Civic Club Forum about news after Trump.

Beyond these presentations, many of our ideas about what news could (and should) look like after Trump have been percolating in the background of the many other research projects we have undertaken during the past five years. Seth spent the 2019–2020 academic year on research leave at the University of Oxford as a visiting fellow with the Reuters Institute for the Study of Journalism, with much of his time dedicated to understanding the value proposition of news from the audience's point of view—particularly given how disorienting and overwhelming the news could feel during a 2020 year marked by pandemic, partisan division, and economic hardship. Seth wishes to thank Reuters Institute director Rasmus Kleis Nielsen, research team leader Richard Fletcher, and the research staff—Anne Schulz, Nic Newman, Scott Brennen, Simge Andi, and Silvia Majó-Vázquez—for all they contributed to sharpening his thinking about journalism and opening it up to a more global orientation, even as this book draws on the unique US context.

Some of our original ideas about how the press handled Trump and his attacks on journalism evolved into a 2020 article that was part empirical analysis of tweets and news coverage and part conceptual development about how social media had altered the space for press criticism. That piece, "Digital Press Criticism: The Symbolic Dimensions of Donald Trump's Assault on U.S. Journalists as the 'Enemy of the People,'" was published in *Digital Journalism*, and we are grateful for the helpful feedback provided by the journal's editor, Oscar Westlund, and the anonymous reviewers. That input helped shape the larger ideas presented in this book.

We also want to thank Steven Wang of the University of Wisconsin–Madison, Dennis Major and Nermine Aboulez of the University of Oregon, and Michaele Myers of the University of Minnesota for their work in helping us format the book for publication. We also thank Susan Keith and Leslie-Jean Thornton for allowing us to use the complete data set that Sue helped them collect for the 2018 news editorials featured in Chapter 4.

Matt wishes to thank Elisia Cohen, director of the Hubbard School of Journalism and Mass Communication at the University of Minnesota, for her support for the project. Sue acknowledges support from the H.I. Romnes Faculty Fellowship at the University of Wisconsin–Madison to work on this project, as well as help from the Knight Foundation, which paid for the data set involving interviews with political journalists. Seth appreciates the generous support of the late Shirley Papé and her family through the endowed chair that he holds in her name in the School of Journalism and

Communication at the University of Oregon. Seth's work has benefited immeasurably from the support for research assistants, data collection, and conference engagement—as well as the Oxford research leave—provided by the Papé Chair. He also wishes to thank Dean Juan-Carlos Molleda and Senior Associate Dean Leslie Steeves for their unflagging support of his research.

Finally, we want to acknowledge the support of our families. Matt thanks Curtis, Lizzie, Claire, and his chihuahua Weenie for their endless joy and much-needed distraction from writing a book. Sue could not have endured two years of analyzing intense Trump attacks on journalists without being able to vent to her partner, Dr. Robert Asen, her kids Zachary and Simone, and her cockapoo Bini. And Seth appreciates being able to process the tumultuous Trump years over many long walks along the Thames and spirited dinner conversations with Tiffany and their boys, Jackson, Addison, Preston, and Asher.

Matt Carlson
Minneapolis, Minnesota

Sue Robinson
Madison, Wisconsin

Seth C. Lewis
Eugene, Oregon

Introduction

Decentering Journalism in the Contemporary Media Culture

"Our media is not free. It's not fair. It suppresses thought. It suppresses speech, and it's become the enemy of the people. It's become the enemy of the people. It's the biggest problem we have in this country."[1] These words were spoken by Donald Trump at a rally outside the White House on January 6, 2021. Thousands of Trump supporters had come to Washington, DC, to support Trump and his baseless claims that he, and not his opponent Joe Biden, had triumphed in the November 2020 election. Trump's speech began with him badgering reporters—"the fake news media," he called them—for downplaying the size of the crowd while he simultaneously falsely inflated its size to "hundreds of thousands." As he spoke, Trump continued to denounce journalists as actively working against him by dismissing his fraud claims and suppressing information that would vindicate them. He accused journalists and congressional Democrats of working together (along with "big tech" firms like Google, Twitter, and Facebook). The theme was clear: journalists could not be trusted. As Trump told his crowd of fervent supporters: "The American people do not believe the corrupt fake news anymore. They have ruined their reputation."

By the time of Trump's 2021 speech, his attacks on journalists had become familiar to the point of ritual. Trump had been labeling journalists as the "enemy of the people" since 2017, and the initial outcry over this authoritarian rhetoric had been replaced by numbness. His discounting of news stories as fake news and his conjoining of journalists with the Democratic Party had also become common tropes. They were echoed in scores of speeches and press gaggles, repeated in hundreds of Twitter posts, and echoed in right-wing news outlets. Years of relentless belligerence toward journalists had simply become a standard part of the discursive environment.

Even with these jabs at the news media and other assorted opponents, the January rally was not a normal speech. For the bulk of it, Trump held tight

News After Trump. Matt Carlson, Sue Robinson, and Seth C. Lewis, Oxford University Press. © Oxford University Press 2021. DOI: 10.1093/oso/9780197550342.003.0001

to his claim that he had won and that an election outcome that saw Biden defeat Trump by more than seven million votes with an Electoral College victory margin of 306 to 232 was nothing but a fraud. Trump proceeded to confidently spew dozens of allegations of election malfeasance that had been consistently discredited by election officials and judges at all levels. Most notably, he called on Vice President Mike Pence to refuse to certify the Electoral College results. That this was largely a ceremonial act dictated by law with no chance of affecting the electoral outcome did not matter; the defiance did. It was about asserting authority over reality. Trump ended his speech by urging his supporters to march to the Capitol Building, saying that he would be there with them to support them. His words ignited the agitated mob, already well stoked by prior speakers such as Trump's lawyer Rudy Giuliani, who called for "trial by combat."[2]

What followed was a deadly attack on the Capitol by throngs of Trump supporters fighting their way into the building and sending lawmakers into lockdown. Unimaginable images poured out on live television and through social media, from attackers using steel barricades to break windows and gain entry, to hours later when police and National Guard soldiers cleared the building with tear gas. Journalists struggled with the language to describe what was occurring: was it a "mob," a "coup," "terrorists," a "riot," a "protest," or even an "insurrection"?[3] Reporters intent on covering ceremonial congressional proceedings suddenly became war correspondents risking their personal safety to report on the melee around them. This was more than an idle threat. Attackers carved "Murder the Media" into a Capitol door, and many reporters were accosted.[4] Outside the building, a group of reporters had to abandon their equipment and flee as the crowd turned on them. Someone tied a camera cable into a noose.

The political violence incited by Trump—and the targeting of reporters during the attack—show in starkest terms the consequences of his language. His unwillingness to accept electoral defeat manifested itself as the creation of an alternative reality filled with fraud and conspiracies that had no evidence. His contempt toward the press paved the way not only for his supporters to disbelieve accurate reporting, but to take a hostile position toward most of the profession, outside a few right-wing news organizations. His constant berating of news as fake and journalists as biased had built a wall in their minds, and no well-reported news story was going to break through and convince them otherwise. To storm the Capitol is to be a true believer in Trump and to discount all other voices. After the attack, Trump's speech fomenting violence would result in his impeachment and sharp rebukes even from those inside the Republican Party who had previously been reluctant to criticize the president.[5]

As we look back at this incident, perhaps the question that lingers above all others is, How did we get here? And what do we do about it? These questions are bigger than any single book can tackle, and our part is to ask how the state of journalism has arrived at this point. Trump's four years in office and two presidential campaigns provide ample cases of attacks on journalists, many of which appear in the chapters to come. However, our starting point is not to provide a retrospective of Trump's antics during his time as president, but instead to pose a more basic question: How is the relevance of journalism being challenged in the contemporary media culture? Trump's constant attacks on journalists coupled with his penchant for lying revealed that journalism's model of serving the public is broken in ways that go well beyond the consequence of any single politician. It's broken in ways that may be difficult to recognize in the day-to-day crush of news, and in ways that cannot be easily fixed by tweaking news practices. Of course, journalists still engage in watchdog reporting, churning out resource-intensive, in-depth investigations and challenging dubious official claims on a regular basis. Many people have been outraged by the lies, malfeasance, and incompetence that have been reported. But these accounts also get lost in the crush of news stories and media content that compete for our fragmented attention. They reach an audience numbed by the volume of breaking news stories that never seem to shift the status quo, or are met by jaded readers and viewers who have joined Trump and other conservative critics in judging the "mainstream" news media to be hopelessly tainted by leftist elitism. When journalism can no longer serve the public according to its mandate, when it can no longer muster broad, sustained attention and collective indignation, then we find ourselves in a moment of epistemic crisis and in need of fresh perspectives.

Trump's removal from office did not wipe away the political currents that enabled it. His removal from social media platforms did not reset the media culture that has arisen. And his relative silence since leaving office did not restore trust in news or lessen the populist backlash against pluralism. What we need is an appraisal of Trump's assault on the press and the responses from journalists—an autopsy of what went awry and what might be fixed that is forward-looking in challenging journalism to do better. This book is a reimagining of news after Trump.

Confronting Journalism's Relevance in a Changing Media Culture

When we call journalism's relevance into question, what we mean is that we refuse to take journalism's relevance for granted. Much of the research about journalism shares an unspoken assumption that news is always at the center of social and political processes. Even when journalism is made an object of critique, its social centrality is rarely questioned.[6] Rather than automatically place journalism at the center, we instead treat journalism as one knowledge-producing symbolic system within the more expansive context of contemporary media. We use "media" in its broad sense to include all manner of mediated communication. This pluralistic view acknowledges how our lives are saturated with mediated experience.[7] News is only ever a part of this experience.

We advocate for a broad perspective that locates journalism within what we label the "media culture." While intentionally inclusive of a variety of media phenomena, media culture encapsulates three interrelated aspects. First, it includes the changing technologies, infrastructures, and institutions of media.[8] The materiality of media technology cannot be overlooked, but it must also be understood as embedded within various institutional forms that shape what media "things"—computers, mobile phones, satellites, websites, and so on—look like and how they are used. This aspect of media culture also pertains to the structures that arise, including organizational and economic forms such as social media platforms. The second aspect involves the communicative practices taking place though these various media channels. People use media in myriad ways, and these practices should be understood as both dependent on the materiality of media technology and institutions and as adaptations to these structures. The final aspect is the realm of interpretation about these practices and structures. Media allow us to create particular symbolic forms that are collectively meaningful. The "culture" side of media culture in this sense resembles Raymond Williams's idea of culture as the "structure of feeling" in a time and place.[9] By emphasizing interactions across material forms, practices, and beliefs, the concept of media culture avoids either being technologically determinist or granting undue power to individuals. The media culture is an expansive space of actors and actions, of which journalism is only one part. Even journalism contains its own subcultures, including conservative news cultures.[10] And while *news* remains a focus in the book, it is always embedded among other types of media content with fuzzy, shifting boundaries between them.

The changing media culture is most notable for facilitating a panoply of mediated voices. Given how this process has unfolded over the past decades, it is easy to lose sight of the transformations that have occurred. From the expansion of mass communication forms such as cable television and talk radio to emergent digital channels and social media platforms, the overall shift has been the same: more communicators are engaging in a growing variety of practices through expanding networks of communicative flows. All of this decenters journalism and thus requires a broader conceptual framework attuned to positioning news discourse as just one form among many.[11] Even if journalistic practices are thought to have remained constant, the changing media culture *around* journalism affects how journalism functions and how it is understood. Journalistic content circulates within (but is clearly not exclusive to) a variety of media channels—from television networks and social media platforms to radio stations and mobile apps. Plus, the existence of so many mediated voices alters how journalism is understood through the increasing numbers of alternative formats for conveying information, which in turn provide more spaces for media criticism to flourish.

Invoking the idea of "relevance" is about considering journalism's place within this media culture as well as its broader social influence.[12] In an earlier era, journalism's centrality was at least partly an artifact of the constraints of a mass communication structure that limited the number of mediated voices. These limits concentrated attention on a small number of channels, which had the effect of producing a consensus-based news environment fed by lucrative revenues from advertisers needing to reach consumers. In what Daniel Hallin called the "high-modernist" moment for news, this was

> an era when the historically troubled role of the journalist seemed fully rationalized, when it seemed possible for the journalist to be powerful and prosperous and at the same time independent, disinterested, public-spirited, and trusted and beloved by everyone, from the corridors of power around the world to the ordinary citizen and consumer.[13]

Hallin was already writing in 1992 about the dissolution of this moment for a variety of reasons that remain quite familiar: the collapse of the Cold War consensus ushered in stark political differences; distrust of institutions was rising; news reporting was becoming more adversarial; and the profit motive was overtaking journalistic decision-making. While Hallin was writing about change, his formulation is also telling for how it articulated the resilience with which journalists would see themselves and their social role. A generation later, we can see how this normative imagination of journalism still retains its modernist thinking even as the political, technological, and cultural conditions have continued to shift around it.

The defining characteristic of this modernist model of journalistic relevance is how journalists have staked out a paradoxical social position in which they situate themselves as being culturally central while they simultaneously distance themselves from power. This is most clearly visible when journalists' allegiance to objectivity is rendered in practice as neutrality and detachment, carefully situated "above the fray" of political battles waged by "both sides."[14] Thus, they position themselves as present among the powerful, but not involved in the administration of power. Normatively, this position allows journalists to gain access to power and to place themselves within democratic practices as central actors for the proper functioning of democracy—but this works only so far as journalists also accentuate their autonomy from power.[15] This mixture of centrality and distance has always contained a contradiction that makes it problematic—particularly when journalists try to dismiss their impact or their role in constructing news accounts. But, in years of journalism research, the distance side of the equation has received far more attention than the centrality side. So, while questions have long been asked about whether journalism is truly independent from power, or whether objectivity and neutrality are possible or even desirable, questions of journalism's importance—of its relative centrality in public life—often go unexamined.

Invoking relevance brings the question of journalism's centrality into the spotlight. However, we need to avoid dichotomous thinking that reduces relevance to its presence or absence—the notion that news is either relevant or irrelevant—or reduces it to some sort of measurement. Instead, a beginning point is to ask how a newfound focus on journalistic relevance brings into the open contemporary journalism's contradictions. On the one hand, journalism remains a powerful institution in democratic life and one that supports other powerful institutions. As an institution charged with representing social reality to mass audiences, it shapes collective understandings of the world we share. As an institution with a set of practices, it influences how political candidates act and eventually govern.[16] In short, the power of news to make certain issues salient and meaningful in our collective life still matters a great deal.[17] The endurance of this vision of journalism is evident in the assumptions that appear in critiques of news. Much of the criticism directed at journalists for their political coverage is predicated on the belief that journalists often wield this power rather poorly. Familiar complaints focus on journalists' tendencies to emphasize horse-race coverage over policy substance,[18] overly defer to official sources,[19] reduce controversy to false equivalences about "both sides,"[20] ignore or stereotype marginalized populations,[21] and play up conflict rather than address deeper structural factors.[22] These issues only matter to the extent that journalism maintains significant authority within society through its institutionalized production of symbolic forms. At the core of their jobs, journalists still decide what counts as news and tell us why events matter. By relevance, therefore, we refer to the collective capacity of the American press to fulfill these instrumental, informational, symbolic, and democratic roles of consequence.

To question journalism's relevance is to look broadly at the media culture and ask how shifts taking place at all levels of media consumption and production affect the institutional practices of news. To the factors identified by Hallin we need to add a host of others that have become especially influential in the twenty-first century: the decline of the agenda-setting power of traditional journalism,[23] the scale of partisan news and its outsized impact (exemplified by Fox News—both its unique role in political discourse and in how it set the stage for Trump's rise and accelerated his takeover of the Republican Party),[24] the fracturing of media audiences,[25] the withering of business models for news,[26] and the maturing of digital platforms not produced or controlled by journalists as central sites for information circulation and public commentary.[27] As a result of these changes, journalists' jobs have become more arduous and complicated,[28] journalism in local communities has suffered,[29] coverage of key institutions has waned,[30] some aspects of political engagement have declined,[31] media have become fragmented and polarized,[32] news consumption has been de-ritualized,[33] and once-familiar patterns of mass communication have given way to something more difficult to describe. In the next chapter, we discuss these emergent conditions in more detail, but, suffice to say, they all raise questions about journalism's relevance.

That journalism can be both relevant and irrelevant—that it is both fundamentally broken and yet a considerable force to be reckoned with—reflects the complicated media culture that has emerged. These opposing positions provide indices of the complex social relationships that define contemporary journalism. Discussing one side without the other misrepresents the state of journalism. Speaking only of journalistic relevance as precarious downplays the still rather considerable power of news to mediate events to the public,[34] and denies journalism's role to either amplify or ameliorate the intense polarization of US politics or its role in challenging the words and actions of powerful actors. Conversely, treating journalism as unchanged by seismic shifts in the media culture uncouples news from its very real struggles. Taken together, these positions on journalistic relevance suggest a time of confusion and fragility, but also a period of readjustment.

Ultimately, what we gain from foregrounding journalistic relevance is greater recognition that journalists do not control the conditions in which they operate. They do not create new technologies, or govern media economics, or dictate that they be listened to. Instead they must respond to the swirling conditions in which they find themselves, beset by fundamental challenges while also reckoning with journalism's own problematic patterns—including its multitude of mistakes. Digital networks alter communication flows, allowing for new forms of interactivity that compete with news (think of the ocean of time spent online—on YouTube, Instagram, Netflix, TikTok, and so on—and how only a tiny fraction of it is spent on anything resembling journalism);[35] shifts in advertising models result in financial woes for news organizations; the rise of polarization and changing news audience habits give rise to news fatigue and consequently news avoidance; and sustained, orchestrated attempts at undermining journalism abound all around the world. These transformations, which we will delve into throughout this book, are tense, conflicted, and ongoing. They are not uniform or consensual. They have deep roots, and their consequences range from shifts in the everyday experience of how news gets made and consumed to debates over what kind of normative footing journalism should have in this political and media environment.

How Does the News *Know*? Epistemic Contests Surrounding Journalism

We have argued that focusing on relevance as a conceptual lens for thinking about journalism decenters journalism by placing it as one communicative practice among others within a larger media culture.[36] But the question that hasn't been asked is *why* we should care about journalism's relevance. Certainly many have a vested interest in the continued relevance of journalists, from working journalists to journalism educators to scholars of journalism like us. But our chief concern is not the well-being of journalists or the perpetuation of the news industry for its own sake. Rather, our interest lies in the status of news as a form of collective knowledge and how this knowledge has power to shape collective thinking about the world we inhabit.

News has long been recognized as distinct from other domains of knowledge that tend toward the systematic and the esoteric.[37] It is closer to an everyday form of knowing; news texts offer contextualized information through plain language and/or images with the aim of reaching broad, nonexpert audiences. This divergence from other, more formalized forms of knowledge generation (such as science and medicine) should not minimize the importance of journalism as a way of knowing, but instead direct our attention to the interpretive structures of news narratives. How journalists produce knowledge can be examined through Mats Ekström's definition of the epistemology of news as the "rules, routines and institutionalized procedures that operate within a social setting and decide the form of the knowledge produced and the knowledge claims expressed (or implied)."[38] This decidedly pragmatic conceptualization of news-as-knowledge accentuates issues of practice and context over philosophical understandings of truth. It directs attention to *how* news is assembled as a knowledge form[39] while also positioning these forms within the *where* of their social settings. News cannot be understood apart from this cultural context; it makes no sense without it. Journalists cannot force anyone to accept their stories as valid and true. Instead, they rely on what Thomas Gieryn calls "epistemic authority" or "the legitimate power to define, describe, and explain bounded domains of reality."[40] And this authority is not guaranteed. It is the product of ongoing legitimation strategies meant to establish, maintain, or repair the status of journalism in the face of contestation. Understanding, then, how journalists come to be acknowledged as authoritative storytellers in society (or not) is an essential element in investigating how journalism and its knowledge claims gain or lose relevance in a media culture in transition.

Our interest is not in any single news story, journalist, or incident, but rather how they amalgamate into a larger struggle over systems of public knowledge. Ultimately, these epistemic contests are conflicts over what truthful accounts ought to look like and who ought to create them. *What journalism is* becomes the object of these contests. This focus on epistemic contests eschews more abstract philosophical questions about the status of truth and whether we exist in a "post-truth" age to instead examine the conditions that surround the production of news. Put another way, our interest is in how journalists justify and defend their reporting as what we might call "truthful accounts" that are broadly accepted as a viable representation of reality. This focus sidesteps questions of truth to instead emphasize news as a type of epistemic accomplishment occurring within a social space.

When we speak of relevance within the framework offered by the epistemology of news, what we are concerned about is the status of news as an institutional form of knowledge production.[41] The institutional level of analysis comprises a focus both on the "occupational ideology" of journalists, as Mark Deuze discusses it,[42] and on the organizational and material aspects of the news industry. The view encompasses both what journalists do (their practices) and what journalists value (their norms), and it suggests an interorganizational perspective, encompassing journalism's orientation beyond any single newsroom. It directs attention to journalism as an idea—a way of thinking about how to communicate accurately, systematically, widely, and legitimately about events in the world. In this way, an epistemic view of journalism helps dispel any notion that news is simply a recitation of facts devoid of normative assumptions. Rather, clearly in its representational practices, the news always communicates values about the world in how it identifies what is good or bad, worthy of inclusion or able to be ignored.

The focus on epistemic contests also helps us connect discussion of journalism with larger issues of power. In a society in which the public relies on the mediation of current events through media channels—we all can't *be there*, so we rely on media to take us there vicariously—questions of what forms these accounts take and who ought to produce them are intertwined with larger political questions about what liberal democracy ought to look like and how information about public life should be produced and circulated.

Foregrounding questions of relevance also speaks to the difficulty of using "journalism" as a collective noun.[43] To speak of "journalism" as an entity is to conjure up something more cohesive and bounded than what actually exists.[44] This is not a new problem. "Journalism" has always been a slightly messy term and a problematic signifier; what would be considered typical of journalism has varied in both time and place. When objective news emerged as the symbolic core of US journalism in the past century, it coexisted with partisan and alternative news formats (from tabloid newspapers to political blogs) that defined themselves against this core whether by engaging in advocacy-based journalism or in alternative storytelling practices deliberately contrasted with staid news discourse. Because "journalism" covers such a diverse range of outlets, actors, expectations, and normative commitments, its use to denote something exact is always only partial. Moreover, the experiences of news organizations vary widely; at a time when the *New York Times* and *Washington Post* pursue aggressive, nationally based digital growth strategies, many local news outlets struggle with declining audiences and lost revenues. Digital news startups rise and fall with promises of improvements and innovation,[45] while local television news wedded to familiar formulas continues to reach millions of daily viewers. The nightly network newscasts continue to sum up the day with their anchor-led gravity, while MSNBC, CNN, and Fox News carve out their pundit-led, partisan niches in their competition for eyeballs.

Although the boundaries of journalism are no doubt fuzzier than ever, it's also hard to argue that professional journalism no longer exists in any recognizable form.[46] Indeed, there are still routines, patterns, norms, ideals, and other signals of occupational orientation that are recognized (by journalists and by most everyone else) as being distinctly associated with this thing people call journalism.[47] Does this mean that journalism is only done by professionals at traditional news organizations? Absolutely not, and in the book we talk about both the multifaceted nature of journalism as it exists now and, importantly, the broader conceptions of journalists and journalism that might emerge in the future. But it does mean that it's fair to acknowledge that certain commitments and impulses—such as accuracy, fairness, independence, timeliness, and ethics[48]—have been and still are associated with capturing an essential characteristic of journalism as a meaningful "thing" in the world.

In this book, we refer to the well-established vision of journalism as fact-based, neutral, and autonomous as "the standard model" because of its prominence within the collective imagination of what journalism is. This is the model of journalism taught in introductory news writing courses or conjured when one is asked to think about news. That its symbolic value is disproportionate to its actual existence speaks to both its resilience and its weakness. How this normative understanding shapes the ways in which journalists approach questions of who, what, when, where, why, and how reveals visions of how democracy ought to operate. Ultimately it is the *struggle over journalism*—the fight to define it, defend it, and demean it—that forms the heart of this book, and so how different actors portray journalism differently is more important than any particular definition that we ourselves might try to impose on "journalism" as a collective concept. The stakes of this struggle are not just what happens to journalism, but what happens to our communities—politically and logistically, but also socially, culturally, and morally.

What the Presidency of Donald Trump Meant for Journalism

The seemingly improbable rise of Donald Trump as a viable candidate for president, his eventual surprise electoral victory in 2016, his tumultuous, scandal-filled four years as president, and his loss to Joe Biden in 2020, provide a prism through which to examine issues of journalistic relevance and epistemic contests around journalism. Even if Trump did not create the conditions that made all of his actions possible, how he exploited them reveals fissures within the present media culture. Trump, with his knee-jerk antagonism toward journalists and his flagrant departure from the behavioral norms of the presidency, allows us to see more clearly how the forces of fragmentation, polarization, illiberalism, and demagogic populism have planted themselves in this media culture, while simultaneously serving as a warning sign of their consequences. His presence continuously amplified public discussions around the role of journalism, which led to a moment for reflection and reform.

This book is not a history of the Trump presidency as a whole, but it goes where other history books might not: developing a close examination of Trump's relations with journalists, his use of social media to promulgate his own messages outside of news channels, and reactions to him and his attacks from across journalism. Trump's attention to journalists waxed and waned over his time in the political spotlight, sometimes drawing his full wrath and other times taking a back seat as Trump attacked his many other foes, including Democratic politicians and candidates, government officials investigating him, two impeachment inquiries, and so on. But even as this book reveals the character and consequences of Trump's assault on the press, it also does not pretend to be a comprehensive account of every Trump tirade against the news media—there are far too many such moments to fit into a single book. Instead, we identify key points that define Trump's relations with journalists, ones that provide insight into larger shifts taking place within the media culture and how journalists are debating their future.

As a result, this book devotes much attention to *how* Trump continually attacked journalists and *why* such efforts could be so politically effective. In one sense, there is nothing sophisticated about Trump's offensive against the news media. He did not craft arguments, assemble evidence, or offer pro-longed diatribes. Instead, his attacks on the news media were shallow and repetitive. Yet while Trump's tweets, taunts, and rally slogans may have appeared spontaneous and unrefined, they represent in aggregate an orches-trated effort to undercut the power of the Fourth Estate, as Trump himself has admitted. As the chapters in this book document, Trump took advantage of journalistic conventions to increase his presence in the news; he used press-bashing as a type of political performance commensurate with his populist rhetoric; he demonstrated the expansiveness of the contemporary media cul-ture through his use of social media, political rallies, and right-wing media to reach the public; he boldly invented or misrepresented facts in ways that strained reporting norms; and, in doing all of this, he challenged the institu-tional character of journalism.

While all politicians spin facts and pander to their bases, Trump's pen-chant for polarizing rhetoric intent on inflaming emotional appeals while showing disdain for facticity or comity crossed over to demagoguery. Demagogues exhibit paranoia, engage in scapegoating, and base their au-thority on a unique ability to lead—all characteristics of Trump's discourse and his actions.[49] Traditional journalistic modes—the neutral, objective style of the standard model of news that dominates the journalistic imaginary—are not well equipped to confront the excesses of demagoguery. The epi-stemic nucleus of news reporting is a quotation from an official source; it may be presented with some context, but that quotation is accorded a cer-tain legitimacy as a factual statement, even if it is a self-serving one. Trump's fiery rhetoric, preying on prejudice and divisiveness, clashed with these working assumptions, forcing journalists into a position of uncertainty over whether they are irresponsible in amplifying such claims through the simple act of reporting what was said or whether they are irresponsible if they ig-nore them.[50] But demagoguery is also difficult to ignore. When such rhet-oric violates expectations and breaks unwritten rules of political conduct, it generates compelling stories. Trump's propensity for lying, his over-the-top personal attacks on anyone who crossed him (including journalists), and his unwillingness to concede any mistakes were simultaneously repulsive and irresistible to the journalists covering him up until his final days in office in January 2021.

Trump's effectiveness as a demagogue can be recognized in his ability to turn all eyes to him as the center of the story. Years before taking office, Trump had already cultivated a substantial public image and celebrity status, including as a reality-television star. He was often characterized as exceptional, in-charge, and independent. Trump's ego and braggadocio were well known, as he often took credit for ideas that weren't his own.[51] Moreover, Trump's habits of communicating independently of his aides through social media, giving off-the-cuff answers to journalists' questions, and offering extemporaneous ad-libs during prepared speeches altogether supported the perception of Trump as a stand-alone force. The resulting focus on day-to-day skirmishes and absurdities pulled attention away from the larger policy changes that benefitted the wealthy at the expense of the working class, the environment, and democracy itself. He kept himself planted in the center of public consciousness through a combination of bluster and theatrics, and it would be tempting to focus on him as an individual with singular actions, thus allowing us to relegate him to the past at the end of his presidency.

Trump may have lost the 2020 election, but he still received nearly seventy-five million votes. While a portion of the electorate surely supported Trump as a preferable choice for specific policy reasons (like self-interest in preserving tax cuts or limiting regulations), for many who voted for Trump a second time in 2020 it was a matter of social identity. Trump represented a valuable and rare authenticity, an emotive yearning for things to be better for them, and a different kind of moral code. Despite all that transpired over his first term, many millions saw themselves as a loyal part of Trump's "us" in the us-versus-them dynamic that so defined his discourse. In saluting Trump for speaking up for the individual American, they were rewarded with a feeling of connection over their shared anger and frustration, resentment and fear.

Such intense feelings and the cult of personality associated with them will not simply vanish, just as Trump himself resisted exiting the White House—continuing to argue, even long after the Electoral College vote was confirmed, that the election was stolen from him. What Trump harnessed was a right-wing populist vein in American politics, one particularly skeptical of journalists and other elites, that predated him and will persist after him. As such, any narrative that individualizes Trump's actions, successes, and failures—that acts as if he and he alone were responsible for everything described in this book—is shortsighted. To fully recognize the implications of Trump for the news media requires situating him within networks of actors that propped him up, spoke for him, shaped his image, challenged news reporting critical of him, and carried out his policy changes.[52] This includes institutionalized actors such as the White House communications team, his press secretaries, advisers like Reince Priebus, Steve Bannon, Stephen Miller, and Kellyanne Conway, and other appointed officials called upon to toe the Trump line. But it especially includes vocally supportive pundits on the Fox News Channel as well.[53] As we explain further in Chapter 3, Trump's attacks on perceived enemies—including the press as the "enemy of the people"—often were instigated by things he first watched on morning programs such as *Fox & Friends* and evening shows hosted by the likes of Tucker Carlson, Sean Hannity, and Laura Ingraham. In turn, the same cadre of Fox News anchors, personalities, and guests—and, later into his presidency, the pro-Trump sycophants on the far-right Newsmax and One America News networks—served to echo Trump's talking points. All of this gave the president a continuous circle of reinforcement: a prepackaged set of grievances ready to "publish" against his enemies, and a preestablished network of supporters ready to "spread" those messages far beyond Trump himself. Even more broadly, Trump rode a wave of global populist politics upending democratic norms and conventions in numerous countries.[54] Trump is not responsible for Trump alone.

We argue that Trump remains a symbol of a larger phenomenon characterized by identity-driven politics, political polarization, and a news industry struggling to adapt to a changing media culture. We are concerned less with Trump the man than a broader set of transitions happening not only politically but also culturally, economically, symbolically, and technologically—all shifts that have been long-standing and yet exacerbated, accelerated, and made abundantly visible in our present moment. Evaluating how these deeper shifts affect the information environment and, ultimately, democratic functioning needs to take precedence over any single barbed tweet or personal jab. We do not excuse Trump or downplay the damage that his rhetoric caused during his presidency. But nor do we see him as the chief agent of his success, or accord him generative power for shaping the conditions that allowed him to succeed.

There is also much to criticize about news reporting in the Trump era. As we review in the chapters of this book, early news reporting failed to put Trump in an appropriately critical and contextual light. Too often, news reporters focused on the latest, loudest comment instead of explaining the larger picture of Trump's claims or evaluating the impact of his administration's policies. Journalists simply regurgitating Trump's specious claims ended up normalizing them. Journalists have been accused of playing stenographer to an administration prone to lying, or of failing to call out racist language directly. A consistent theme is the lack of attention to deeper trends that would position Trump to be less of an aberration and more of a culmination of forces that are not so easy to dismiss.

We also recognize that there was no shortage of well-reported, hard-hitting investigative stories about Trump. Just before the inauguration, *Politico* media critic Jack Shafer called the Trump administration "journalistic spring" for the abundance of news stories waiting to be unearthed.[55] Journalists covering the Trump administration responded with a flood of news stories critical of the Trump administration, including Pulitzer Prize–winning investigations regarding Trump's charitable giving (by the *Washington Post* in 2017), Russian electoral interference (by the *Post* and the *New York Times* in 2018), and Trump's payoffs to women to hush up affair allegations (by the *Wall Street Journal* in 2019). But, of course, Pulitzer Prizes are given to journalists by other journalists. The ability of investigations to exact change relies on other mechanisms, and the failure of any reported controversy to sway public opinion or spark bipartisan outrage speaks to the array of forces that have come together in this particular moment.

Consider, for example, when in the weeks before the 2020 election the *New York Times* obtained and published Trump's income tax documents after years of his deflections and stonewalling. Through careful, long-form reporting augmented with cutting-edge data visualization, the *Times* exposed Trump's gigantic personal losses, the extraordinarily small amount of federal taxes he paid, and looming enormous debt obligations to unknown entities.[56] Yet the story did not move the political needle and was swiftly overshadowed as the campaign wore on. What does it mean for journalism when such a story—perhaps the most sought-after story involving Trump—seemed not to matter at all?

News after Trump: Developing a Moral Voice for Journalism

The Trump presidency has since ended, but the reckoning for journalists remains. Caught between outmoded reporting routines and their need to innovate and survive, journalists waffled in their response to Trump between 2015 and 2021, sometimes adhering to institutional norms and other times experimenting with collective efforts to call out lies and racist statements—but all the time trapped in a vortex of volatility, struggling to translate their professional sense of purpose into a social and cultural sense of permanence. This public anguish within the journalistic community reveals deep fissures in what had been a more cohesive, shared set of norms and protocols during the stabler times of the mass communication era. Journalists confront fundamentally altered functions and identities, as people clamor for them to be democratic activists, righteous moralists, civic therapists, and political strategists in response to this environment of dark money, demagoguery, foreign infiltration, and an altogether intensifying fear that democracy is dying on our watch. Amid such scrambling, the news media enterprise is seeking not only to find a sustainable business model in the digital era, but, as this book explores in detail, journalists are questioning *how* they should operate in a world where they have such incredible tools for reaching broad audiences with quality news and where they are simultaneously distrusted and dismissed as never before in modern times.

In contemplating news after Trump, this book offers both an empirical investigation of what happened and a normative intervention for a way forward. We argue that modes of journalistic objectivity that have been crafted to support journalism as both central and detached no longer work effectively. When Trump would single out journalists, such as in the January 2021 speech recounted at the beginning of this chapter, his intention was to make journalists part of the news story that they were covering. Trump's constant critiques pulled journalists into the spotlight, resulting in a dance between Trump's attacks on the press's trustworthiness and journalists' corresponding defenses of their credibility and utility. Yet this mode of centralized detachment is so ingrained in how journalism imagines its legitimacy that it is difficult for journalists to rewire their normative underpinnings.

In laying out a normative vision, we offer no nostalgic vision of journalism. This is not a rear-facing book. We are not offering a paean for a nonexistent golden age of journalism, nor are we blindly espousing classic journalism norms. Journalism has always been caught between moments of delivering on its promise of holding power to account and moments of failing its audiences. Historically, newsrooms have been too white, too male, and too beholden to the powerful.[57] We do not call for a restoration of this environment, even if such a thing were possible. Nor do we take the approach of blowing it all up and starting over again. We agree that the uncertainty and the unpredictability of the present moment provide an opportunity for voices that have traditionally been left out of power to take advantage of digital media and a weakened institutional identity for journalism. The problem is that these voices are not only marginalized groups that deserve to be amplified, but also those who perpetuate extremism, divisiveness, and xenophobia—people who seek to subvert and ultimately smash the old media regime and delegitimize the mainstream press out of a desire to promote their own self-serving, exclusionary narratives.[58] Just as we cannot turn the clock back, we cannot wipe the slate clean and hope that the wisdom of the crowd prevails.

We also do not assume that journalism alone can and should be the dominant voice in the contemporary media culture. Reconstructing the relevancy of journalism starts by recognizing journalism as decentered within the present media culture. As "journalism" becomes more complex and encompasses more variety and a less unified voice, so too are journalists existing in a communicative landscape in which they compete with other public voices ranging from elite officials to anonymous commenters. Social media platforms usurp the role of news gatekeeper and, thus, alter the flow of information, reinscribing news stories in myriad ways.[59] All of this complicates the circulation and reception of news while also expanding the range of participants in creating public affairs content.

But we are also not willing to let go of journalism as an important institution. We advocate, then, for overhauling journalism's foundational value system and especially its norms and routines that have contributed to the problematic political situation in the first place. Stripping away entrenched, unhelpful norms and routines gets back to foundational aspirations of journalists producing truthful accounts, but ones built around the amplification of diverse voices, a commitment to democratic processes and their preservation, and the facilitation of community discourse. In other words, we suggest opportunities for journalism to develop a more explicitly moral orientation to its work, grounded in broadly shared values such as democracy, decency, civic participation, and a pluralistic society. Journalism must be at once more assertive in speaking in a moral voice on behalf of communities, more comfortable in rendering judgments, and more self-aware of its shortcomings. This does not mean giving up facticity. Rather, it recognizes that an overwhelming focus on the production of isolated facts alone is neither adequate nor particularly useful on its own—in part because such antiseptic procedures may isolate journalists from a fuller understanding of the communities they are supposed to help.

Our vision is informed by an argument that James W. Carey offered nearly a half-century ago.[60] Writing in the heyday of mass communication, Carey looked critically at a media culture in which news organizations were able to "centralize and monopolize civic knowledge and as importantly the techniques of knowing" while reducing the audience to a passive client.[61] Carey warned that as journalists encased themselves in the mantle of professional distance and privileged autonomy over communal attachment, they were losing connection with the people they were meant to serve. Today, we find echoes of Carey's critique: professionalism has rendered news paternalistic and morally distant within a media culture that prizes authenticity, and the populist critique sees the press as an elite interest group favoring self-protection above public service.[62]

Carey argues for an alternative vision of journalism that trades the protection of professionalism as paramount for a normative footing situated within a sense of the larger communal good: "We would, in short, all be better served if professionals, including journalists, were to see themselves less as subject to the demands of their profession and more to the demands of the general moral and intellectual point of view."[63] We take from Carey's arguments the need for a healthy communicative environment that can present the diversity of viewpoints that exist in a pluralistic society. This viewpoint is not incommensurate with a longing for shared facts, but it recognizes that facts are not a simple output coming off the journalistic assembly line like a bunch of toasters. Rather, they are cultural artifacts shaped by relations among various actors: reporters, sources, and the news audience as well as our organizations, institutions, and systems.[64] And, as such, the profession is subject to the same power dynamics, hierarchies, and biases. Reconsidering journalism's claims to relevancy also requires confronting the representational power of news and how it positions certain actors as "authorized knowers"[65] or "primary definers"[66] while rendering the less socially powerful as victims, perpetrators of violence, or invisible. The ethos of detachment has staved off vital questions about how journalism connects to its audiences, how it creates enduring value in people's lives (or not), and how diversity needs to be understood holistically at the level of production, text, and audience to rebuild trust.

To be clear, even as we critique journalism's shortcomings, we are not letting off the hook those who would denigrate the press out of cynical self-interest. Our normative focus supports our contention that calling a news organization an enemy of the people is abhorrent and dangerous, and Trump's actions will find no endorsement in these pages. His attacks will be called out for the nakedly self-serving utterances that they are. Journalists deserve to work without fear of physical endangerment, particularly at a time when the press faces growing hostility in the United States[67] and around the world.[68] But many journalists also like to believe they can remain above the fray, particularly in the space of politics. They may favor an externalist perspective about their social role in which they stand on the sidelines of political happenings to observe and report back. But this view ignores the role that journalists play in deciding who gets in the news and how they are covered.

When embracing their role as moral agents, journalists occupy a space that allows them to tackle fundamental issues of right and wrong while eschewing political statements. We are not advocating for reporters to dictate and judge differing partisan viewpoints. Rather, we wish to enable them to call out violations of widely held moral standards such as telling brazen lies, using power to harm people, and engaging in racist discourse and actions. Philosopher and ethicist Stephen Ward might call this "democratically engaged journalism" because it adopts a moral code around human rights, poverty reduction, social justice, tolerance for difference, and other grand virtues.[69] We recognize that such broad transformation is difficult and even unlikely, but it remains necessary to imagine how journalistic relevance could be rethought and what might be done to achieve such change. At the same time, this is not just an academic exercise of romanticizing what might be; newsrooms across the country already are having uncomfortable conversations about what they should be doing differently.[70] We underscore the need for journalists to connect with the stories, contexts, histories, and facts for millions who have turned away from news and tuned into falsehoods that mesh with their ideologies. Journalism, like any other social institution, must be held to account and asked to do better, particularly in this opportune moment of reckoning.

Plan of the Book

This is not a book about the few years that Trump dominated political discourse. Rather, it is about how overlapping forces resulted in a period of news media turmoil, the end result of which—in the years and decades to come—may mean an entirely reconfigured information landscape for public affairs. The chapters that follow explain for media watchers, scholars, and citizens alike what this dynamic landscape looks like, illustrating the most salient shifts and why they matter as well as how we might move forward toward more collective truths.

A challenge is the familiar problem of writing about events without the comforting distance of time to understand their lasting implications. Writing a history of the present, as it were, is difficult. The legacy of Trump, both for politics generally and for government-press relations more narrowly, will take years to sort out. It could be that his presidency was a blip resulting from an alignment of various factors unlikely to so perfectly come together again. Had 79,646 people in Michigan, Wisconsin, and Pennsylvania—0.025% of the total US population—voted differently in November 2016, this book may not exist at all.[71] Nevertheless, the election of Trump made visible a media politics fueled by ideological fervor, partisan identity, and distrust of institutions, chief among them the press. It seems certain that the political news environment of the future will not look like the past. Instead, journalism, long disrupted and challenged in various ways, has encountered a confluence of forces that together are more destabilizing to the institution than what has come before. The gravity of this moment makes it all the more important to jump in and begin unraveling these forces to propose a way forward.

This book draws on a range of sources of evidence, with an emphasis on public discourse about Trump and the news as primary sources. Trump's social media output and utterances during interviews, speeches, and rallies provide a record of what has been said. But this record also extends to others in Trump's orbit of formal and informal supporters. For the news media, we examine the many places where journalists speak about themselves, including within news content or commentary, books, speeches, and the journalism trade press. We analyze more than six hundred editorials in which news organizations across the country formally responded to Trump's attacks and the environment that enabled such accusations to gain momentum. We also draw on research about the political and media landscapes, including trends in public opinion surveys as well as data from surveys and in-depth interviews with journalists across the country. These data help identify the short-term consequences of the moment as well as connect to longer-lasting patterns.

The chapters in this book examine the struggle over who gets to provide truthful accounts and what these accounts should look like. Chapter 1, "Where We Are: The Media and Political Context," sets the stage by looking at how a host of factors have come together to give rise to the conditions that facilitated Trump's political ascendency. It provides an overview of the key issues confronting contemporary journalism in the present media culture, many of which have been decades in the making. It then turns to the global rise of populist anti-institutional movements and their implications for journalism theory and practice. Trump's demagogic tendencies are unpacked to help make sense of why he went after the press as often as he did.

The next two chapters focus on what Trump's attacks on journalism looked like. Chapter 2, "The Trump Campaign: Outsized Coverage from the Press, Outsized Attacks on the Press," examines how the institutional trappings of political journalism allowed Trump to benefit from disproportionate news coverage, particularly in the primary stages of the 2016 presidential contest. As the campaign progressed, press-bashing became a political performance that was an indelible part of Trump's electoral success. In these ways, a confluence of long-simmering cultural factors came to demand newfound attention to the symbolic decentralization of journalism in contemporary life. More broadly, Trump's success lays bare the disconnects between institutions, communities and citizens, ubiquitous polarization, and intense animosity for any "other," all of which leads to questions about the relevance of mainstream journalism. Chapter 3, "The Trump Presidency: Four Years of Battling and Belittling the Press," shifts the focus to the period of Trump's presidency, when his attacks on the press became even more extreme, and more central to his own maintenance of power. By calling journalists the "enemy of the people," he simultaneously amplified the power of the press and undermined its authority. For Trump, "the media" became one of many established elite institutions hostile to the experience of everyday Americans. This message became a fixture of his rhetoric as he turned to communication channels outside of traditional journalism, such as social media, political rallies, and conservative media outlets. In this chapter, we explore how the far-right media ecosystem became a propaganda machine churning out lies that helped Trump and others not only achieve power but formulate a dichotomous and competing alternate universe of facts.

Journalists did not ignore Trump's constant badgering. Chapter 4, "The Press Fights Back: Reclaiming a Story of Relevance for the Press," looks at how a coordinated, collective effort in August 2018 to produce newspaper editorials defending journalism provided a rare public moment of focused attention on the press's roles and identities. In this response, journalists fell back to the grand—yet flailing—narrative placing journalism at the heart of democracy. Behind their facade of unity, we find a fracturing of this narrative—reflective of a broader change that has been occurring for quite some time. We argue that journalists' efforts to bolster their relevance must downplay their institutional ties and focus on community relationships to build trust with groups they have long ignored. Such actions demand rethinking what a relevant press is *for*. This is taken up in Chapter 5, "Journalistic Moralities: Confronting Trump's Lies and Racism." As their professionalized practices were challenged by Trump's frequent lies and his racist statements, journalists debated how to respond. Some prominent journalists advocated for the traditional values that have propped up journalism for the past century, while others argued that journalists needed to be more willing to render judgments explicitly to avoid being the handmaidens of Trump. In all of this, we refocus the news media toward a pro-democracy, pro-connection stance.

The conclusion, "What Relevant Journalism Looks Like: Developing a Moral Voice," draws from across the book to make a case for how journalism can move forward after Trump. To rebuild its relevance, the journalistic community needs to adapt to a changed media culture in which its centrality is no longer guaranteed. When journalism becomes just one voice among others, it becomes necessary to question whether long-standing objectivity norms hamper its ability to make judgments and act morally. Journalists must turn toward relationship-building to establish the necessary trust and legitimacy to pursue the institutional production of news knowledge. However, fixing journalism cannot be done merely from within journalism; media consumers must support their news outlets (financially and otherwise) in a concerted call for fact-based truths. A serious appraisal of the systemic patterns that enabled this moment means looking more constructively at what journalism *can* become by confronting reporting patterns that turn people away from news. Many of our conclusions might seem unsettling or anathematic to journalists. But we end this book on an optimistic note, showcasing opportunities for journalists to become connected to citizens in more authentic and productive ways. Providing a brighter future starts by looking at these outcomes critically and carefully to envision what could be different and why that matters for public life.

1

Where We Are

The Media and Political Context

On the day of the 2016 US presidential election, the data journalism-centric "Upshot" section of the *New York Times* ran a story titled "Who Will Be President?"[1] Under the headline, Hillary Clinton's and Donald Trump's disembodied heads were accompanied with the odds of winning calculated as 85% and 15%, respectively. In keeping with sports metaphors popular with political reporting, the lead paragraph concluded: "A victory by Mr. Trump remains possible: Mrs. Clinton's chance of losing is about the same as the probability that an N.F.L. kicker misses a 37-yard field goal." The field goal was, in fact, missed. Trump's election came as a surprise to many—even to Trump, according to Bob Woodward's account of election night.[2] Over the course of the evening, as the improbable tipped over to the inevitable, journalists scrambled to rewrite stories. The *New York Times*' front-page story, "Trump Triumphs," was so hastily assembled that it ran with the wrong bylines.[3] But with the election called for Trump, attention immediately turned to how it had happened. It was clear that a lot had been misunderstood—about the shape of polity, about discontentment among groups of voters, and about how journalism works.

Before untangling the forces that put Trump into office, an important caveat is recognizing that Trump's election margin was not overwhelming. Clinton outperformed Trump in total votes—65,853,514 to 62,984,828—but lost the Electoral College because of *where* these voters were. Trump eked out victories in Wisconsin, Michigan, and Pennsylvania, giving Trump an ultimate Electoral College advantage of 304 to 227—a stunning result for what was otherwise a Trump loss in the popular vote. The 2016 presidential election was notable for pitting two candidates who had both rabid fans and equally passionate detractors. This book does not rehash the factors that led to Trump's victory, nor do we speculate on how it might have gone differently in some parallel universe where Clinton campaigned more in Rust Belt states she assumed were hers.[4] Instead, we focus on the political rise of Trump as a

News After Trump. Matt Carlson, Sue Robinson, and Seth C. Lewis, Oxford University Press. © Oxford University Press 2021. DOI: 10.1093/oso/9780197550342.003.0002

particular moment that illuminates general themes about the state of journalism as a source of institutional knowledge production in the contemporary media culture.

To truly comprehend Trump's rise and to derive what this means for journalism, we need to first establish the forces that coalesced to make this moment possible. Trump may position himself as the chief actor, and his demagogic style is well known. However, we contend that rather than give in to Trump's own image of his outsized efficacy, his actions need to be recognized as contingent on a host of factors. Trump's 2016 victory sparked introspection across the academy about what we know and what we expect of the polity, about how political, media, and technological trends connect with one another, and about where this is all going. Trump will receive ample attention for his actions throughout this book, but at the outset he needs to be positioned not as an actor single-handedly controlling political destinies, but as a symbol marking the confluence of seemingly disparate factors that have made Trump's political career possible. Trump did not *cause* the conditions through which he became an unlikely president. And his 2021 departure has not led to the dissolution of the trends that put him there in the first place. When revisiting the constant whirlwind of breaking news and fresh outrage and strong emotions that was the hallmark of the Trump presidency, we need to be sure that we do not lose track of the longer view of how we got here and what these actions indicate about the broader failings of journalism.

This chapter offers a contextual snapshot of the media and political trends enabling Trump. The first half of this chapter considers the media context. Journalists turned out to cover the 2016 campaign and Trump's presidency much as they had in the past—embedding journalists on the campaign trail, attending rallies, showing up to press conferences, and working top sources for new angles. Yet they did so in a way that was unprepared for a media culture that had changed. Long-building incremental shifts in media and technology had, by the time of the 2016 election, become more visibly recognizable and more structurally significant, altering the playing field of politics. As media have gone digital, an explosion of choices vying for a finite amount of attention and the rise of new intermediaries like social media platforms have altered how news circulates and who gets to speak. The news industry has struggled with lost advertising revenues and questions about its future. These structural shifts are coupled with long-running trends pointing to declining public trust in journalism, much of this owing to a growing partisan divide in how journalism is viewed. Journalists have long been accused of harboring political biases, and public opinion surveys indicate how entrenched this view has become. But journalists have also drawn the ire of other communities who feel they are not fairly represented in the news.

The second half of the chapter takes up how various political forces have aligned in a way that provided an opening for Trump. This includes the polarization of the voting public and a hardening of political identity. These conditions made a right-wing populist movement possible, in line with populist developments around the world. Through demagogic rhetoric placing himself in opposition to adversaries ranging from immigrants to journalists, Trump propped himself up as a defender and advocate for a portion of society largely built around working-class white identity. Furthermore, he offered an alternative morality based on individual advantage that fed long-simmering resentments between "us" and "them."

Bringing these factors together positions Trump not as the powerful actor he has so often claimed to be, but as the realization of overlapping forces resulting in this particular moment. This broader view is essential if we are to chart the ways in which journalists have to reckon with their social position, normative attachments, and news-making practices. We need to know how we got where we are and recognize that these trends are deep and resilient, speaking as much to entrenched matters of identity as they do to new digital platforms. Only by acknowledging the various strands that make up the contemporary context can we seek to provide insights about journalism.

Journalism in the Trump Era

In 2008, when Barack Obama won a historic election to become the first African American president of the United States, total advertising revenue for US newspapers was nearly $40 billion (down from a 2006 peak of nearly $50 billion), and the total number of US editorial positions at newspapers stood at seventy-one thousand. The tally of newspaper journalists had remained somewhat consistent, and newspapers had rebounded in recent years after suffering through the recession of the early 2000s. By the fall of 2008, a new, more pernicious recession fueled by the collapse of the housing market and related financial instruments portended a new round of decline. Other forces added further headwinds for journalism: the iPhone was beginning to shift online access to mobile, Google's search-based advertising revenues were growing apace, and social media sites such as Twitter and Facebook were gaining users in huge numbers. Online commerce was beginning to erode brick-and-mortar stores that had been mainstay advertisers for newspapers for decades. All of this introduced uncertainty into the news business.

Nine years later, during Trump's first year in office, total advertising revenues for US newspapers had cratered to $16 billion, a decline of 60% in a decade.[5] Total newspaper staff stood at thirty-nine thousand.[6] In the same period, the number of news personnel at digital-native news sites nearly doubled, to thirteen thousand, but this rapid growth does not begin to make up for the reductions at newspapers.[7] Even within the newspaper industry, nationally focused outlets like the *New York Times*, *Washington Post*, and *Wall Street Journal* have in recent years grown thanks to burgeoning digital audiences and online subscribers. Meanwhile, local newspapers have suffered, leaving fewer reporters to cover large geographical areas. At the extreme end, news deserts—spaces with no local news—spread to many rural parts of the country, while many communities within urban areas also go uncovered.[8] Newspaper circulation has continued to drop, with many newspapers cutting circulation days or closing altogether. For local news, digital subscriptions have been slow to make up for losses in print.[9] Since Obama's victory scarcely more than a decade from the time of this writing, there are simply far fewer people producing news, and scant positive indicators about the health of the news industry as a whole.

Parenthetically, we should note that journalism—as we indicated in the introduction—is not exclusive to nor defined by the news industry, nor is it the sum of the organizations that collectively produce much of what qualifies as "news" to most people. Indeed, "journalism" is something of a leaky social container, with fuzzy boundaries and porous lines of demarcation. This is made all the more complicated in a contemporary media culture where news may seem to be everywhere and nowhere at the same time. The likes of CNN and other legacy news media still maintain a persistent ambient presence, whether on television in public spaces such as airports and hotels or in the private spaces of people's social media newsfeeds and smartphone lock screens. And yet the "standard model" of what has traditionally been classified as news, such as that produced by professional journalists and concerning public affairs, makes up an increasingly tiny fraction of most people's media diets, and otherwise seems lost amid the mountain of everything else that people find more interesting online.[10] Journalism, therefore, is not nearly so straightforward as people might have once imagined.[11] However, even in its perpetually unstable form, journalism as a signifier can point to something meaningful nonetheless: an assemblage of people, practices, and institutional relationships that still manages to bring forth, day to day and hour to hour, stories and images and audiovisuals that have a certain "news-ness"[12] about them, whether in tone or topic, style or substance, or some combination of it all. And, in that respect and in the United States at least, the newspaper industry and its fortunes are often used as a kind of shorthand to represent the ups and downs of journalism as a profession or institution, in large part because newspapers, even now in their diminished state, remain the primary engines of original reporting in most communities.[13]

Alongside these forces of change, journalism has also experienced questions about who it has worked for and who it has failed. Candis Callison and Mary Lynn Young refer to the reckoning happening as journalists confront their role in maintaining the social order that they purport to merely represent through their news stories.[14] In a theme emerging across this book, the rise of Trump and his anti-press rhetoric combined with growing critiques from marginalized communities coalesce into a critical juncture for journalists assessing the basis for their continued authority. For this reckoning to occur, journalists must avoid seeing themselves only as victims of external attacks and negative economic trends, and instead begin to recognize their responsibility for cultural conditions and their capacity to imagine different futures.

The sections that follow set the stage for examining epistemic contests regarding journalism as a form of institutional knowledge through the example of Trump and his allies. We do so by placing journalism within the broader media culture, a term that encapsulates three aspects: industrial, organizational, and material conditions; media practices; and modes of thinking about media. In the present media culture, journalists find themselves struggling with economic uncertainty, divided over what kinds of practices are appropriate, and questioning how their normative guideposts fare amid so many changes. Before turning to what this looks like in reaction to Trump and his allies, the following sections set the stage by examining three trends that have affected what US journalism looks like and how news is consumed. The first trend is digital disruption. As audiences have migrated online, news consumption patterns have morphed, and advertising revenues have shifted away from news outlets. These changes eat away at journalists' control of public communication and the resources that make this role possible. The second trend is a longer-term decline in journalistic credibility, as measured by public opinion surveys. In particular, the persistent critique that journalists harbor either implicit or explicit liberal biases has taken root in a significant portion of the public. The third trend goes beyond assessments of credibility to the question of journalists' safety as the political conditions we have described spill over into violence against journalists. The picture that emerges is of journalists struggling to respond to larger technological, political, and cultural shifts of which they are both a part of and apart from. It provides much-needed context that avoids an oversimplified narrative of Trump versus the press.

How, When, and Where People See News

Having the ability to look up and consume as much political news as one desires has become so ordinary that it's easy to forget how different it used to be. We get a faint glimpse of the past when we get shut out of a paywalled news site or abandon a fruitless search to recover some story we remember but can't find. Otherwise, we have a plethora of news that exceeds the one resource that we have not been able to extend: time. Just as the amount of news has opened up, so too the temporal rhythms of digital news have shifted by being unmoored from rigid broadcast and print delivery schedules. How, when, and where people see news has changed.

To use the term "news" is to invoke a variety of media forms, from print publications and radio broadcasts to mobile apps. The coexistence of a diverse array of forms spread across different types of media makes it difficult to capture the entire news industry. Yet there is a clear shift toward digital forms of news. When people were asked for their preferred manner of accessing local news content, the Pew Research Center found that online (37%) trailed television only slightly (41%), and was well ahead of print (13%).[15] But what "online" or "digital" news means is much more complex than the uniformity of traditional news media like newspapers. Digital audiences can visit a news site, subscribe to newsletters or alerts, or follow news outlets and journalists on social media. In these ways and others, digital news consumption involves new types of intermediaries. This includes the presence of algorithms at many levels, from ordering search results or social media feeds, to personalizing news content, to even authoring news stories.[16] On social media, the spread of news is driven not just by journalists but by opinion leaders.[17] In addition, news aggregation sites work in the space between news producers and consumers by repackaging news.[18]

To make matters more complicated, news consumption increasingly occurs through smartphones. Mobile phones challenge a medium-agnostic view of news content that privileges news story content over the mediated means by which stories appear in front of audiences. Greater emphasis on the technology of news shifts the focus to how medium differences shape what news stories look like and how they are used. In other words, we use a phone differently than a television.[19] Mobile news collapses space and time by fostering access to media content anywhere, both in how news users can access news wherever and whenever and in how news alerts or news embedded in social media feeds can find the news user.[20] One effect of this has been that mobile news consumption has become an activity more akin to snacking—digesting bits here and there in the course of other activities—rather than a "meal" of more in-depth engagement.[21]

As the technologies of news consumption change, a renewed scholarly interest in news consumers has blossomed. News use spreads across media and inserts itself into the fabric of mobile communication, spurring research that gets away from examining the use of any single news medium to instead investigate everyday repertoires of media use.[22] This approach helps capture not only habitual uses of news, but more transitory moments of incidental news exposure.[23] Efforts to measure news repertoires have been accompanied by an interest in how news audiences interpret the news environment. News audiences often make sense of the diversity of the ways and places they encounter news through their own "folk theories." These folk theories—such as ideas that "I can just Google it" or "the news will find me"—become ways of coping with the confusion of so many media choices, but they also indicate audiences' overestimation of their ability to stay up-to-date.[24]

The ability to find news is also the ability to avoid it. This is not a new development; Markus Prior demonstrates how, over time, more television options translated into declining audiences for the nightly broadcast news.[25] Digital media exacerbate this trend with their flood of content. Even what people mean by "news" is fluid enough that what one person considers news, another might find to be entertainment. More recently, the so-called "news finds me" perception names a way of coping with the flood of digital content and a belief that curated systems of social media will circulate the important news of the day. Yet the evidence so far suggests that this loose attachment to the news has negative consequences for actually knowing what goes on.[26] While research on news avoidance is developing, findings indicate that there are deeper cultural cleavages around news use. For example, women news avoiders articulate a host of gender-based differences around news use and expectations about political processes.[27] Likewise, younger people are also more likely to avoid news.[28] And people in Black and Brown communities have long turned to ethnic publications rather than mainstream outlets where they are portrayed as either athletes, perpetrators, or victims.[29] What's needed is more attention to how societal stratifications feed into news use, and how this relates back to feelings of political efficacy or helplessness. All of this provides more reason for taking a deeper look at how journalists' normative commitments hinder their ability to connect with audiences in a high-choice media culture.

Expanded access to news corresponds with a greater diversity of news content. Perhaps most prominently, partisan media channels expand the range of what news discourse looks like. The long view reveals a shift from a media landscape defined by a limited number of options for news consumption to a high-choice media environment.[30] When fewer choices were available, news organizations hewed to centrism to attract large audiences. But as media proliferated, first through cable television and talk radio and later through digital sources, adopting political niches became feasible and profitable. This availability allows for partisan selective exposure as a way of avoiding disconfirming viewpoints.[31] Polarization is often ascribed to the rise of partisan news media, but the familiar question of causation rears its head: Do partisan media drive the electorate to be more partisan, or does a partisan electorate seek out confirming views by flocking to certain media outlets? The picture is somewhat muddy,[32] and many choose to use media abundance as a way to avoid political news.[33] Although the causality of whether partisan media make partisans or partisans seek out partisan media is difficult to discern, partisan media can amplify partisan beliefs and depress the ability to consider counternarratives.[34] Even more fundamentally, media content types appeal to partisans differently.[35] Putting causality aside, the links between the political moment and the media moment are strong and intertwined.

In sum, journalism in the present media culture should be understood as not just about new ways of repackaging old forms of content, but about new means of experiencing news, with new actors standing between content creation and consumption. News audiences can certainly be active, whether in small ways like appending comments to the end of news stories or sharing articles on social media,[36] or in more visible ways as citizen journalists.[37] But news consumption is also shaped by technological actors like algorithms, infrastructural affordances and constraints, the rise of social media platforms, and cultural shifts about what it means to be a news consumer. All of this suggests a time of transition that unsettles entrenched journalistic and political processes, as will be evident throughout this book.

Fragmenting Attention, Disappearing Dollars

Of all the innovations of nineteenth-century US newspapers, perhaps most understated was the shift from high-priced subscriptions to cheap prices offset by robust advertising revenue. Scholars of journalism rarely venture into the history of advertising, but this funding model coupled with improvements in printing technology helped transform newspapers from elite goods to popular, inexpensive reading materials. Fights for newspaper circulation doubled as competition to lure advertisers happy to pay for growing numbers of readers. Later, the decline of newspaper competition resulted in a news landscape of only one newspaper in all but the very largest urban areas. These surviving newspapers were able to exact high prices from advertisers, and the newspapers served as the preeminent mass-produced informational hub. Local television news took attention away from newspapers, which, while resulting in the decline of evening newspapers, left morning newspapers a healthy spot in the news diet.[38] In short, the twentieth century proved to be the heyday of advertising-supported journalism, particularly at the local level. Newspapers and magazines charged for circulation, but, on average, this was only a small portion of where the money came from. Broadcasting was all advertising-supported, with even public broadcasters collected underwriting fees indiscernible from advertising.[39] This system worked within the confines of mass communication, when a smaller number of outlets could amass large audiences. Newspapers were especially profitable, with their high levels of reach within set geographical areas. Local advertisers had no real alternative but to pay newspapers to advertise their goods and services. At the close of the century, in the year 2000, the newspaper industry earned $4.62 in advertising for every dollar it earned from circulation.[40] Advertising kept circulation costs lower, brought in enormous profits for newspapers, and stifled future innovation.

Digital media quickly sliced into the news industry's advertising advantage. This happened in direct ways. For example, the classified advertising segment, which accounted for $20 billion in 2000,[41] evaporated as these ads moved online, often to free spaces like Craigslist or specifically targeted spaces like Monster.com. But more indirectly, the proliferation of online pages meant more spaces for advertisers. When the shift from a scarcity of venues for advertising gave way to an abundance of sites, the cost of placing an advertisement plummeted. Advertisers trying to reach consumers no longer needed newspapers, disrupting a stream of money that had allowed newspapers to be both civically minded and profitable. On the consumption side, the newspaper as a compendium of information—movie times, weather forecasts, stock market prices, sports scores, and so on—became far less important thanks to the ease and speed with which such information could be found online. The all-things-to-all-people newspaper bundle simply wasn't designed for a digital environment of hyperspecialization.

Shifts in advertising are not only about where advertising dollars are going, but how advertising works. Programmatic advertising allows advertisers to target potential customers by responding to users' online behavior and demographics. Data become more important for connecting advertisers and potential customers. So, while newspapers have flagged in their ability to attract advertisers, Google and Facebook as relatively new entrants to the media landscape have come to eat up a large portion of the overall advertising revenue pie, including 77% of local digital advertising—leaving very little left for newspapers to vie for.[42] These patterns are only accelerating as mobile devices become the dominant platforms for accessing digital content.

The news industry is a tale of contrasts. For example, the *New York Times* has managed declines in print circulation by attracting nearly 7 million paying digital subscribers, and it now earns more money from digital ads than print ones. As a result, in 2019, the *Times* employed more than sixteen hundred journalists, the highest number ever for its newsroom.[43] In cable news, Fox News, CNN, and MSNBC have seen their revenues more than double between 2008 and 2018, to a combined $5.3 billion.[44] One measure of the health of national news is that 22% of journalists live in Washington, DC, New York City, or Los Angeles.[45] Yet local journalism has suffered, reaching what a PEN America report calls "a state of crisis."[46] Even as newspapers have invested heavily in their digital presence and the economy has rebounded from the Great Recession, the newspaper industry as a whole has seen its revenue shrink by an average 4.3% each year between 2014 and 2019.[47] Such shrinking is unsustainable, and raises real concerns about where local news will come from in the future. If the advertising model is broken, some new forms will have to emerge, perhaps involving philanthropy, membership models, or public funding.[48] Yet thus far the number of people paying for digital news—both in the United States and in other countries—has been low, and the tendency to pay for more than one news service is even more rare.[49]

These trends, although well known within the news industry, have been less recognized by the public.[50] Perhaps this is because of the perception that we are awash in media. On television, CNN, MSNBC, and Fox News provide a steady diet of content, shifting between factual reporting and opinion programming throughout the day. In becoming national news outlets, the *Wall Street Journal, New York Times,* and more recently the *Washington Post* have amassed huge subscription-paying digital audiences to augment their print products. In these ways, the traditional press is still powerful. It still draws wide swaths of the public's attention. Its decisions about what to cover and how to cover it still shape understandings of social reality. Digital news spreads into many online spaces, including on social media platforms, as news outlets aggressively seek to find audiences where they are—a far cry from the audience seeking out the newspaper or tuning into a broadcast. Scrums of reporters still appear on the White House lawn to shout questions at the president. All of this gives an appearance of robustness that masks deeper losses, particularly at the local level, that have plunged much of journalism into serious financial danger.

Public Perceptions of the Press

The economic turmoil of the news industry is accompanied by disturbing divisions in how the public perceives the credibility of the press. Journalists cannot compel audiences to consume and accept the news they put out. They require some degree of acceptance that what they report is factual. This is easier to achieve for certain types of stories—that fire most certainly did happen or this sports game clearly did occur—and more difficult for complex stories involving disagreement or denouncements. As a result, journalists find that their reporting does not always have the effect that they think it will, in part because public opinion of journalists is shifting in increasingly partisan ways that work against journalism's traditional reporting norms.[51] This is made more complicated given that what "journalism" means is open to different interpretations rather than some fixed, agreed-upon definition.

The story of public perceptions of the press is one of a long, slow decline. Since the 1970s, Gallup has asked people about their "trust and confidence" in journalists to "fully, accurately, and fairly" report the news. The percentage of respondents saying that they have a "great deal" or a "fair amount" of trust and confidence has steadily eroded over time, reaching its nadir in early September 2016. Less than two months before a hotly contested presidential election, only 32% showed any significant confidence in the news, with 68% expressing little or no confidence.[52] This historically low score for the press suggests widespread frustration with reporting during the closing months of the campaign, perhaps uniting Trump supporters unhappy with what they saw as widespread bias against Trump with Clinton supporters unhappy with what they experienced as journalists failing to hold Trump accountable while unduly amplifying unfounded suggestions of Clinton's malfeasance. By September 2019, the percentage of respondents expressing at least some confidence inched back up to 41%, a level that has been fairly consistent across the 2010s.

It is unlikely that trust and confidence in the press will rebound wholesale in any sustainable way. What is more difficult is divining what these surveys indicate. Certainly, declining positive views of journalists are by no means novel.[53] They tend to track with a general decline in trust of major institutions occurring since the Vietnam War and the Watergate scandal. A general cultural shift toward openness, while providing new tools for the press, pushed the public toward skepticism, if not cynicism.[54] For the news media, this is partly self-inflicted, as a more cynical approach to political reporting has ensnared journalists as well.[55] Ultimately, expressing trust in institutions has become more uncommon, and respondents contacted by polling organizations to gather their opinion might feel obliged to show some incredulity as a way of demonstrating their independence.[56]

The shift toward skepticism toward the press is not, by itself, negative. We expect powerful public institutions to be held accountable, and the press is not exempt from this demand for scrutiny. Just as journalists take it as a normative duty to shed light on the powerful, so too should media criticism examine journalism. As recounted in the introductory chapter, much of journalism research targets the news for its failings to live up to the aspirations that journalists set for their work. Such scrutiny is commensurate with a belief that the news remains powerful in its ability to define social reality. Criticism and skepticism are warranted.

The greater concern is not the presence of criticism but its increasingly partisan divide. Perhaps such partisan differences should not be surprising, given the summary of polarization we have given, but the differences are stark. A Pew Research Center survey asked people about journalists' efficacy in fulfilling their watchdog function—a role central to the mission of journalism—by inquiring if they believed that journalists "keep political leaders from doing things that shouldn't be done."[57] As Figure 1.1 shows, in the past, self-identified Democrats and Republicans both tended to answer this question affirmatively, with supporters of the party out of power usually seeing more value in the news media. In 2016, during the presidential election between Trump and Clinton, both Democrats and Republicans assessed the watchdog value of the press equally, with Republicans very slightly agreeing with Pew's watchdog statement by a margin of 77% to 74% (notably at a time when they were out of power in the executive branch). A year later, with President Trump regularly lambasting the press and Republicans in control of all three branches of government, a forty-seven-point partisan gap formed, with Democrats overwhelmingly supporting the watchdog role (89%) while fewer than half of Republicans (42%) showed support. Democrats' support for the watchdog role rose by 15%, while Republicans abandoned it by a stunning 35% year-over-year. Overall assessments of journalists' watchdog role declined in 2018, but the partisan gap between Democrats (82%) and Republicans (38%) remained at forty-four percentage points.

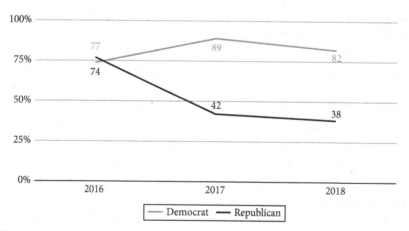

Figure 1.1 Percent Saying News Media "Keep political leaders from doing things that shouldn't be done," by Party Identification.

This partisan divide also shows up in Gallup's surveys of trust in news. While the percentage of Democrats expressing trust in the news has long remained higher than that of Republicans, this gap began to widen after 2016. By 2020, 73% of Democrats expressed either a "great deal" or a "fair amount" of trust in the news media, compared to only 10% of Republicans—a sixty-three-point partisan gap.[58] This was the fourth year in a row that the Gallup survey showed a widening divide.

It's not clear exactly what this partisan division in attitudes toward journalism means in the long run, but in the near term it confirms that the heated, partisan polarization of the present political moment has swept up news organizations. The persistence of this gap in 2020 suggests that these findings are more than a post-election fluke. Journalistic work, even with its normative orientation toward objectivity and political detachment, is seen by large parts of the population as a partisan activity imbricated in the partisan contest to control governing. The asymmetrical perceptions of Democrats and Republicans provide further evidence that this divide is part of the trend discussed later, in which politics has become more about identity than policy preferences. Attitudes toward the press are part of the same process. As we will see in the next two chapters, Trump activates these anti-press sentiments when he criticizes reporting in ways that strike at the foundations of journalistic legitimacy.

Scholars of journalism and political communication have to ask what happens if and when assessments of the news media become predictably partisan—if they haven't already. The Gallup poll referenced earlier found that 42% of respondents found the national news media to be too liberal.[59] While it is unclear who these respondents are, the fact that more than four in ten identify the news as having a left bias points to the success of years of accusations of liberal media bias repeated regularly in conservative media outlets such as Fox News and echoed by Republican politicians.[60] It has become so pervasive and normalized that it primes news audiences to expect press coverage to be one-sided.[61] Scholars studying the hostile media effect find that this priming becomes particularly salient as one's beliefs deepen.[62] Perhaps with Democrats retaking federal power in 2021, this assessment will flip back in accordance with historical patterns. Or it might be the new normal: a substantial portion of the public is locked in to believing that journalists are hopelessly biased—a view that echoes Trump's persistent accusations.

Journalists under Attack

As the news industry has stumbled through the opening decades of the twenty-first century, the assertion that journalism is "under attack" has been used metaphorically to describe new forms of competition and criticism. But there is a literal side too to this language that deserves to be addressed. A final troublesome aspect of the contemporary media culture concerns the growing threats that journalists face in the course of their work. Even in supposedly "safe" places of the developed world that have historically prized press freedom, such as the United States, journalists find themselves under siege as never before—whether facing harassment from agitated crowds, being targeted by police, or, in the most common form, receiving voluminous messages of hate from angry audiences and online trolls. "A constant drum of verbal attacks," Silvio Waisbord notes, "is the new normal in newsrooms around the world."[63]

The fear is that the animosity and hostility regularly directed at the news media by Trump and others will turn more severe. For example, reporters covering the unrest following the police murder of George Floyd in Minneapolis in May 2020 were targeted by authorities through arrests and violence—with some journalists blinded as police took apparently deliberate headshots with rubber bullets to chase away reporters and photographers along with the protestors.[64] Physical violence has up to now been relatively rare in the United States, but many journalists report facing constant threats to their safety. At Trump rallies, supporters were spotted wearing a shirt that advocated lynching journalists, with the words: "Rope. Tree. Journalist. Some assembly required." The shirt was even sold through the website of Walmart, before outcry caused the retail giant to cease its sales.[65]

Threats to journalists in the United States have become so common that, in April 2019, the international press freedom group Reporters Without Borders downgraded the status of American journalists to "problematic," adding: "Never before have US journalists been subjected to so many death threats."[66] This type of targeting cannot be divorced from verbal assaults by Trump that go as far as labeling the news media as the enemy. These are more than empty threats. On June 28, 2018, a man upset with *The Capital* newspaper in Annapolis, Maryland, for printing a negative story about him years earlier walked into the newspaper's offices and shot and killed four journalists and a sales assistant.

Even while such violence against journalists remains more common in other parts of the world,[67] the trend lines in the United States and other developed democracies are concerning.[68] They point to worse things to come as antipathy toward journalists grows apace, suggesting that today's verbal harassments are tomorrow's physical confrontations, as "harassment online can represent the leading edge of abuse that may become more vicious and pernicious offline."[69] Women journalists, especially, appear to face a larger share of the worst forms of abuse. A survey by the Committee to Protect Journalists that polled female and gender non-conforming journalists in the United States and Canada found that 85% of respondents felt that journalism had become less safe. More than 70% had experienced threats to their safety at some point.[70] The International Women's Media Foundation found similar results, with more than half of the women journalists surveyed experiencing threats in the previous year.[71] Other studies have documented what these deteriorating safety conditions mean both for the physical safety of women journalists and for their mental and emotional health—not to mention their likelihood of sticking it out in a profession that feels increasingly hostile to their involvement in it.[72] Female journalists, particularly those in broadcast television, often face a greater share of harassment (e.g., in-person disruptions, abusive treatment, unwanted sexual advances, and threats to safety) than their male colleagues. But because of socialized gender roles and cultural expectations, they also often feel obligated to perform a significant degree of "emotional labor"—that is, the work of managing other people's emotions to keep them happy, much like flight attendants and other service workers do—as they attempt to deal with hostile publics even while simultaneously trying to maintain their composure and ward off future assaults.[73]

Online harassment, in particular, has become a disturbingly regular part of the job for many journalists. Waisbord argues that such harassment—often motivated by populism of the kind described later and directed primarily against women, journalists of color, and LGBTQ journalists—is more than trolling for the fun of it, and it's not press criticism in any legitimate sense. Rather, such online abuse is a "political struggle to control speech." It's a form of mob censorship that is chillingly coordinated in its efforts to silence journalists in ways that are distinct from censorship campaigns by the state or markets, raising complicated questions about where democratic speech rights end and hate speech begins.[74] Even as the average journalist—working at a smaller, locally oriented news organization, mostly under the radar—may not face voluminous online abuse, it's nevertheless apparent that encounters with harassment are still common enough that they appear to have a meaningful and deleterious impact on how journalists think about and act toward their audiences.[75]

It's true that journalists have always been unwelcome by many who wish to avoid the publicity that news brings or who have sought to communicate independently of the press. In many cases, such animus toward journalists is understandable. But the ratcheting up of threats to safety impinges on journalists' basic ability to be able to report the news. It is a symptom of a deeper antagonism, perhaps most flagrantly discernable when Trump attacks journalists as the enemy of the people (discussed in Chapter 3).

Journalistic Scrutiny

The preceding sections point to the ample struggles that journalists face. Media fragmentation, political polarization, economic anxiety, and threats of violence all define the news media in the Trump era. It is a time of contrasts for the press. Journalists often turn out very good journalism through news stories that expose wrongdoing and lead to change. Although this is a book about journalism, the chapters that follow barely scratch the surface of the legions of news stories looking into all aspects of the Trump administration. Digital media tools allow for these stories to spread widely and rapidly. But it is also a time of reflection in which journalists have to address their faults and question their strategies for reporting in an era when facts are contested and journalists can no longer count on support from large swaths of the public. Perhaps the picture painted here overly portrays journalists as victims of a changing world. We end this section by looking more critically at journalism to better understand how the populist politics described in what follows reflect failures of the news industry.

The more critical story of journalism we wish to tell examines a turning away from news from two different directions. Both started well before Trump came on the political scene, both are affected by shrinking local newsrooms and widespread economic uncertainty, and both call out journalists for what they view as harmful or absent news representations. The first connects back to the conservative critique of news discussed earlier in this chapter. In rural America, resentment toward political institutions and urban places has long been simmering. In her study of Wisconsin, Kathy Cramer shows how a keen sense of disappointment—in how life had turned out, in perceptions that "other" groups "got more," in the lack of appreciation and interest shown by public officials—has come to permeate the political identity of people in rural places.[76] When people perceive their public and social institutions to be failing them, they lose the generalized trust that had existed over time. This includes viewing journalists·as one more distant elite. As mainstream journalism came to seem remote, conservative media machines such as Fox News catered to emotions of fear and anger and promoted a populist viewpoint. Reece Peck describes this "populism as narrative" as working for the regular people, ("the folks," "the real Americans") who felt ignored and left behind economically and culturally.[77] This narrative, promulgated by Fox News and others, weaved notions of freedom from tyranny in the way it situated regular folks as standing against the liberal elites, drawing on personal, first-person accounts that uplifted the working class through a shared sense of community and identity. This only fed distrust of the traditional press, which has been accused of pandering to political elites, flirting with advertisers, and bending toward sensationalism. Journalists, in this view, were dismissive or absent, and promoted a value system that seemed to exclude rural Americans. Instead, people sought the feeling of justification and the focus on individuality that Fox and others offered.[78]

The second group of skeptics comprises Black and Brown communities that have long distrusted journalists. Even as journalists defend their reporting of minority populations, many in these communities view journalists as perpetuating racism through their stereotypes, in-built assumptions, and patterns of reporting that marginalize non-white voices.[79] Black and Brown citizens register their discontent as they disengage from journalism. As a Black Facebook poster wrote on the site, "They talk nice, and sometimes they do good. But their interests are not your interests. The media is rarely your friend."[80] This is not a personal grievance but a structural one: Journalists, in their adherence to norms of professionalism that often give credence to elite sources, tend to prop up systems that are often harmful for disempowered groups. Yet journalists have cultural power in how they represent these groups to a wider public—a condition that makes many in marginalized communities wary of reporters, wishing for something better.[81]

As journalists hew to a center that they create,[82] many in society feel marginalized, excluded, stereotyped, and stigmatized by the news accounts that emerge. When journalists fall back on professionalized norms of distance and objectivity, privilege powerful elites in their coverage, and organize news according to institutional beats, they have few mechanisms for ameliorating this situation. Journalists may defend themselves by arguing that they cannot cover all the people all the time, particularly with increasingly scarce resources. But a defensiveness within journalism obscures the degree to which so many in society have found disfavor in the news they see, leading them to look elsewhere for information.

Within newsrooms, a lack of diversity has been a perpetual issue. As journalism professionalized in the early twentieth century, it was largely an occupation for white males, and increasingly one dominated by educated, middle-class, white males writing for a white audience. This adherence to white values can delegitimize or ignore other voices. And even though journalism doesn't generally pay well, its relatively high cultural status attracts people of higher-income or educated backgrounds. This includes those who can afford to work a few no-pay or low-pay internships when climbing the career ladder. Today the profession in the United States remains mostly homogenous. Even as the minority population of the United States has reached 40%, only 17% of staffers at newspaper and online news outlets are non-white.[83] These numbers ebb and flow over time, but the consistent result is that US journalists, particularly on race and ethnicity, generally do not reflect the demographics of communities they cover.[84] The issue extends to journalism education, which also has been marked by whiteness.[85] This leads to difficulty recruiting Black and Brown students to journalism schools. A 2015 study showed that "minorities made up 21.4 percent of graduates with degrees in journalism or communications between 2004 and 2014, but less than half of minority graduates found full-time jobs, while two-thirds of white graduates did."[86] For minority journalists who do get newsroom journalism jobs, many find themselves to be the only person of color on staff— an isolating and complicated experience. As *Atlantic* editor Gillian B. White noted, the lack of minority journalists "can lead to news coverage that is incomplete, tone-deaf, or biased. Those possibilities are especially troubling as the country's complex and often ugly relationships among people of different races, cultures, ethnicities, and religions are pushed to the forefront of the American conscience."[87] The issue of diversity in newsrooms is not merely about who works at a news organization, but more broadly about how the makeup of journalists as a group affects which news stories get told as well as how they get told.

As journalists promote a normative vision of their work as democratically and culturally important, they encounter many people who scoff at this narrative out of anger for how they are represented or because they are being left out of the image of society perpetuated in news stories. This is paired with an expanding media culture in which news seems less universalizing, and less like a monolithic institution with some kind of pervasive and ubiquitous authority. Trust then becomes siloed as well, scattered among a crowd of producers with varying agendas and motivations. Given the external economic and technological factors that have hampered the news industry, journalists have been slow to recognize the extent to which many of the problems they face are of their own making. The Trump years spurred a conversation about what these failures are and, as we see at the end of this book, what futures are possible.

The preceding pages have laid bare journalism's struggles in confronting both familiar issues about their representational practices and unfamiliar ones regarding a shifting media culture that has left them increasingly decentered amid a host of other mediated voices and platforms. These struggles pop up throughout this book as journalists wrestle with what the future of journalism should be. They also set the stage for considering complementary shifts in the political environment, particularly with regard to the rise of right-wing populism. This means delving into the political currents that elevated Trump to the White House.

Charismatic Paranoia: Populist Politics in the Time of Trump

When Trump announced a US military withdrawal from northern Syria in October 2019, he immediately received bipartisan condemnation. Trump's actions paved the way for an imminent attack by Turkey on Kurdish forces that had been loyal to the US military effort since the start of the Iraq War— an outcome that many saw as a betrayal. Trump took to Twitter to defend his actions, not by mounting a defense on strategic grounds, but by pointing to his own sagacity. He sought to reassure his critics that he would not let Turkey overrun the Kurds:

> As I have stated strongly before, and just to reiterate, if Turkey does anything that I, in my great and unmatched wisdom, consider to be off limits, I will totally destroy and obliterate the Economy of Turkey (I've done before!).[88]

The phrase "great and unmatched wisdom" became a target of ridicule, but its use here to mitigate criticism, and the familiarity of such boastfulness,[89] deserves more scrutiny with regard to how Trump constructed the grounds on which he governed. Such regularly espoused egotistic statements supported his decision-making in a way that prized individualistic characteristics over procedural or institutional qualities. It stressed Trump's agency above all else.

What is clear is that Trump absorbs attention—whether in the form of the adoration of his supporters or the scorn of his detractors. His Twitter feed stirred up fresh controversy regularly, shaping what the news coverage would be.[90] He campaigned and governed off his personality and presence, dispensing with the carefully crafted public utterances common from politicians sensitive to the always-watching cameras and a commentariat ready to seize on the whiff of a gaffe. For Trump, campaigning and governing are really the same thing. It's always about him: his battle to control the narrative, his appetite for verbal brawls, his quest for approval, his constant hawking of his personal brand. Trump's penchant for naming everything after him, his insistence on being a public face, and even his fabricating a fake *Time* magazine cover with his picture on it, speak to his megalomania.[91]

One way of thinking about what Trump sought to accomplish with such language is to turn to what Max Weber called "charismatic authority." His tripartite model draws a distinction among traditional authority, which refers to legitimacy gained by dint of a continuity of belonging; rational-legal authority, or the suprahuman legitimacy of the bureaucratic system; and charismatic authority, or legitimacy through personality. Weber defines the latter as an individual "set apart from ordinary men [*sic*] and treated as endowed with supernatural, superhuman, or at least specifically exceptional powers or qualities."[92] Such claims of exceptionality do not matter unless they are recognized by a significant number of people. That is, charismatic authority is not an isolated attribute; rather, it is the product of a particular kind of relationship that exists within a social system. Weber wrote about ideal types, such that he does not address a situation like Trump's, where a high percentage of the population dismisses his charismatic authority. Yet even as Trump's detractors poked fun, his ability to have been elected and to have maintained power as president despite copious examples of controversy, mismanagement, and absurdity indicates accordance from some significant portion of the electorate.

Weber attributes the power of charismatic authority in part to a longing for security among supporters of a particular leader.[93] This need to feel secure is a basic need that persists across civilizations. It points to a deep-seated desire to bring some sort of order and sense to the world. The operation of charismatic authority, then, is not merely self-aggrandizement on the part of the leader, but a form of public service based on the promise of the restoration of order. Trump's slogan of "Make America Great Again" espouses an emotional goal that is at once rooted in the past and intent on forming the future. Its connection to charisma is the assumption—spoken or not—that only Trump, with his unique talents, can accomplish this.

Unlike the timelessness of traditional authority or the impersonality of rational-legal authority, Weber's coupling of charismatic authority to the individual limits this authority to their timespan. Charismatic leaders depend on their relationship with their followers, but always under the threat that this charisma effect will dissipate. Charismatic authority always exists in the present, reproducing leaders' authority through their interactions. This is applicable to Trump in his constant use of social media and political rallies as public spectacles intended to rile up supporters. But it also distracts from larger shifts discussed in this chapter.

Trump's particular performance of charismatic authority demands a more specific categorization than Weber's idealized scheme accommodates. To capture the power of Trump's message requires positioning his rhetorical style as that of the demagogue. As argued in the introductory chapter, Trump mixes fear-mongering with a tribalist conception of community. In this way, the exercise of charismatic authority rests not only on the elevation of the speaker, but the dismissal of everything outside the orbit of the speaker. The demagogue does not press a rational case, but an emotional and reactive one. The point is not to equate emotional appeals with demagoguery,[94] but to critique a particular appeal to emotions built on presenting outsiders as dangerous invaders and the root of social ills. This appeal is presented as an alternative moral system whose adherents feel not only justified in following, but proud and righteous to do so. Political scientist Sigmund Neumann, who was driven out of Germany with the rise of the Nazi Party, reflected on the rise of political demagogues in 1938: "The most powerful modern demagogues are sincere and fanatic believers in their mission as 'saviors' of their people. They are not tortured by skepticism or self-doubt. This very defect in self-valuation makes them the heroes of the masses who are harassed by uncertainty."[95] Neumann taps into a combination of forces, including the rise of mass politics, mass communication, and the unsettledness of rapid social change. Such assessments throw into question the viability of liberal democratic governance in the face of susceptibility to such divisiveness from political demagogues.

Right-Wing Populism in the United States

By taking a broader perspective, we can place Trump alongside other American demagogues who have espoused populist politics. Many examples of American populists exist, from William Jennings Bryan to Huey Long to Ben Tillman.[96] In his study of the long history of American populism, Michael Kazin defines populism as "a language whose speakers conceive of ordinary people as a noble assemblage not bounded narrowly by class, view their elite opponents as self-serving and undemocratic, and seek to mobilize the former against the latter."[97] Intentionally neutral, this definition is capacious enough to admit a long progressive march toward the expansion of democracy to more and more of the populace. It is tinged with a mistrust of elites and a celebration of the ordinary citizen deeply woven into an egalitarian vision of the United States. Kazin notes that, by the 1940s, populism shifted its political provenance to take on a conservative bent of shrinking rather than expansion, and looking backward rather than forward.[98]

One emblematic example of the rise of an exclusionist populism is Father Charles Coughlin, a Roman Catholic priest who shaped US politics in the 1930s through a radio audience measuring millions of listeners. Much as Trump benefited from the economic uncertainty following the Great Recession and years-long declines in manufacturing, Father Coughlin took advantage of the tumult of the Great Depression. Much as Trump availed himself with the new medium of Twitter, Coughlin used the new medium of radio. As Marshall Fishweek argues: "The Crux of Coughlin's appeal . . . was not love but hatred. He sensed, and took advantage of[,] the neurotic anxiety all around him. He provided a conflict in which angry members of his audience could know and confront their real enemies."[99] Coughlin's enemies were a mix of communists and socialists as well as establishment politicians and businesspersons, and he positioned himself as speaking to everyday Americans confused by a system that seemed wholly outside of their control. He preached isolationism and dismissed elites as globalists—a stance that eventually tipped over into anti-Semitic attacks and support for fascist governments in Europe. When Coughlin responded to the Kristallnacht attacks in Germany by defending the Nazi regime for standing up against the Jewish population, this hardening of Coughlin's position led to his eventual condemnation.[100] The point is not to draw too fine a connection between Coughlin and Trump; this would erase how each adapted to his time and place. Rather, invoking Coughlin as a precedent—and only one example out of many—demonstrates that there are particular moments in which populists gain power by feeding off anxiety and uncertainty. From the Know-Nothing Party[101] through Coughlin and on to Trump, nativist-themed populism is a familiar sight within US politics, but one whose power ebbs and flows as conditions change. Trump's political rhetoric as candidate and as president places him in this lineage.

The politics of populism has emerged to emphasize not collectivism but division. How this division manifests itself is the foremost question for confronting the damage wrought by such ideologies. Cas Mudde defines populism as "an ideology that considers society to be ultimately separated into two homogeneous and antagonistic groups, 'the pure people' versus 'the corrupt elite,' and which argues that politics should be an expression of the *volonté générale* (general will) of the people."[102] His emphasis on the sense of righteousness held by the pure people underscores the moralistic elements of populism. Any populist call to exclude particular groups is defended on the grounds that this exclusion is morally justified. Those left out deserve it. What's difficult is that, at its origin, populism was meant to increase political participation among non-elites, but in latter instantiations populist movements have become associated with xenophobic attitudes targeting, in particular, non-native or non-white populations.[103] This evolution raises hard questions about proper political discourse and the role of distrust in liberal democracies.[104]

The familiarity of Trump's demagoguery can be further historicized by recalling Richard Hofstadter's classic 1964 essay, "The Paranoid Style in American Politics." Written in the shadow of Cold War fears and the candidacy of conservative Republican Barry Goldwater, Hofstadter grasps for a broader perspective to explain the burgeoning tumult of the 1960s. From a historian's perspective, he explains that those who support demagogues do so from a standpoint of open suspicion:

America has been largely taken away from them and their kind, though they are determined to try to repossess it and to prevent the final destructive act of subversion. The old American virtues have already been eaten away by cosmopolitans and intellectuals; the old competitive capitalism has been gradually undermined by socialistic and communistic schemers; the old national security and independence have been destroyed by treasonous plots. . . . [T]he modern radical right finds conspiracy to be betrayal from on high.[105]

Hofstadter connects populism with an essential struggle over the heart of democratic governance. Democracy's appeal to reason as a means of making wise choices, as we explore next, runs up against political reactionaries who find gain in stoking division. Fractionism is a powerful force.

Populist rhetoric built on an exclusionary framework of us versus them has always had an ugly history. It builds community and comity through othering and animus. Yet such ugly populist rhetoric shrouds itself in ideas that, when stripped of their context, sound benign—such as following the rule of law or upholding tradition. This point was made salient during the Unite the Right rally in Charlottesville, Virginia, in August 2017. Despite the banal name, the event was a white nationalist spectacle of torch-bearing marchers chanting racist and anti-Semitic slurs. The rally ended in violence capped off by a white nationalist ramming a car and killing a counter-protester. During a press conference following the aftermath, Trump waffled on denouncing the white supremacists and instead proclaimed there to be "very fine people on both sides." He also spread the fault around: "I think there is blame on both sides."[106] Trump was widely condemned for these statements as protecting white supremacy, either out of his personal feelings (Trump has been a leading "birther," with his public suggestions that President Barack Obama was born in Africa rather than Hawaii), or out of his allegiance to a significant bloc of white voters. It was a moment that made clear what populism looks like when it tips over into pronounced malice. But it is also a reminder that while Trump fanned the flames of hatred and benefited as a candidate, these forces have long been in place in American culture.

A Polarizing President for Polarizing Times

Why does Trump's demagoguery function so well—or well enough to have gotten him elected—in this present moment? The tools of the demagogue do not alone determine their effectiveness. Instead, understanding Trump requires looking at a political moment in which heightened partisanship is connected to increased polarization across the electorate. Although partisanship is not a new condition, the election of Trump has brought more attention to the rise of affective polarization. In contrast to issue-oriented polarization, affective polarization denotes a dislike for those in the other party and a preference for those within one's preferred party.[107] It is affective because it is about emotional response and social identity rather than just an ideological preference for this or that policy. While there are debates about how pervasive affective polarization is, the trend has clearly been toward identity-based sorting in politics. As Lilliana Mason finds, cross-cutting identities, in which people's various contradictory positions put a damper on extreme partisanship, have waned.[108] Politics and identity, it turns out, have become closely intertwined.

The connections between social identity and political identity emerge as well in examinations of people's experiences. Kathy Cramer's study of rural Wisconsin voters reveals that those who would seem to benefit from certain political policies prized their social identity above all else.[109] Rural voters felt neglected by what they felt was a distant ruling elite. This sense of exclusion became a central part of Trump's campaign through the activation of fear. In particular, John Sides, Michael Tesler, and Lynn Vavreck argue that Trump's unlikely ascension among more traditional Republican candidates owed a lot to his ability to tap into racial anxieties among white voters. They found that those voters with general economic anxiety did not necessarily favor Trump, but those concerned with losing jobs to minorities did favor Trump. This prejudice existed before Trump, but he "leveraged it to his advantage."[110] This resulted in what the authors call "racialized economics," or "the belief that undeserving groups are getting ahead while your group is left behind." In a recurring theme, non-whites were cast as the "undeserving group."[111] This language fits well with the populist literature discussed earlier, but its success relied on the growth of affective polarization that fosters distrust of those on the other political side. It means that Trump's success has been more deeply personal and identity-based than it has been about policy choices.

The escalation of polarization to the level of one's social identity raises concerns about how to find common ground when dislike of the out-group becomes deeply felt and attached to individual morals. Mason calls it "the American identity crisis" because it leads not to mere disagreement, but to feelings of intolerance.[112] Similarly, Shanto Iyengar and colleagues warn what happens when partisan social identity leads to a prioritization of one's beliefs over communal-mindedness: "Partisanship appears to now compromise the norms and standards we apply to our elected representatives, and even leads partisans to call into question the legitimacy of election results, both of which threaten the very foundations of representative democracy."[113] This ominous warning suggests that polarized politics are not so much disagreements over policy as they are a moral chasm separating different views about the fundamental rules of the game.

Populism around the World

This chapter has so far focused on the US experience to contextualize Trump's populist tendencies, but we gain much by looking abroad as well. Trump's political rise is paralleled by other leaders who have assembled populist coalitions by challenging establishment elites and journalists and by concocting enemies out of the unfamiliar. The Tony Blair Institute for Global Change, a London-based nonprofit organization, identifies forty-six instances of populist candidates or parties gaining power in thirty-three democratic nations between 1990 and 2018.[114] This is a global phenomenon, visible in such prominent populists as Jair Bolsonaro in Brazil, Viktor Orbán in Hungary, and Rodrigo Duterte in the Philippines. Corralling right-wing populists into a single category unduly wipes away nuances, but the usefulness of looking broadly at these trends is to defuse claims of American exceptionalism. The Blair Institute report identifies two commonalities across time and place: a belief that a nation's core is under threat from outsiders and that this core has a right to assert its will politically. Added to this is an emphasis on direct communication; as the report's authors put it, "Populism emphasises a direct connection with its supporters, unmediated by political parties, civil-society groups or the media."[115] This makes it all the more important to attend to the language choices and symbols that are employed to advance populist projects and the media channels used to spread them.

Demagoguery finds fertile soil in the rise of right-wing populist movements sprouting up around the world. The European experience provides lessons for examining Trump's success in the United States. In his analysis of the rise of right-wing populist parties in Europe since the 1970s—including the National Front in France, Lega Nord in Italy, and the Danish People's Party—Hans-Georg Betz characterized these parties as not rejecting democracy, but instead as questioning the ethic of social equality

at the heart of liberal postwar European politics. The result has been political movements that capitalize on the feelings of alienation common to
wide swaths of the populace. Populist parties turned to the "unscrupulous
use and instrumentalization of diffuse public sentiments of anxiety and disenchantment and their appeal to the common man [sic] and his allegedly
superior common sense."[116] Parliamentary systems created spaces for these
parties to gain some political power among centrist parties that are argued to
be ignoring the wider public.[117] Chantal Mouffe makes a similar argument
when she attributes European populism to a dominant political consensus
with narrow thinking that left space for populist parties to accumulate authority as the voice of non-elites. Mouffe writes, "We should realise that, to
a great extent, the success of right-wing populist parties comes from the fact
that they provide people with some force of hope, with the belief that things
could be better."[118] Such hope, Mouffe goes on to note, is always damned
by the exclusionary vision of populist politics. But what's more troubling
to Mouffe is that politics becomes a matter of moral outrage rather than a
sphere of respectful debate. When politics becomes a competition between
good and evil, there is little space for compromise.

Furthermore, these populist politicians all over the world have similar
communication strategies that, one, offer news outlets a flamboyant spectacle that is irresistible to cover and, two, tap into widespread media criticism and distrust in order to speak directly to the people, expressing disdain
for the established press corps in the country. Accordingly, the news media
directly help to drive the popularity among certain constituents—which
Gianpietro Mazzoleni in Europe, Khadijah Costley White in the United
States, and Kurt Weyland in Latin America argue amounts to media complicity in the rise of these politicians.[119] Incorporated into these strategies
are consistent and aggressive attacks on the press, which these politicians
strive to control. Ultimately, many scholars have documented how effective
this anti-journalistic rhetoric is across the globe in making mainstream news
media irrelevant at the expense of free and accurate information flow.

A Trumpian Populism

How charismatic authority, demagoguery, and populism come together
starts with acknowledging the conditions supporting Trump's rise. For many
white, middle- and working-class voters, economic anxiety has festered since

the 1980s, when the equitably distributed prosperity of the postwar boom gave way to a stratified growth with those at the top reaping the most.[120] That this shift occurred within the neoliberalist framework espoused by conservative politicians such as Ronald Reagan and Margaret Thatcher gets lost as this anxiety instead becomes wedded to a xenophobic logic whereby white citizens come to see their loses as caused by minority gains.[121] Ronald Inglehart and Pippa Norris connect this development to the decline of class identity as driving electoral decision-making and the rise of voting based on values. Economic insecurity—a root case of populism—gets refracted as a clash of competing values.[122] The populist call to restore power to everyday folk is a redistribution of values rather than of income. This is resonant in Trump's pledges to make America great again as a vaguely economic but assuredly cultural promise.

What this populistic rhetoric looks like can be made clearer by examining two of Trump's most prominent speeches. The first is the speech announcing his entry into the presidential campaign on June 15, 2015. The event was notable for Trump's awkward trip down an escalator on his way to the podium, supported by actors hired for $50 to show up and cheer.[123] The speech was filled with populist and nationalist sentiments that would become the hallmark of his campaign, and instantly drew condemnation for Trump's negative portrayal of Mexican immigrants: "When Mexico sends its people, they're not sending their best. . . . They're sending people that have lots of problems, and they're bringing those problems with us. They're bringing drugs. They're bringing crime. They're rapists."[124] Months later, Trump echoed criticisms of non-European immigrants through his call for "a total and complete shutdown of Muslims entering the United States."[125] These pronouncements employed classic right-wing populist rhetoric, and they were not empty statements. Within weeks of coming into office, Trump issued a travel ban to prevent citizens of seven predominantly Muslim nations from entering the United States while also restricting the flow of refugees into the country.[126] In 2018, after forcing a government shutdown in a bid to procure funding for more barriers along the US-Mexico border, Trump declared a highly controversial state of emergency to reallocate federal funds.[127] In 2019, he suggested that US congresswoman Ilhan Omar, the first female Muslim congressperson and a refugee herself, leave the United States and return to Somali. These words and actions are polarizing rather than consensual and indicate the depth of Trump's appeal to a large swath of the white voting population. Trump also flaunted his wealth and putative business acumen to support his fitness for the presidency, but it is his Make America Great Again populism that most marks his politics.

A second speech that deserves scrutiny is Trump's inauguration address.[128] Unlike the political nature of a campaign announcement, an inaugural address is a particular moment of presidential speechcraft aimed at consensus-building. Yet Trump used the milestone event to reiterate the populist themes he espoused throughout his campaign. In positioning himself as an outsider, Trump accosted the political establishment, noting: "Washington flourished—but the people did not share in its wealth. Politicians prospered—but the jobs left, and the factories closed. The establishment protected itself, but not the citizens of our country." Continuing on, Trump tagged his inauguration as "the day the people became the rulers of this nation again. The forgotten men and women of our country will be forgotten no longer." The speech struck a nationalist tone in proclaiming "America first" as a guiding policy and promising protectionism.[129] Trump presented himself as a savior.

The speech offers a distillation of Trump's populism. It feeds off the disenchantment and resentment particularly found among white, working-class voters left behind by urban growth and cosmopolitanism.[130] Trump reached out to communities experiencing population decline and the harsh effects of the opioid epidemic.[131] Populist rhetoric and policies provide a means of firing up and turning out voters, which served Trump to great effect. With regard to rural voters, journalist Al Cross remarked: "I have never seen a candidate who generated the reaction, depth of support, and enthusiasm as Donald Trump."[132] Indeed, Trump's advantage with white voters without a college education was thirty-nine percentage points over Clinton—the biggest split of all available elections going back to 1980.[133] Two years after Election Day, Trump boasted an approval rating among rural voters of more than 60%, even as his overall rating remained consistently in the low forties.[134] His rural support stayed strong, even during his 2020 election loss.[135] Trump tapped a nerve and found a pocket of voters to support him with great fervor. The 2016 and 2020 elections were, of course, more complicated than these matters of identity politics alone, but these forces need to be acknowledged both as stirred up by Trump and as long-standing beliefs awaiting activation.

While Trump's rhetoric positioned him as a populist, whether he governed like one remains a subject of debate. His Tax Cuts and Jobs Act, passed at the end of 2017, has largely benefited wealthy elites, with billionaires enjoying a lower tax rate than working people.[136] Trump also surrounded himself with other elites and was notorious for his time spent at his golf courses during his presidency. Yet Trump also followed up on the nativist pledges of restricting immigration, curtailing refugee resettlement, separating migrant families, reallocating funds to build border walls, and engaging in trade wars. He responded to the coronavirus pandemic by placing blame on China and engaging in nativist discourse. Up until his last days in office, he continued to strike the same populist chords he initially ran on, and his demagogic tendency to situate himself as the lone savior persisted. He may not be a textbook populist (if one could be said to exist), but he still oriented himself in a populist manner, particularly in his attacks on the press, as will be seen in Chapters 2 and 3.

The emphasis on populism as a recurring theme in American politics is useful not only for supplying a historical backdrop, but also as a reminder to avoid playing into the legend of Trump the individual. That path only leads to a decontextualized view that is as mythologizing as it is inaccurate. Moreover, it is dangerous in that it shifts agency to Trump while downplaying the underlying structural shifts in politics and media culture that enabled Trump. Trump cannot and should not be treated merely as a cause that has an effect, but rather understood as an effect stemming from broader causes. Understanding Trump and his relationship to the news media requires placing him within the context of converging forces that marked this particular moment, including the headwinds affecting journalism.

Conclusion: What Trump Means for Journalism

To end this chapter, we need to return to the opening question of just how to position Trump. On the one hand, he clearly possesses agentic power. His executive branch declarations, legislative actions, and judicial appointments directly affected millions of people. His military decisions altered the balance of peace and security around the world, and his ability to rile up supporters with anti-democratic sentiments—as when he refused to concede the 2020 election without any evidence of fraud to support his claims—is felt throughout the culture. But at the same time, Trump has to be seen as a symbol of an array of forces on a global level coalescing to result in a particular moment. Mistakenly granting Trump too much responsibility for his rise to power has many faults: it assumes an ephemerality based around one actor instead of looking at longer time frames. It obscures deeper trends that persist beyond his presidency.

While Trump did not start the political fissures that put him into office, the phenomenon of Trump—and the incredulity many felt when he was elected—unleashed a torrent of attention on the connection between politics, identity, and the polarization of the electorate. This book vacillates between focusing on Trump and taking a deeper dive into the trends that elevated him. We take a long-term perspective by positioning Trump as a way into larger discussions about the state of journalism now and in the future. This moment is both one that has been coming for some time and a rupture, a way of seeing the media culture that now exists.

2

The Trump Campaign

Outsized Coverage from the Press, Outsized Attacks on the Press

A CNN poll conducted at the end of May 2015, weeks before his official campaign announcement, put Donald Trump in eleventh place—just behind former New York governor George Pataki and well behind such party stalwarts as former Florida governor Jeb Bush and Senators Ted Cruz and Marco Rubio.[1] Yet less than two months later Trump would become the Republican frontrunner, a position he would not relinquish for the rest of the primary campaign. How did Trump, an outsider with no record of public service and who was most known as a reality television personality, so quickly rise to prominence and maintain this position against an onslaught of criticism first from Republican rivals and later Democrats?

The rise of Donald Trump has been read through many social lenses—as an assertion of white, working-class voters, as a backlash against Barack Obama's two terms as the first African American president, as a response to global cosmopolitanism and a growing urban-rural divide. As we argue in the previous chapter, all of these explanations connect support for Trump with deep rifts within the US public around such identity issues as race, class, education, region, and gender. In this chapter, we add to this conversation by confronting what the ascension of Trump as a political agent has indicated about our current media culture. We have proposed media culture as a concept that encompasses media institutions and infrastructures, media practices, and the meanings that arise around how these are understood. All three of these elements matter. When Trump emerged as a candidate in the middle of 2015, he did so in a media culture with a greatly expanded number of public voices increasingly involving social media platforms as intermediaries to speak to a fragmented audience. Trump was able to utilize social media to promote his candidacy, as did his supporters. Yet journalistic practices around covering campaigns remained consistent with past elections, largely built around summarizing the actions of candidates and

News After Trump. Matt Carlson, Sue Robinson, and Seth C. Lewis, Oxford University Press. © Oxford University Press 2021. DOI: 10.1093/oso/9780197550342.003.0003

analyzing their performances in a competitive frame. These news practices hearken back to an earlier media culture when journalists retained more communicative control, rendering them ill-suited for the present. Finally, the contemporary media culture is marked by a deep distrust of journalists, albeit one that is increasingly asymmetrical and partisan. Taken together, Trump's approach to journalism in the 2016 campaign demonstrates how a confluence of long-simmering cultural factors coalesced to propel Trump to victory while also marking the symbolic decentralization of journalism in contemporary life.

Trump received outsized media coverage not by charming journalists or forming an outwardly chummy relationship with reporters, but through openly fighting with the press. While all politicians bristle at their media coverage, for Trump bashing the press increasingly became part of the campaign as he progressed from longshot outsider to Republican nominee. Given the centrality of Trump's attacks on the press, this chapter argues that they cannot be dismissed as self-serving, casual retorts or secondary to his other rhetoric, but rather as indispensable to his ability to construct the political coalitions needed to get elected, maintain support, and push through policies. That such attacks on the news media were so pervasive and baked into his rhetoric provides support for our argument that Trump only succeeded when he was able to neutralize journalistic accounts by instilling doubts about journalists. Confronted with news that easily disproved his lies, fact-checked his questionable evidence, investigated his business dealings and personal life, and challenged his fitness for office, Trump engaged in an epistemic contest meant to undermine the news as a whole by situating journalists as elites obsessed with preserving their power rather than serving their audiences.

The argument that we are making does not position journalists as passive victims. We offer no blanket defense of journalists for their coverage decisions. Rather, we aim to show how Trump was able to take advantage of a combination of news norms that reward the unusual and abnormal and a reluctance by reporters to offer their own judgment out of a fear of being branded as biased. Trump's ability to engage in an epistemic contest that so prominently featured press-bashing as a key part of political performance indicates the failure of journalism to learn from its past or to adapt to a media culture changing around it.

The elements explored in this chapter—the angry tweets, the raucous rallies, the attacks on journalists—are all familiar by now. But by looking back at how Trump interacted with the press—both practically and symbolically—as he made his bid for the presidency, we can hope to provide a deeper understanding of what these elements tell us about the status of journalism as an institutionalized way of knowing and how journalists' efforts at producing truthful accounts are being contested on a fundamental level.

Trump's Outsized Coverage

Trump's electoral success can be traced, to no small degree, to his outsized news coverage. After he became an official candidate, Trump quickly absorbed a disproportionate amount of attention from journalists. Initially, Trump benefited from recognition because of his celebrity status. While other candidates enjoyed fame within the political sphere—Jeb Bush's father and brother had both been presidents—Trump's celebrity owed to his long tenure in the public eye, including a recent decade-long run hosting *The Apprentice* on NBC. Trump's fame instantly set him apart from the pack of candidates. Before Trump, Ronald Reagan had previously worked as a successful actor, but he was long out of the entertainment business by the time he ran for president. In contrast, Trump's final appearance on the *Apprentice* was February 16, 2015, only a few months before his campaign announcement. Trump entered a crowded field of candidates with the advantage of name recognition that went well beyond the political sphere, which is an asset when vying for the spotlight against a field of seasoned candidates.

While this household name recognition benefited Trump, he quickly set himself apart through his willingness to ignore the conventions of political gentility. In contrast to scripted, gaffe-averse professional campaigns, Trump's freewheeling style introduced an element of unpredictability into what he might say on any given night. In leveraging his celebrity status and adding in the component of capriciousness, Trump quickly gamed the system, so to speak, of how to become news. The dynamics Trump was able to exploit are not new. A frequent complaint levied at campaign coverage is a pack journalism mentality in which journalists coalesce around certain assumptions and frames for a given candidate.[2] As journalists embedded with campaigns are exposed to the same speeches day after day, pack journalism suggests not just sameness of news content, but a boredom caused by the sameness of the political content they cover. Trump upended convention in his willingness to stray from prepared remarks, grabbing far more attention for his deviations and asides than the repetitive messages forming his platform.[3]

With little initial elite support, fundraising, or campaign infrastructure, Trump benefited from an unorthodox campaign style that kept journalists interested. Thomas Patterson connects Trump's style with journalists' constant need to generate fresh and appealing content: "Journalists are attracted to the new, the unusual, the sensational—the type of story material that will catch and hold an audience's attention. Trump fit that need as no other candidate in recent memory. Trump is arguably the first bona fide media-created presidential nominee. Although he subsequently tapped a political nerve, journalists fueled his launch."[4] Reporters tired of monotonous speeches and litanies of talking points found in Trump someone perpetually newsworthy.

The journalistic community wrestled with this outsized coverage, even as it continued unabated. NPR's David Folkenflik commented in the weeks before the Iowa caucuses: "The media have been along for the ride, thankful for the ratings, reveling in a colorful character charting an unpredictable course atop the polls, and fearful of missing what might come next."[5] This combination of factors encouraged further coverage of Trump. Trump's uniqueness may have been a story journalistically, but it also became about journalism's struggles to maintain its place in a media culture crowded with choices. As a *New York Times* story put it: "The presence of Mr. Trump can be irresistible, especially in an election in which viewership and advertising rates have soared, generating tens of millions of dollars in additional revenue for an industry threatened by digital competition."[6] It would be difficult to attribute Trump's outsized coverage to purely economic motives by revenue-hungry journalism organizations, even if Trump's rise did coincide with a difficult financial moment for the news industry. Without a doubt, reader metrics offer journalists greater granularity about digital news consumption.[7] But reducing the reason for so much coverage of Trump to the extra clicks he generated is too simple and draws too fine a connection between news economics and content decisions. A more plausible explanation is to ascribe his success at getting coverage to journalists' penchant for the unexpected. Undoubtedly Trump's habit of straying into unscripted and controversial territory—a space that in early elections would have meant potentially campaign-ending gaffes—increased journalists' interest in what he would say. And because time and resources are finite, more coverage of Trump in the early stages of the primary race meant less time and fewer resources for the rest of the Republican field.

The disparity in news coverage is striking. During the first half of 2016, when most primaries took place, there was not a single week when Trump did not receive more coverage than any other GOP candidate.[8] This attention spilled over beyond Trump as the Republican race received nearly double the attention that the Democratic race received—63% of election coverage news compared to the Democrats' 37%.[9] In the first few months of 2016, when the primary races were most contested, Trump received more coverage on the three nightly network newscasts (ABC, NBC, and CBS) than *all* the other candidates combined.[10] Trump's ability to monopolize attention obviated a need for massive spending on television advertising or field offices staffed with expensive operatives. The attention of journalists was much more valuable. Journalists eager to generate Trump exclusives even bypassed their usual policies of requiring on-camera interviews by allowing him to participate via phone.[11] The temptation that Trump might say something notable was too much to pass up. In March 2016, the *New York Times* reported that Trump had accrued the equivalent of $2 billion in earned media.[12] Equating news coverage with advertising is fraught, but the number does provide a measure of the scale of Trump's presence across the news coverage of the campaign. Trump received far more attention than the rest of the field, and attention is what candidates covet most.

These patterns of outsized news coverage of Trump did not change much once Trump became the Republican nominee. As one of more than a dozen contenders for the Republican nomination, Trump's efforts to absorb media coverage made sense. But he continued using the same tactics in later parts of the campaign when it was just him against Democratic nominee Hillary Clinton. Nonetheless, through spectacle and wild statements, Trump remained the dominant news story of the campaign. For example, at an August 2016 rally in North Carolina, Trump suggested that Clinton could be assassinated if she tried to push through gun control legislation as president.[13] Because such a statement was so outside the expectations of how presidential contenders should speak, it was guaranteed to be noticed and repeated by reporters. Trump would also incite crowds with unfounded allegations of Clinton's illegalities, who would then respond on cue by chanting, "Lock her up."

The result of this strategy was attention. For all of 2016, the Trump campaign received twice the amount of network news coverage as the Clinton campaign.[14] A broader study of media coverage by Harvard's Shorenstein Center found that Trump overall received 15% more coverage than Clinton.[15] But the gap is even bigger when considering coverage of Clinton often included Trump talking about her.[16] Media analyst Andrew Tyndall explained this discrepancy as a fundamental difference between Trump's brazenness and Clinton's more orthodox approach: "Compared with her, he is more accessible, more outlandish, more entertaining, more flamboyant, more unpredictable and, by far, a more radical departure from political norms. . . . By contrast to his, her campaign has been so buttoned-down, and covered as such."[17] Trump's ability to generate news through outrageousness helped him fend off attacks as press coverage turned more negative for both candidates. The Shorenstein Center found that the percentage of stories deemed to be negative in tone never dropped below 64% and went as high as 81% in the weeks before the election.[18] Voters bombarded by negative news of both candidates, much of it within an objective news paradigm that stressed balance, were given an unduly symmetrical impression of two flawed candidates.

Ultimately, Trump prevailed and was elected president, albeit unexpectedly. He won with an Electoral College victory while losing the popular vote. On the eve of the 2016 election, the polling aggregate site RealClearPolitics calculated only a 37.5% favorability rating for Trump, with 58.5% unfavorable.[19] How much a role the media coverage played is difficult to isolate, particularly given Trump's populist rhetoric and the heightened role of social identity discussed in the previous chapter. But Trump's swerve away from mundane politics certainly made him a magnet for journalists.

In the end, we argue that the epistemic conditions of political campaign coverage benefited Trump. Journalists deserve criticism for an initial failure to cover Trump as more than a novelty. Yet as the campaign wore on and Trump's success accelerated, plenty of critical reporting did raise serious concerns about Trump's personal and professional conduct. That Trump's support did not collapse under this journalistic scrutiny raises questions about journalists' ability to act as agents of accountability in a liberal democracy. Journalists accustomed to exposing scandals or political gaffes found that they could not just point to Trump's impropriety and expect widespread rebuke and repercussions to follow.

Trump's ability to withstand negative reporting underscores the argument that journalistic epistemology should be understood in relational terms. Journalists produce news, but the meaning and impact of their texts require a broader perspective that accounts for the acceptance (or not) of their legitimacy, and interpretation by others of what ought to be done. It points to the importance of decentering journalism to account for a broader media culture in which conservative media outlets and the circulation of texts on social media offset news reporting in traditional outlets.[20] A plethora of media choices enables the consumption of partisan outlets or the avoidance of news altogether. All of this is complicated by the politics of identity that figured so prominently in the 2016 campaign, which gave further reason for many to look past Trump's foibles or to discount the news reporting as merely driven by bias. Taken together, understanding Trump's success despite the negative news coverage requires connecting the widespread distrust of journalists recounted in the previous chapter with Trump's active work to dismiss journalists, as explored in the next section.

Press-Bashing as Political Performance

Populist politics is built on a pronounced division between an "us" and a "them." Who is the *us* and who is the *them* is the central matter in building a coalition and identifying the target of scorn. These groupings are often vague and flexible. This is done strategically so that the insider and outsider groups can expand or contract for the sake of political expediency. For those in the *us* column, this language is one of connection across unseen masses. Unity is forged through projecting a common experience onto a significant portion of the populace. It becomes an empowering form of political identity, propelling support for the populist candidate who is positioned as the individual solely capable of carrying out reforms that serve the interests of the in-group. Populism pits some conglomeration of the people as the legitimate political force against a *them* that is also a conglomeration of disparate groups. This has included specific groupings as scapegoats, such as Central American refugees or undocumented immigrants. Yet while scapegoats serve an important symbolic role as the object of contempt, they are not positioned as powerful actors. The other *them*—the one more central to this book—is an imagined coalition of elites presumed to possess a highly concentrated and self-interested amount of social power. This group includes elected politicians most visibly, but it also comes to include journalists as an essential part of the ruling elite. As a *them*, journalists are imbricated with these other elites into an amorphous collective that is marked by two assumptions: the amassing of power and disdain for the unseen masses of the *us*.

Trump's populist messaging connects journalists to other types of elites. For example, Trump's speech at the 2016 Republican National Convention, where he accepted the party's nomination, positioned journalists not as reporting on the government, but as actively conspiring with other elites to maintain power. In espousing many of his talking points from the campaign, Trump accused journalists of being active agents working to elect Hillary Clinton:

> Big business, elite media and major donors are lining up behind the campaign of my opponent because they know she will keep our rigged system in place. They are throwing money at her because they have total control over everything she does. She is their puppet, and they pull the strings.[21]

Later in the speech, Trump added:

> Remember: all of the people telling you that you can't have the country you want are the same people telling you that I wouldn't be standing here tonight. No longer can we rely on those elites in media, and politics, who will say anything to keep a rigged system in place.

Such statements locate true power with a cadre of elites that includes journalists who operate clandestinely to preserve their self-interest at the expense of everyday people. In following the populist script, Trump relies on attacking the press as an elite, and therefore an opponent to him and his followers. It is not the substance of any particular news story, but the institutional power of journalism being targeted. This example also demonstrates Trump's tendency to omit specifics and instead speak in generalities when attacking the press.

Trump's attacks on the press are so numerous as to render us numb to their function. To prevent this from happening, it is imperative to step back and look across this discourse to conceptualize what it all does. After all, such attacks are not informational in their construction. They are not careful rebuttals or challenges, but blanket statements, just as the example from the convention did not need to name a specific instance. Trump does attack individual journalists or news organizations, but in ways that lead to a weaving across cases into the larger conclusion that the press is out to get Trump, that it is unfair and inaccurate, and that it is protecting its elite status.

Given these attributes, Trump's attacks on the press should be understood as a type of political performance. The study of social performance has a long history in philosophy, anthropology, and sociology, as manifested in seminal works by scholars such as Erving Goffman, J. L. Austin, Victor Turner, and Judith Butler. These approaches differ, but they share an interest in how discourses and behaviors come to have power in social settings: not because of their specific content or gestures, but because such actions are interpreted so as to create shared meanings that structure the world in particular ways. Broadly speaking, any performance has roles for the performer and the audience and rules about what can be said. Performances, then, are about social integration and the power to constrain or allow what can be said or done. Performances enact social relationships and establish meanings through their continuous repetition.

Political performance, as imagined here, pertains to the sphere of governing and citizenship. Political performances bring groups into being through language. Our interest is not in whether Trump actually believes his own statements lauding working people, blasting immigrants, or bashing journalists. Many argue that he is being disingenuous to further his political ambition. But trying to guess what his actual commitments are is not as important as examining what's manifest. That he said it and has succeeded is what matters. Likewise, the conclusion that Trump is motivated by an obvious desire for political power is also not as important as what gets said.

Political performance should be understood as both ritualistic and intentional. The ritualistic side of Trump's press-bashing is evident in its repetitive nature. Trump attacked journalists hundreds of times with his tweets. He lambastes the news media in nearly all of his speeches, and derides journalists directly in both formal and impromptu press conferences. This matters to the degree that a sense of community arises through the enactment of performance. Trump's attacks come to be anticipated. The repetition constantly reconstructs the us/them dynamic, pulling Trump's community together as his allies align against a collection of opponents that includes journalists. This discourse is also intentional in that the pervasiveness of Trump's attacks strategically directs his supporters' energy and animus while allowing Trump to control the shape of public discourse on his terms.

The value of examining Trump's attacks on the press as political performance lies in pushing past the obvious and expected to ask how such performances construct a shared identity. When Trump communicates, who belongs and who does not in his coalition? Groups are always achievements, and the constant attacks on the press help hold a group together through shared mistrust and antipathy toward the press as an inextricable part of a ruling elite. Press-bashing should be recognized as part of a shared political identity on the right. The implications of this constant anti-press rhetoric will be examined later, but first our attention turns to how Trump was able to build into his campaigning open attacks on the press while also drawing out-sized press coverage that helped him secure the Republican nomination and eventually the presidency.

Press-bashing needs to be understood as a type of political performance whose effect cannot be measured in any individual utterance, but gains influence through a sustained commitment to staking out an oppositional stance to most national news reporting. It does not operate at the level of the news story, but instead takes aim at journalism at an institutional level through repetitive discourse that draws its power from its pervasiveness. In the language of media effects, it primes audiences to discount negative news messages.[22] This cognitive doubt provides news audiences with a schema for challenging the credibility of any news item that threatens preconceived notions. Trump himself has overtly explained his motives for such blunt attacks. CBS News' *60 Minutes* journalist Leslie Stahl alleged that Trump admitted to her that he blasted the press to shield himself, and quoted Trump as saying, "I do it to discredit you all and demean you all, so when you write negative stories about me no one will believe you." The immediate consequences of such a strategy are to undermine the credibility of journalists in order to discredit negative reports. Explaining the deeper consequences requires conceptualizing what these utterances mean and how they become a form of ritual that creates community by constructing a sense of an "us" in response to journalists as an outsider "them."

Rallies as Spectacles for and against the Press

All presidential candidates hold carefully orchestrated rallies aimed not merely at whipping up the support of those present, but attracting a larger audience that experiences the mediated rally at a distance. Rallies are an example of what Daniel Boorstin calls "pseudo-events," a term he invoked early in the television era to identify events concocted primarily for the cameras.[23] Television, with its intimate sensibility and pervasive reach, reshaped how politics worked. The trends Boorstin perceived more than a half century ago are even more fully realized when considering contemporary politics from the vantage point of mediatization.[24] As the realm of politics became one that was filtered through media channels, political parties have had to accommodate by adjusting their organizations and actions. But they do so in competition with everything else that vies for our attention. Particularly for political campaigns, media attention is crucial. As the number of candidates swells, the amount of available attention any candidate can receive decreases. For this 2016 campaign, attention was doubly difficult. With no incumbents running and both parties conducting primaries, the amount of available news coverage was further decreased.

Trump the candidate quickly seized on the rally as a space of spectacle. He would whip the crowd into a particular frenzy, pandering to their interests and engaging in call-and-response type interactions that would regularly result in chanting. The crowd would cheer Trump and boo his adversaries, including the press. Rituals quickly formed, as when the ejection of protestors would be met with copious applause and "U-S-A" chants. Writing in the *New Yorker* about his experiences attending Trump events, author George Saunders pinpointed Trump's success at rallies as his ability to connect on an emotional level: "He is not trying to persuade, detail, or prove: he is trying to thrill, agitate, be liked, be loved, here and now. He is trying to make energy."[25] Journalists would regularly interview rally attendees, many of whom would wait hours to secure a seat. Their reasons for attending and supporting Trump often pointed to an emotional bond arising through his communicative style:

> [Trump supporters] see a person that actually stands for what they've been thinking in their heads but were too afraid to say all those years.[26]
>
> Donald Trump has a straightforward way that he communicates.[27]
>
> "I've been mad. I'm one of the angry voters that they've been discussing for the last year."[28]
>
> "He's not like past presidents who prepare a beautiful speech but it's not coming from the heart. He speaks it like it is."[29]

Rally-goers often spoke not of political positions but of how Trump connected with them on the level of social identity. These reactions serve as a reminder that populist politics is about more than the speaker. It requires a personal level of connection that involves an audience—both the one present and the one watching from a distance.[30]

The rallies also functioned as a mediated space that extended Trump's reach far beyond the arenas and airplane hangars in which he spoke. Their mediation was crucial for reaching a much larger audience, and for conveying the fervor of the event to voters deciding on which candidate to support, if any at all. Yet as Trump's rallies became spectacles *for* the press, they became spectacles *about* the press. Journalists' presence was central to the event itself, and they were not allowed to fade into the background as simply a conduit between the event and the audience. Journalists became part of Trump's rallies both as a rhetorical target and as a kind of prop.

A staple of Trump's campaign speeches was to group journalists with others as part of an elite governing structure. In a speech on August 18, 2016, Trump used the term "establishment media" to make this case, stating: "The establishment media doesn't cover what really matters in this country, or what's really going on in people's lives." Later in the speech he presented his audience as a victim: "Every story is told from the perspective of the insiders. It's the narrative of the people who rigged the system, never the voice of the people it's been rigged against." Similarly, in another speech (September 24, 2016), Trump portrayed journalism as complicit in maintaining elite power: "We're trying to disrupt the collusion between the wealthy donors, the large corporations, and the media executives. They're all part of the same political establishment." If taken out of context, these statements parallel a long-running contention within critical journalism research that corporate-owned media serve existing power interests.[31] In this view, journalists have become too close to the powerful sources they cover, while the for-profit model that dominates US journalism privileges the sensational over the substantive.[32] These assertions strike at journalistic authority by challenging journalists' normative positioning as distant from the political process they cover, undermining journalists' assertion of representing the world neutrally, and situating the press as occupying a social space outside the lived experience of non-elite voters. Yet Trump twisted the argument that journalists' interests are not voters' interests in a way that promoted a demagogic belief that only he could alter this system precisely because he listened to and understood the forgotten masses. The only structural change necessary is the election of Trump.

A second theme in Trump's rally discourse is that the press has an agenda it actively works to support. Rather than tied to specific instances of perceived bias, these claims were often broad and vague. For example, toward the end of the campaign as negative stories about him proliferated, Trump began to attack journalists more forcefully and extensively. In a speech on October 13, 2016, Trump alleged that journalists were violating their core norms: "Let's be clear on one thing, the corporate media in our country is no longer involved in journalism. They're a political special interest no different than any lobbyist or other financial entity with a total political agenda, and the agenda is not for you, it's for themselves." In the same speech, he baselessly accused the *New York Times* of working with his opponent: "Hillary Clinton is also given approval and veto power over quotes written about her in the *New York Times*." A week later at an October 21, 2016 rally, Trump assigned a particular ruthlessness to journalists: "For them, it is a war—and for them, nothing is out of bounds." Journalists were not just elites, but active opponents of the campaign and, by extension, adversaries to a wider populist movement. The language of war would foretell Trump's accusation of the press as the "enemy of the people," discussed in the next chapter. Furthermore, Trump's use of "media" as a singular noun collapses disparate news organizations and journalists into a singular entity. At the same time, these attacks allowed Trump to argue that any negative reporting about him was invalid on the grounds that it was motivated by journalistic bias.

The press was not only a part of Trump's speeches, but also came to be used as an unwitting prop through journalists' physical presence at rallies. As with any political rally, journalists covering Trump are cordoned off in a specified area from which to report. This consolidation provided convenient access for journalists, but it also made them visible targets for Trump. They became a physical space to which Trump and thousands of rally attendees could direct their anger when he got to the usual parts of his speech bashing the press. The division between attendees and journalists made material the symbolic division between an *us* of Trump and his supporters and a *them* of elites that included the journalists in the rally space. And it did so on Trump's terms.

As part of the press-bashing at his rallies, Trump would explicitly turn journalists who were present to cover the rally into objects of collective scorn. At a campaign rally in South Carolina on December 7, 2015, Trump went on an extended rant about his perceived mistreatment by journalists after they allegedly underreported the crowd at a recent rally. Trump targeted journalists, stating that "70%, 75% is absolute dishonest, absolute scum. Remember that. Scum. Scum. They're totally dishonest people." Trump then returned to pinpoint a specific story by NBC reporter Katy Tur: "You know, everybody knew it was false. . . . She's back there. Little Katy. She's back there. What a lie it was. No, what a lie—Katy Tur. What a lie it was from NBC to have written that. It was a total lie. And they did a story where they—I didn't know they had a group like this, where they actually criticized the media, and they said it was a total lie. . . . Third-rate reporter." Throughout this part of the speech, the crowd turned toward the press pen to directly boo Tur. In her memoir, Tur described the moment: "They turn all at once, a large animal, angry and unchained. I force a laugh."[33] She continued to cover the event, a particularly notable one because it was there Trump called for a ban on all Muslims from being allowed entry into the United States. After the rally, Tur and her crew were escorted out with extra security. This was not unusual; Tur admitted that nearly every news organization had a security detail, except Fox News.[34] Trump's singling out of Tur spilled out beyond the rally to further harassment online, including death threats. In a segment on MSNBC, Tur read out some of the threats she had received, including "I hope you get raped and killed."[35] Tur would continue to attend Trump rallies, and recounted the persistent vocal assaults that journalists faced throughout the campaign.

More routinely, Trump drew attention to journalists present at the rally by accusing them of refusing to show the size of the crowd. Trump made this claim at a Pensacola, Florida, rally on November 2, 2016: "They never show crowds like that—look at that, it goes all the way back. They never show crowds. They don't show crowds." Such accusations provided Trump with a staple opportunity to attack the journalists present at the rally and direct attendees' anger to the penned-in reporters. But these censures lacked substance.[36] The press pool designated one camera, creating a single feed to be shared among news organizations. The responsibility of this camera was to stay on Trump as he spoke, only moving to follow him as he entered and exited the stage. When Trump would implore the cameraperson to pan the crowd, which could not be done, he turned the lack of panning into further evidence of press bias. For example, at a rally in Biloxi, Mississippi, on January 2, 2016, Trump taunted the camera operator: "Look at the guy in the middle. Why aren't you turning the camera? Terrible. So terrible. Look at him, he doesn't turn the camera. He doesn't turn the camera."[37] As Trump makes this attack, he transforms the camera and its operator from an unobtrusive mediator into part of the performance of the rally. The point of view of the camera, something largely unnoticed given our familiarity with television, becomes a politicized object. The camera becomes a metonym of the press at large, allowing the crowd to direct its collective anger to a single spot. Moreover, despite Trump's complaints, news coverage of his rallies always included plenty of crowd shots from other journalists, and rally sizes were regularly reported. That Trump was wrong or lying didn't matter ultimately, as the accusations were enough to remind both the in-person and television audiences of news bias.

The rally remained a consistent part of Trump's political identity as he has moved from being a candidate to being president and back to candidate again in 2020. Trump even spent the day he was impeached, December 18, 2019, at a rally in Michigan in which he pointed to the journalists covering the event and accused them of being active members of the Democratic Party.[38] Trump's fondness for rallies is not surprising given his background as an entertainer, his need for approval, and his desire to control the spotlight. Rallies provided moments of collective aggrandizement for a president whose approval rating remained consistently in the low forties. They allowed the president space to vent against his enemies, which routinely included journalists. These were heated events. In a rally in El Paso, Texas, on February 11, 2019— two years into his presidency—a Trump supporter attacked the press pen, shoving a BBC reporter and yelling obscenities while being dragged away by security. Trump paused his speech during the incident, and restarted after the attacker had been removed. Later in the speech Trump returned to his usual attacks on the press, stating, "We have suffered a totally dishonest media and we've won and it's driving them crazy. It's driving them crazy. It's driving them crazy but look at them, they still come [to cover the rallies]."[39] The familiar themes of journalists as out-of-touch elites, as promulgating an anti-Trump agenda, and as inept were invoked, even after the attack. The persistence of such charges demands their continual recitation, as Trump could only maintain his demagogic position by delegitimizing the journalists that challenged his claims and governing record through the everyday act of reporting.

Tweeting against the Media Establishment

Trump's well-covered rallies were complemented by his much-discussed use of Twitter as a platform for bypassing journalistic channels to reach a mass audience. Twitter serves as an even more direct route than rallies, which have to be embedded in news broadcasts or summarized in news stories to reach beyond the attendees. Trump could tweet from his phone, knowing that his short missives would instantly reach a large audience and often spark news coverage. Unsurprisingly, the platform provided Trump with one more avenue to attack journalists during the campaign while simultaneously attracting copious attention for such attacks.[40]

Echoing his rallies, Trump used Twitter to situate the press as a foe working against his campaign. He made this position clear in a tweet on August 6, 2016, shortly after Trump turned his attention to the general election: "I am not just running against Crooked Hillary Clinton, I am running against the very dishonest and totally biased media—but I will win!"[41] This tweet offers a clear distillation of the strategy we have discussed, in which Trump conflates the press and other actors as an amorphous elite working against the best interests of non-elite Americans. Trump also defended his use of Twitter as necessary precisely because of press bias. On June 15, 2016, Trump tweeted: "The press is so totally biased that we have no choice but to take our tough but fair and smart message directly to the people!"[42] The claim here is that openly partisan, direct communication is superior to putatively objective but actually biased news.

Unlike the performative stage of a political rally, with its ample time for long arguments, Twitter's space constraints—with tweets limited to 140 characters at the time of the 2016 campaign—shaped and constrained what political messages could look like. Trump's tweets were necessarily parsimonious, which also meant that they were easier to produce in large numbers, more direct in their language, quicker to read, and faster to spread. As digital messages, tweets are easily embedded in all manner of political discourse: they circulate outside the space of news through retweets and algorithmic selection, provide space for comments (both supportive and derogatory), and are easily searchable and spreadable. And they gain greater reach outside of the platform when reporters embed them in news stories or when they appear on television as images or as part of the text of chyrons that scroll across the bottom of cable news. But, fundamentally, they were fully controlled by Trump (and occasionally his aides), requiring only a mobile phone to instantly reach millions. That Twitter—and social media more generally—have become so mundane is to forget how much of a transformation this has been for political elites.

To illustrate how Trump used Twitter to critique and cajole the news media, an insightful case is how he has treated CNN. The long-established cable news channel was a popular target for Trump throughout the campaign. Between his official campaign launch on June 16, 2015, and Election Day 2016, Trump sent 178 tweets that mentioned CNN, or slightly more than a tweet every three days.[43] This focus on CNN owes to several factors. As an all-news channel with both left-wing and right-wing pundits, CNN produces a lot of content to catch the eye of Trump the candidate. CNN also provided a forum for Trump, and he appeared regularly on CNN programs during the primary stage of the campaign. But CNN competes with the right-leaning

Fox News Channel, which Trump largely supported over CNN, although not without exceptions. CNN also has long been a target of conservatives for its supposed liberal bias; its "Clinton News Network" nickname popularized during the presidency of Bill Clinton had a resurgence with the candidacy of Hillary Clinton.

Looking at how Trump tweeted about CNN is valuable for exposing how Trump's treatment of journalists shifted as the campaign moved from the primary stage to the general election. At first Trump tweeted about mainstream news outlets to help him secure the Republican nomination. This included promoting his television appearances, touting polls that showed him doing well, and supporting his campaign surrogates as they attacked other Republic candidates. Once the general election began, Trump's tweets became much more negative toward CNN and the press more broadly. This pattern becomes clearer if we examine how Trump tweeted about CNN specifically. Table 2.1 breaks down when and how

Table 2.1 Trump Tweets about CNN during the 2016 Campaign

Month	Tweets mentioning CNN	Tweets promoting a Trump interview	Tweets criticizing CNN
July 2015	15	2	2
August 2015	6	1	0
September 2015	15	3	1
October 2015	11	4	1
November 2015	8	2	3
December 2015	38	7	7
January 2016	9	3	3
February 2016	10	4	1
March 2016	6	1	1
April 2016	2	0	1
May 2016	9	3	5
June 2016	7	0	7
July 2016	9	0	8
August 2016	16	0	15
September 2016	10	0	10
October 2016	7	1	6
Total	178	31	71

Source: https://www.thetrumparchive.com/.

Trump mentioned CNN each month between his campaign launch and the election. The first column indicates the total number of tweets mentioning CNN. The numbers here fluctuate quite a bit. The high number of tweets in December 2015 reflects Trump's exuberance after being named the front-runner for the Iowa caucuses in a CNN poll. Of his thirty-eight tweets about CNN in December 2015, nineteen were about the CNN poll. The second column indicates the times when Trump promoted an upcoming or completed appearance on CNN. The final column indicates a tweet containing some sort of criticism of CNN, whether directed at an individual journalist or commentator, a program, or the network generally.

In the eight months between July 2015 and February 2016, Trump tweeted twenty-six times promoting his own appearances on CNN,[44] while offering up eighteen tweets critiquing CNN. The promotional tweets were upbeat and informational to entice viewers. For example:

> I will be doing a major sit down interview on State of the Union With Jake Tapper at 9:00 A.M. on @CNN. Enjoy! (October 25, 2015)[45]
>
> I will be interviewed by Anderson Cooper at 8pm on @CNN from New Hampshire. Should be very interesting! (February 4, 2016)[46]

During this period, Trump did attack CNN in general ways. For example, in a rather tame tweet, Trump encouraged the network to improve its reporting:

> @CNN has to do better reporting if it wants to keep up with the crowd. So totally one-sided and biased against me that it is becoming boring. (November 29, 2015)[47]

But Trump also zeroed in on commentators he disagreed with. He used the platform to attack S. E. Cupp, a conservative CNN analyst often critical of Trump:

> Watching @CNN and consider @secupp to be one of the least talented people on television. Boring and biased! (December 22, 2015)[48]

Charges of being "boring" seem rather mild in comparison to the other accusations reported in this chapter and the next. In addition, his use of "bias" here is more personal than partisan, considering that these comments came as Trump vied against other Republicans.

Trump also used CNN to compliment commentators with whom he agreed. This included former Obama strategist and advisor David Axelrod as well as Trump supporter Kayleigh McEnany (who would later become his press secretary):

> Thank you @davidaxelrod for your nice words this morning on @CNN. It was a good night! (December 16, 2015)[49]

> Fantastic job on @CNN tonight. @kayleighmcenany is a winner! @donlemon (January 11, 2016)[50]

These tweets reflect Trump's close attention to CNN and his use of Twitter as a means to attack individual commentators while promoting himself, his surrogates, or others that made positive comments about him or his chances of winning. This fits with Trump's overall effort to dominate the press coverage of the primary stage in order to starve his competitors of media attention. These tweets reveal Trump's close attention to how he was covered on television, which he would seize on as a marker of success while attacking detractors.

Once Trump was assured the Republican nomination, his treatment of CNN on Twitter changed considerably. Of the forty-nine instances in which Trump tweeted about CNN between June 2016 and the November election, forty-six were attacks. Regarding the three non-attacks during this time period, one was the addition of a CNN tag at the end of an attack on Clinton, another was a reference to a positive CNN poll, and the last one promoted an appearance by Trump's wife, Melania, on Anderson Cooper's program:

> My wife, Melania, will be interviewed tonight at 8:00pm by Anderson Cooper on @CNN. I have no doubt she will do very well. Enjoy! (October 17, 2016)[51]

The remainder of the tweets attacked CNN, most often accusing the network of bias. While Trump's earlier tweets during the primary period of the election contained more specific critiques aimed at individuals for particular stories, the tweets during the general election were more sweeping and blunt. Examples of his Twitter attacks on the cable network include the following:

I am watching @CNN very little lately because they are so biased against me. Shows are predictable garbage! CNN and MSM is one big lie! (June 5, 2016)[52]

I am watching @FoxNews and how fairly they are treating me and my words, and @CNN, and the total distortion of my words and what I am saying. (June 13, 2016)[53]

@FoxNews is much better, and far more truthful, than @CNN, which is all negative. Guests are stacked for Crooked Hillary! I don't watch. (July 17, 2016)[54]

CNN is unwatchable. Their news on me is fiction. They are a disgrace to the broadcasting industry and an arm of the Clinton campaign. (September 9, 2016)[55]

Wow, just saw the really bad @CNN ratings. People don't want to watch bad product that only builds up Crooked Hillary. (October 1, 2016)[56]

Wow, @CNN got caught fixing their "focus group" in order to make Crooked Hillary look better. Really pathetic and totally dishonest! (October 10, 2016)[57]

These tweets connected to familiar themes of how Trump bashes journalists: positioning CNN as emblematic of all news media, the superiority of Fox News as an alternative, suggestions that the news media favored Clinton and actively worked with her campaign, and accusations that news stories critical of Trump were shoddy and incorrect. The lack of nuance and specificity in these tweets combined with their pervasiveness worked strategically to keep salient a deep-seated belief among many that journalists should not be trusted. Twitter gave Trump a vehicle for press-bashing that worked outside of news channels, allowing him to stave off this negative reporting, at least to his Twitter followers. CNN remained a popular target of his vituperation. Coupled with the discourse from the rallies, these tweets show how disdain for the so-called mainstream news as epitomized by CNN was so closely tied to the political identity of many conservatives.

Trump continued to use Twitter to attack CNN after becoming president. His first tweet as president that mentioned the network came less than a week after the inauguration in a message lauding the Fox News Channel while appending, in all capital letters, "FAKE NEWS" in front of the CNN tag:

Congratulations to @FoxNews for being number one in inauguration ratings. They were many times higher than FAKE NEWS @CNN - public is smart! (January 24, 2017)[58]

This tweet set a tone that would continue. As president, Trump mentioned the network 293 times on Twitter, overwhelmingly as attacks.[59]

It's worth pausing to ask, however: just how influential is Trump's megaphone on Twitter? One study by Chris Wells and colleagues explored how different dimensions of the US media system as a whole—from far-left to far-right sources to plenty in between—allocated their attention among the four leading candidates (Trump, Ted Cruz, Hillary Clinton, and Bernie Sanders) during the primaries for the 2016 election.[60] This is not about how the candidates were covered, but rather their ability to muster media attention—to get noticed relative to their competitors. For all the talk about media fragmentation these days, the study found a surprising level of uniformity in how media organizations across the political spectrum allocated attention to the candidates. But importantly, however, they also found a similarly surprising consistency in the factors that drove Trump's particular advantage in gaining attention, with the volume of his retweets playing an outsized role—even as other candidates saw no comparable boost in coverage from retweets they received. What's more, "Trump tweeted more at times when he had recently garnered less of a relative advantage in news attention, suggesting [that] he strategically used Twitter to trigger coverage."[61]

In effect, Trump used Twitter to play journalists like a fiddle during the campaign—dialing up the shock value of tweets at just the right moments to elicit retweets, keep journalists engaged, and ensure his prominence in the news cycle.[62] Just as live cable TV coverage of Trump's rallies provided an unprecedented degree of "free advertising," as we discussed previously, the voluminous press coverage *about* Trump's tweets ended up being far more consequential than the tweets themselves—and that pattern held true from his initial campaigning on through to his time as president. Indeed, it's worth reinforcing this fact about Twitter: Trump's tweets appear on a platform that, even in 2021, relatively few Americans use all that much—about one in four US adults are on Twitter, but most are not particularly active, let alone likely to see any or all of the president's messages at any given moment.[63] But because political journalists have so readily taken to Twitter and spend so much time on it, they are prone to blow the platform and its personalities out of proportion[64]—doubly so when a powerful individual deftly uses the space to orchestrate maximum attention.

Between his tweets and his rallies, Trump engaged in a number of high-profile spats with specific journalists. The media watchdog group Media Matters for America kept a running list of Trump's attacks, which in mid-October 2016 included sixty-six individual journalists and media pundits, and twenty-one news organizations.[65] Two notable encounters occurred in August 2015, months before the first primary voting would begin. First, Trump attacked Fox News Channel's Megyn Kelly for asking a question about his treatment of women during a debate. Soon after, Trump began insulting Kelly in various other news outlets. On CNN, he laid into Kelly, saying, "She gets out and she starts asking me all sorts of ridiculous questions. You could see there was blood coming out of her eyes, blood coming out of her wherever. In my opinion, she was off base."[66] The Trump campaign denied that his insult pertained to menstruation, but the quote circulated widely and a usually friendly Fox News demanded an apology.[67] Later that month, a heated exchange between Trump and Univision anchor Jorge Ramos over Trump's immigration policies resulted in Ramos being ejected by security.[68] Ramos challenged Trump publicly as a means of exposing the contradictions and impracticalities of Trump's immigration plans, but the incident likely only heightened awareness of Trump's anti-immigration policies as a part of his right-wing populist message. While some viewers may have found Trump's actions detestable and xenophobic, others likely interpreted Trump as saying what they already believed.

Another incident in which Trump would deny what he was clearly doing occurred at a November 2015 rally, where Trump mocked *New York Times* reporter Serge Kovaleski through a series of jerking physical gestures. Kovaleski has arthrogryposis, a congenital joint issue that affects his movement, and clearly Trump was making fun of him through an imitation. Trump denied knowing Kovaleski or his condition, despite a long history of the reporter covering Trump.[69] Trump was upset that Kovaleski had challenged his false claim that thousands of Muslims in New Jersey were seen celebrating as they watched the World Trade Center collapse during the September 11, 2001, attacks. Trump also attacked ABC News's Tom Llamas in person during a press conference as "this sleazy guy right over here from ABC; he's a sleaze in my book" after Llamas ran a critical story on Trump lying about how much money he raised for military veterans groups.[70] Other fights included Trump banning or threatening to ban reporters, as well as his personal attacks on NBC News' Katy Tur at a rally. Given that there are dozens more examples, the totality of these personal attacks fits with the wider strategy of press-bashing outlined in this chapter. In many of these cases, Trump's battles with the journalist overshadowed the substance of whatever news story prompted Trump to make a personal attack. This supports Trump's ongoing claims that journalists are out to get him personally, fitting in with his demagogic positioning. Instead of diminishing Trump's standing in the eyes of his supporters, these battles came to symbolize his toughness and commitment while providing Trump with fodder to claim that the press was working against him and, by extension, his populist movement.

When an Election is a Mandate on the News Media

Elections are important moments for journalism, not just because of heightened interest in political campaigns, but also because of the symbolic role that election news plays for journalistic authority. The provision of election news most overtly lines up with journalism's democratic normative ideal. This mode of legitimation places the purpose of journalism as a handmaid to democracy, bringing citizens the information they need to make informed choices in a liberal democracy. This role is made more important in a mediatized society in which most voters only access candidates through media. The ideal is a seemingly contradictory position in which journalists are prominent participants in the political system while also disappearing behind the reports they produce for the public. The ideal here is the journalist as conduit rather than powerful political actor.

Yet just as election news brings out the normative soul of journalism, it also reveals its failures. The lofty rhetoric of journalism's democratic ideals opens up the profession to warranted critiques.[71] A persistent—if not fully ritualized—lament has been the propensity of journalists to eschew policy frames supplying information to voters in favor of horse-race reporting more narrowly focused on who is ahead or behind and on strategy decisions.[72] Politics becomes about the contest rather than the content of what politicians pledge to do. The rise of Trump during the 2016 election not only as a viable candidate, but as the one receiving the most attention, portends a deeper issue that indicates the failure of journalism as an institution. This argument asks that we move beyond merely critiquing the framing practices of journalists to look more broadly at how journalism became so much of the story of the 2016 campaign.

In all major elections, the performance of the press becomes its own story. Campaign metacoverage is a staple of election news.[73] But the 2016 election was one in which political journalism earned particular condemnation from many different directions. Although this chapter has largely zeroed in on how Trump battled journalists, this is only part of the picture. Outside of Trump, journalists received criticism for how they covered other aspects of the campaign, including charges of being overly dismissive of Hillary Clinton's chief primary opponent, Senator Bernie Sanders.[74] Later, in the general election, the amount of news focused on Clinton's handling of emails as secretary of state was also regarded as inappropriate. One study found that the *New York Times*—a newspaper regularly regarded by conservatives as a paragon of elite liberal bias[75]—ran more stories on Clinton's emails in a week than the *total* number of policy-based stories in the final two months of the election.[76] The email story, which amounted to nothing, received more attention than any of Trump's scandals.[77] And, in keeping with recent trends, journalists favored horse-race jockeying over substance, following a familiar trend in political reporting.[78]

Dissatisfaction with journalists was evident. When a Pew Research Center survey asked voters to grade the election coverage, 38% gave the press an F, with 59% giving it a D or F. These were much higher percentages than in any election since Pew began asking the question in 1988.[79] Similarly, Gallup found only 32% of poll respondents had any confidence in journalism in the final weeks of the election.[80] Even with the harsh reporting on Clinton and the focus on her emails, 90% of Trump supporters alleged a bias against Trump. This was predictable given the centrality of press criticism in contemporary conversative politics.

Trump's attacks on the press in the 2016 campaign should be understood both as a continuation of long-expressed beliefs in liberal bias and an escalation of these attacks to strike at something more fundamental about the institutional role of journalism in US life. The degree to which Trump in his diatribes wove journalism into a web of elite forces said to be running the country undermined claims to journalistic authority in a foundational way. In Trump's argument, it wasn't just a slanted story angle, but a more widespread inability of journalists to understand his supporters, if not an outright derision for them. Trump did strike back at news outlets about particular stories he deemed unflattering, but he also roundly critiqued journalism in a general sense.

Trump's press-bashing corresponds to a growing divide in perceptions of journalists between Republicans and Democrats that has persisted past the 2016 election and shows how closely linked partisan identity has become with perceptions of journalists. In an effort to tease out the effects of partisan identity on how people assess the news, the Pew Research Center found striking divides.[81] When asked about the ethical standards of journalists, 79% of those identifying as or leaning toward Republicans judged them to be low or very low, compared to 35% of Democrats or Democratic leaners. The numbers were even more stark for Republicans who strongly approve of Trump: 85% of this group found journalists' ethical standards to be low or very low. The same study also found large differences when combining partisan identification with political awareness and news knowledge. Among highly politically aware Republicans, just 16% expressed "a great deal/fair amount of confidence that journalists will act in the best interests of the public"—compared to 91% of highly politically aware Democrats.

These are big divides. A word of caution is needed about causality. Certainly decades of right-wing attacks on journalists as biased has led to entrenched positions that Trump was able to tap into. Trump draws on these sentiments while escalating his attacks, driving a self-confirming spiral among overlapping forces that drags down confidence in the press. Democrats have gone the other direction, putting more faith in journalism during a time when they had little power at the federal level.[82] But the big picture is a public fractured by partisan identity in how they perceive journalism. This growing asymmetry in evaluations of journalism implies that trusting news has become a partisan activity. This is different from having a news landscape marked by openly partisan outlets. These sites do exist (and will be discussed in more detail later in the book), but the majority of news in the United States still displays a centrist bias as it adheres to the tenets of classic objective journalism that we call "the standard model"—an epistemological mode of providing professionally verified facts to the populace. When this activity is taken to be either shot through with liberal bias or overtaken by shoddy practices (often assumed to be driven by bias), it calls into question where information comes from. This is not to defend journalists as impeccable truth-warriors unmarred by any motives aside from public service, but it is to question what happens when all "straight" news is seen as crooked.

The epistemic contests surrounding news accounts point to the need to examine such foundational questions.

It might be that this argument is overstated. People may profess to distrust news but still consume it as providing an accurate *enough* account, the election of Joe Biden might invert feelings toward press coverage, or polarization might ebb with some newfound spirit of comity. But the causes of this division run deep, and the attacks on the press are relentless. The seed has been planted—a whole field of seeds—in the minds of the news audience that the facts of any news story can be dismissed. The implications go beyond even the day-to-day political stories to larger questions of journalism's ability to tell stories about society to itself. This comes at a time when we need help navigating complex social issues like income equality, racial inequity, public health, and the climate crisis that affect all regardless of their party identification or their feelings about the news. But, in the end, it is up to the journalistic community to formulate a response that goes beyond falling back on a normative framework more attuned to a different era. As we argue later in the book, this response needs to confront journalism's own failings to help explain the wide gaps that have formed in opinions about journalism.

Conclusion: The Perpetual Campaign

Trump's ability to rocket up from a group of also-ran candidates to become the Republican nominee and eventually the president capitalized on a combination of fame and outrageousness that separated him from establishment politics and gave him control over the news cycle. Fighting with the press became an indelible part of the campaign—not as a marginal activity but as a core part of a messaging strategy that identified journalists as elites whose interests are in conflict with Trump's supporters. However, when the dust cleared and Trump emerged victorious, it quickly became clear that there would be no transition from candidate Trump to President Trump. Instead, Trump remained in a perpetual campaign throughout his presidency, even hinting at running again in 2024 after he was out of office. The rallies would continue, with little tonal variation from the past. The anti-press rhetoric would also continue and even deepen, as the next chapter chronicles.

Presidents are always campaigning in the sense that they require public approval to provide a mandate for their policy goals, not to mention to bolster their re-election chances and advocate for their party's candidates. The battle for public opinion is always ongoing. Yet Trump's perpetual campaign moved beyond this into continuously selling Trump as a brand. He did so by constantly engaging with political enemies, stirring up crowds, and instilling a victim mentality. This is the continuation of a demagogic mindset that perpetuates the us/them dynamic so central to Trump's campaign rhetoric.

Trump's success owes to his ability to bash the press as not worth listening to, while also using the press to spread his populist message (even while crowding out media attention that otherwise could be paid to his opponents). Trump's ascent required news coverage, and the coverage of Trump outpaced all other candidates throughout the election, from the primary season on through the general contest. Through his rallies and his tweeting, Trump was able to use his unpredictability and uncouthness to garner more coverage. This pattern continued in the 2020 election, and even as the covid-19 pandemic limited Trump's ability to hold rallies, he held as many as he could anyway.

Trump's ability to exploit journalists' penchant for conflict and newness also points to how normative limitations hamper their reporting. Journalists may not have consciously or collectively decided to devote so much attention to Trump, but it was an outcome destined by standards of newsworthiness. As John Sides, Michael Tesler, and Lynn Vavreck argue, "There need not be any cabal at all—only a set of news outlets that, though not identical, made many decisions based on a common set of economic incentives and news values. In 2016, those incentives and values aligned nicely, and Donald Trump was the beneficiary."[83] Journalists had become caught in patterns of covering Trump that normalized his antics. And when journalists pushed back, they encountered both the limits of their normative defenses and the persistence of Trump's press-bashing. These patterns solidified early in the 2016 campaign and have only strengthened afterward.

Trump's 2016 victory highlights how journalists have placed themselves in a difficult position through entrenched campaign reporting practices that amplify the sensational while downplaying policy. Journalists face two dilemmas. First, they find themselves operating in a media culture in which they are increasingly decentered with the rise of other mediated actors and a fracturing of journalistic actors. Journalists recognize a need to adapt, but lack a consensus on what this should look like, as we see later in the book. Second, journalists find that their preferred position of claiming to be outside of politics looking in falls away when they are thrust into political debates as actors, or even as political adversaries. When all news becomes filtered through the lens of political polarization, journalists become part of what they cover. This is an uncomfortable position for journalists to be in, as their defense of utilizing objective practices to ensure accuracy fails to convince critics. As we will also see later in the book, it has led to a great deal of introspection about what journalism ought to do. Getting to that point requires first facing both external assaults continually targeting journalists and how journalists' own actions have contributed to this moment.

3

The Trump Presidency

Four Years of Battling and Belittling the Press

At 5:35 in the morning on June 13, 2017, Donald Trump sent millions of followers this message:

> The Fake News Media has never been so wrong or so dirty. Purposely incorrect stories and phony sources to meet their agenda of hate. Sad![1]

Before most Americans had rolled out of bed, Trump had started the day with a swipe at the press. Although the message is both short and familiar, it still deserves attention to understand just what this tweet is doing. Notably, it does not target a specific journalist, story, or outlet, but instead identifies its target of scorn as an ambiguous amalgamation identified as the "Fake News Media." The use of capital letters gives the appearance of a proper noun marking some sort of collective or organization churning out a stream of false stories—Fake News Media Incorporated. This ambiguity is perhaps the most important feature of Trump's message: it provides ample flexibility for anyone reading the tweet to fill in whatever example they see fit. This ambiguity continues with the nonspecific entity being accused of two nonspecific charges: that the news has been inaccurate and that it has been unethical. The second sentence amplifies the charges by insinuating that the intention of journalists is to mislead, and that this intention is fueled by hate. The object of hate is left open for interpretation, whether it be a personal animus toward the president, his supporters, or a general enmity toward the nation that persists across the journalistic corps. The addition of "Sad!" at the end locks in the tone of the message; it is hard not to read it without Donald Trump's voice resonating in our heads. Two hours later, at 7:48 a.m., Trump added a second tweet: "Fake News is at an all time high. Where is their apology to me for all of the incorrect stories???"[2]

These tweets are just two examples of hundreds of attacks that Trump as president made against the press, often working outside of traditional sources

News After Trump. Matt Carlson, Sue Robinson, and Seth C. Lewis, Oxford University Press. © Oxford University Press 2021. DOI: 10.1093/oso/9780197550342.003.0004

of political news through Twitter, press conferences, speeches and rallies, and interviews with conservative news outlets. These messages refuted any expectations or hopes that Trump would temper his press-bashing once he was sworn into office. Instead, the opposite happened. The implications of these escalated attacks go beyond the familiar desire of presidents to shape news coverage to instead signal a deeper assault on the relevance of journalism in the contemporary media culture. Trump did not stop at questioning specific reporting or quibbling over story frames. He also targeted journalists' fundamental epistemic legitimacy as producers of truthful accounts. Trump supported his own power by directly striking at the relevance of journalists.

Trump's ability to attack the press owed much to his occupation of the presidency. The office of the president of the United States is endowed with tremendous political power, and no doubt many studies are being written about the administrative fallout after Trump weakened important governmental institutions, politicized the diplomatic corps and the Department of Justice, refused to cooperate with congressional oversight, and challenged judicial independence. But our attention in this chapter is fixed on the symbolic power of the presidency, and more specifically on how Trump wielded it to threaten journalism's institutional role. Decades ago, Herbert Gans identified the president as the most important news source because everything a president says is made newsworthy by the fact that it comes from the president. The journalists whom Gans spoke to regarded the president as speaking for the nation.[3] The media environment has changed dramatically since Gans was studying journalists in the 1970s, but the president still has the privilege of gaining the public's attention at a time when attention is more segmented across a growing number of media choices. And Trump used the symbolic power of the presidency and his uncanny ability to generate attention to go after journalists at every turn.

Why Trump bashed the press so frequently and so viciously should be explained not as merely a knee-jerk reaction, but rather because Trump fundamentally needed journalists to be seen as a powerful and malevolent force countering his own power as president. He needed the press to be his perfect foil. While the previous chapters showed how Trump made attacking journalists a cornerstone of his populist campaign rhetoric, these attacks became even more important as a strategy of maintaining power once Trump himself became a ruling elite. By elevating journalistic power to be on par with presidential power, Trump could then explain away political failures as simply an unavoidable consequence of journalists working against him. It wasn't his fault—it was theirs. But journalists could only work as a scapegoat of such magnitude if they were thought to be strong enough to wield sufficient power to impede Trump. They had to be understood as on equal footing with the power of the presidency. Thus, even as he bashed journalists and sought to delegitimize their reporting, Trump simultaneously accorded them power and legitimacy. He walked this line in part by agglomerating journalists into an ambiguous mass, united in their opposition against him. In keeping with his demagogic rhetoric, Trump then situated the press as part of the elite "them" working against his populist "us." Targeting journalists as biased and acting unfairly strengthened Trump's claims to victim status for both himself and his supporters—a persecution complex about conniving elites that was laid bare in a December 2020 rally in Georgia where Trump declared, "We're all victims. Everybody here, all these thousands of people here tonight, they're all victims. Every one of you."[4] This claim to victim status, including victimization at the hands of nefarious journalists, was not a marginal activity but a defining political strategy throughout his tenure as president.

Even after the events of January 6, 2021, when a mob of Trump supporters made a deadly assault on the US Capitol in an effort to overthrow the free-and-fair 2020 presidential election, "The mood in the pro-Trump world became one of profoundest self-pity," David Frum explained in *The Atlantic*.[5] Trump supporters, in some cases deplatformed like the president himself for encouraging violence, sought to compare themselves to the unpersons of George Orwell's *1984* or to victims of Soviet purges banished to digital gulags. In particular, they sought to blame everyone else for the assault—including the press. "Is the mainstream media—especially places like CNN and MSNBC—outrageously biased? Of course! One hundred percent," Senator Marco Rubio of Florida said in a video statement that initially condemned the Capitol riot and then proceeded to blame journalists, among others, for creating the conditions that led to it. Rubio added, "This kind of blatant bias, this double standard, that's one of the reasons why so many Americans have sought political shelter in divisive political movements and in conspiracy theories that offer them the promise of fighting back against it. . . . We can't allow our anger at all that stuff to turn us into them."[6]

Against that backdrop, this chapter takes up three ways in which Trump attacked the press throughout his presidency. First, Trump's press-bashing discourse is examined for how he elevated his attacks against journalists, including regularly referring to journalists as "the enemy of the people." He was able to engage in this verbal assault through channels outside of traditional news—namely through Twitter, rallies, and conservative media channels. Second, we consider Trump's skirmishes with individual journalists as a type of performance connecting to populist rhetoric that characterized journalists as self-interested elites. These actions allowed Trump to turn his confrontations with journalists into exhibitions of his political power that were not substantively about political issues. Finally, the third section expands outward from Trump to consider how he has been aided by a conservative media infrastructure. Conservative media actors—from individuals to institutions, Rush Limbaugh to Fox News—provided ready-made material for Trump to take up in his battles with the press while also protecting the president through the safe media spaces they afforded him. The cumulative effect of these three areas has been to unsettle the role of the press in covering the White House, which has then spawned questions about how journalists ought to respond in the face of such grave threats to their relevance.

Naming and Shaming: Journalists as "the Enemy of the People"

The annual Conservative Political Action Conference, abbreviated CPAC, has long been an important stop for politicians eager to demonstrate their conservative bona fides. Established by the American Conservative Union in 1974, CPAC had its first keynote delivered by Ronald Reagan as he sought to establish himself as the standard-bearer of American conservatism. Over the years, the number of attendees has swelled to more than ten thousand annually, and the event has gained greater influence within the Republican Party. Politicians clamor to speak to the growing crowds, and presidential hopefuls seek victory in its presidential straw polls.

Trump first spoke at CPAC in 2011, shortly after Republicans regained control of Congress in the 2010 midterm elections, buoyed by the right-wing Tea Party movement. Trump burrowed into conservative politics in part through pernicious accusations that President Obama's birth certificate was a forgery and that he was in all likelihood born outside the United States and therefore ineligible to serve as president. Trump became an annual fixture at CPAC conferences, including with a 2015 speech preparing the way for his presidential run later that year. But he abruptly pulled out of the 2016 conference after conference-goers threatened to walk out during his talk.[7] It was a gambit that fit with Trump's narrative during the primary as a political outsider running against the Republican establishment. The move angered many, relegating Trump to a third-place finish with only 15% of the votes in the presidential nominee straw poll.[8] Meanwhile, Trump's spat with CPAC did little to slow his ascension to the top of the Republican ticket.

A year later, in February 2017, Trump was a little more than a month into his presidency when he returned to the conference, now in need of building a coalition of conservatives to help him govern. Trump's first few weeks had been full of controversy as the Trump administration struggled with the reins of power. This gave rise to ample news coverage of the goings-on within the White House, much of it embarrassing for the new president. Trump pushed back at the reporting, escalating his rhetoric beyond denials to instead impute that journalists conspiring against him were, in fact, enemies of the people:

> The FAKE NEWS media (failing @nytimes @NBCNews @ABC @CBS @CNN) is not my enemy it is the enemy of the American People! (February 17, 2017)

Trump's tweet was an obvious provocation. First, it co-opted the term "fake news," which in its earlier use denoted fabricated online stories most often designed as clickbait. Instead, Trump began using the term to describe news reporting created by established news organizations that he accused of being erroneous. In this tweet, he refers more broadly to a cadre of national news organizations as belonging to the "fake news media." More egregiously, he shifts attention away from himself as an individual being victimized by the news media to instead situate the press as an implacable foe of the country as a whole—indeed, *the* "enemy of the American people." Such an escalation is instantly worrisome. Identifying the press as an enemy justifies all sorts of retribution against journalists. It uses the language of war, and places the press against the rest of the population. Unsurprisingly, it drew instant and loud condemnation from journalists.[9]

It is with this backdrop that Trump stepped up to the podium at CPAC a week later on February 24. Trump's speech was an extension of his campaign rhetoric, echoing the bombast of his campaign rallies and lambasting a series of perceived adversaries.[10] Yet the CPAC speech was notable for how much time it devoted to attacking journalists. Trump used a sizable portion of his high-profile speech to offer an extended rant against news reporting. He began this section of the speech by picking up from his earlier enemy tweet:

> And I want you all to know that we are fighting the fake news. It's fake, phony, fake. A few days ago I called the fake news the enemy of the people. And they are. They are the enemy of the people.

Trump did not shy away from his earlier attack, despite the outcry. Rather his words were met with loud applause at CPAC, an audience that had long been familiar with accusations that the press harbored a strong resentment toward conservatives and conservative ideas. Trump then delved into negative news stories employing unnamed sources as evidence of journalistic fabrications:

> Because they have no sources, they just make 'em up when there are none. I saw one story recently where they said, "Nine people have confirmed." There're no nine people. I don't believe there was one or two people. . . . And somebody reads it and they think, "Oh, nine people. They have nine sources." They make up sources.

Trump proceeded to critique journalists' complaints regarding his enemy claims, arguing that he was speaking only about a small sliver of journalists:

> They're very dishonest people. In fact, in covering my comments, the dishonest media did not explain that I called the fake news the enemy of the people. The fake news. They dropped off the word "fake." And all of a sudden the story became the media is the enemy. . . . So I'm not against the media, I'm not against the press. I don't mind bad stories if I deserve them. . . . But I am only against the fake news, media or press. Fake, fake. They have to leave that word. I'm against the people that make up stories and make up sources.

He returned to his dislike for unnamed sources and argued that they should be disallowed.[11] Trump moved on to opinion polling as another site where he imagined journalists fabricating results in a conscious effort to attack him. After calling out polling at CNN, CBS, ABC, and NBC, Trump argued that the polls were misleading the public:

They're so bad, so inaccurate and what that does is it creates a false narrative. And we have to fight it, folks, we have to fight it. They're very smart, they're very cunning and they're very dishonest.

Trump's reaction to the polling reflects his high disapproval rating early in the presidency. By day 33 of his administration, roughly when he gave the CPAC speech, FiveThirtyEight.com's poll aggregator gave Trump a disapproval rating of 50.2% and an approval of 43.7%. Very quickly this pattern locked in, and continued throughout Trump's presidency.[12] But at the time, Trump argued that the polls were being manipulated by the journalistic organizations that conducted them.

Trump ended his attacks on the press by reaffirming his First Amendment right to critique journalists before returning to the populist, anti-elite rhetoric that was at the core of his campaign:

And many of these groups are part of the large media corporations that have their own agenda and it's not your agenda and it's not the country's agenda, it's their own agenda. They have a professional obligation as members of the press to report honestly. But as you saw throughout the entire campaign, and even now, the fake news doesn't tell the truth. . . . So just in finishing, I say it doesn't represent the people, it . . . never will represent the people, and we're going to do something about it because we have to go out and have to speak our minds and we have to be honest.

The speech highlights the nuances of how Trump's attacks on the press shifted once he had gone from candidate to president. Certainly, Trump regularly condemned the press after he secured the Republican nomination, but his way of talking about journalists changed when his policies and actions as president became the focus of reporting. Journalists that had during the campaign been seen first as useful and then as a nuisance now became an obstacle to governing that had to be confronted. Trump's heightened combativeness worked to inoculate him and his administration from criticism not by refuting the factual claims of journalists but by attacking journalists' own normative arguments that they act as neutral chroniclers working on behalf of the public interest.

Journalists responded in horror at Trump's language. The *New Yorker*'s David Remnick raised alarm against Trump's enemy accusations as he defended his profession: "This is not a matter of the press seeking to pro-tect itself as an interest group. The interest group in question is the United States."[13] What emerges then is a fight to define the interests of unseen masses amalgamated alternatively as the people, the public, or the nation. Both Trump and journalists assembled these symbolic allies to defend their position and cast the other side as dangerous.[14] The extremity of these two positions elevates the consequences beyond any particular story or moment to indicate a deeper struggle over who has the authority to communicate truthful accounts.

After declaring journalists to be enemies of the people, first on Twitter and then in expanded terms in the 2017 CPAC speech, Trump refrained from using the enemy wording for well over a year. This period corresponded with Trump's efforts at governing while maintaining majorities in both houses of Congress and instituting a solid majority on the Supreme Court. This restraint ended in summer of 2018 as confidence mounted that Democrats would likely regain control of the House of Representatives in the November midterm elections. Democratic candidates for office loudly condemned Trump, and the narrative that emerged was of the elec-tion as a referendum on his presidency. Once the midterm election ended, newly empowered Democrats began to investigate Trump, most visibly resulting in Trump's impeachment trial in early 2020. These investigations meant more legal and legislative clashes within government, but they also portended a greater degree of negative news coverage directed at Trump. Trump responded to all of this by stepping up his attacks on journalists, calling them the "enemy of the people" thirty-seven times on Twitter be-tween June 2018 and November 2019, which comes out to about once every two weeks over that span. After a hiatus during the impeachment and the early days of the coronavirus outbreak, Trump began using it again as the 2020 election heated up, tweeting eleven times that journalists were ene-mies of the people between March 2020 and Election Day and using the phrase during his campaign rallies.

This repetition both heightens and dulls the impact of the terminology. Certainly the labeling of journalists as "enemies of the people" is severe and frightening. Most immediately, it suggests that news coverage can be dis-counted as the product of a combative press corps. But the "enemy" label also shortens the distance to more dangerous calls for violence and state censorship—staples of autocratic governance. And yet the repetition of the statement, often through terse tweets, renders such accusations mundane to the point of being widely ignored. While the first instances of Trump's use drew loud condemnation, the reactions had dampened as the charge was made more often.[15]

Looking at the tweets afresh demonstrates their disturbing qualities. In early August 2018, roughly two months before the midterms, Trump offered one of the more robust tweets making the enemy claim:

> The Fake News hates me saying that they are the Enemy of the People only because they know it's TRUE. I am providing a great service by explaining this to the American People. They purposely cause great division & distrust. They can also cause War! They are very dangerous & sick![16]

Trump, as usual, positions himself as a democratic savior uniquely suited to exposing the truth not merely for his supporters but for an audience more broadly constituted as the "American People." In keeping with his previous attacks on the press, his accusations are both severe and vague. No specific story or journalist is invoked, but instead broader accusations of "division & distrust," causing war, and being "very dangerous and sick." Interestingly, all these accusations were regularly made against Trump through critiques of his polarizing populist rhetoric, his penchant for lying, and questions about his mental fitness.

Trump's frequent use of the enemy language allowed him to reiterate his charges, but a closer look shows how the semantic flexibility of this line of attack meant it could expand to all of journalism or it could contract to pinpoint some subset. An example of the former came two years after his initial tweet attacking the press as the enemy of the people, when Trump blasted out an all-capital letter Tweet that simply read:

> THE RIGGED AND CORRUPT MEDIA IS THE ENEMY OF THE PEOPLE![17]

This tweet is notable for its lack of any specifying language regarding the "fake" media and instead seemed to suggest that, generally, all journalism is the enemy of the people. The term "media" is expansive, and it is unclear how much of a modifier "rigged and corrupt" is supposed to be. The capitalization lends it an air of urgency and thoroughness. By contrast, Trump has also used the term in more specific targeting. For example, he used it to vent anger at book authors:

I just cannot state strongly enough how totally dishonest much of the Media is. Truth doesn't matter to them, they only have their hatred & agenda. This includes fake books which come out about me all the time always anonymous sources and are pure fiction. Enemy of the People![18]

In the final months of the 2020 campaign, Trump reiterated his past patterns with periodic enemy tweets. Some were more detailed, such as a May 5, 2020, tweet that collapsed journalists and the Democratic Party, although inverting the usual claims of journalists working for Democrats:

The Do Nothing Democrats and their leader, the Fake News Lamestream Media, are doing everything possible to hurt and disparage our Country. No matter what we do or say, no matter how big a win, they report that it was a loss, or not good enough. The Enemy of the People![19]

Here the "enemy" tag at the end seems to apply to a fuzzy conglomeration of journalists and politicians, but specificity isn't the point. Trump also stuck to more simple messaging, tweeting out in all-caps "FAKE NEWS IS THE ENEMY OF THE PEOPLE!" on August 3, 2020.[20]

Trump's enemy claims also made it into his political rallies. The previous chapter showed how candidate Trump treated the reporters present at the rallies as a prop, singling them out as an object of derision for the thousands of supporters present in the same space. In keeping with the above tweets, Trump similarly ratcheted up his attacks on journalists covering the rallies. At a West Virginia rally on September 29, 2018, Trump pointed to the press pen and began to excoriate the reporters in attendance:

And the number one enabler of the Democrats is the fake news media right back there. And they really do, they stoke the fires of resentment and chaos. They report incorrect news. They report phony news, and you know, when I say—when I say and come out with very, very strong statements about media, I'm talking about the fake news media.[21]

Trump hedged by insisting he is only referring to the "fake" news, yet his statement easily slides to include all of journalism. The ambiguity here is whether he is referring to the specific journalists at the rally as the "they" in his statements or treating them as synecdochic of the larger journalistic community. This confusion of just whom he is targeting aside, Trump continued on by returning to the enemy rhetoric:

> They are truly an enemy of the people, the fake news, enemy of the people.
> They really are. They are so bad. . . . This November 6, you have a chance to
> reject these disgraceful political hacks, but you can only do it, you got to
> vote Republican, I mean, we have good people.

Trump equates voting for Republican candidates with countering journalists, which again collapses all of Trump's opponents into an amorphous mass.

Even as Trump's ability to hold rallies was curtailed during the 2020 election, he still used them to attack journalists as enemies. A week before the election at a rally in Tampa, Florida, as Trump complained about how the *New York Times* was covering him, he again called journalists an enemy: "Look, we are in big trouble with the press. They are truly the enemy of the people. They are the enemy of the people."[22] During this rant, Trump singled out CNN along with the *Times* as actively working against him by fabricating negative stories and ignoring positive ones. Trump would go on to win Florida again, even as he lost the election.

The close connection between journalists as the enemy and journalists as a political entity can also be seen in Trump's references to the press as the "opposition party." While in isolation this term may appear less egregious than the "enemy of the people" claim, it was used to suggest that journalists operated as an organized body. At a time when Trump was regularly uttering the enemy phrase, his use of oppositional party augments his efforts to construct a unified opponent:

> THE FAKE NEWS MEDIA IS THE OPPOSITION PARTY. It is very bad
> for our Great Country. . . . BUT WE ARE WINNING![23]

Although short, the tweet contains several familiar populist elements: the excoriation of journalists as opponents while suggesting an ambiguous collective by using the language of "our" and "we." This extends the target of the putative harm away from merely Trump or his administration to the entire public. The declaration of victory fits with the timing of the tweet in the months before the 2018 midterm elections in a bid to suggest momentum for Trump while rallying voters with the assertion that voting for Republicans equated to defeating journalists.

Trump invoked the "opposition party" language again several months later, after Democrats had taken control of the House of Representatives, as he explicitly linked specific news organizations with the Democratic Party:

> The Mainstream Media has NEVER been more dishonest than it is now. NBC and MSNBC are going Crazy. They report stories, purposely, the exact opposite of the facts. They are truly the Opposition Party working with the Dems. May even be worse than Fake News CNN, if that is possible![24]

This tweet is notable for its alignment of journalists with the Democratic Party at the moment that Democrats regained control and began to initiate investigations that would eventually lead to the impeachment of the president. Trump was seeking to amalgamate his opponents to suggest the conspiracy against him, fitting with his constant refrain of victimization. This argument continued on throughout his presidency. On October 7, 2020, Trump tweeted, "THE FAKE NEWS MEDIA IS THE REAL OPPOSITION PARTY!"[25]

A final means through which Trump regularly insulted journalists during his presidency was in his use of the term "lamestream" media. As a play on words of the term "mainstream media," the term was made prominent in 2008 by Sarah Palin, the proto-populist Republican vice presidential candidate.[26] After not using the term during the campaign or the first years of his presidency, Trump used the "lamestream" media term ninety times in tweets between July 26, 2019, and Election Day 2020, often as a way of pairing journalists with Democrats:

> Never has the press been more inaccurate, unfair or corrupt! We are not fighting the Democrats, they are easy, we are fighting the seriously dishonest and unhinged Lamestream Media. They have gone totally CRAZY. MAKE AMERICA GREAT AGAIN![27]

Trump's tweet provides several reasons for discounting press coverage by challenging the motives, accuracy, and mental health of journalists. A month later, Trump zeroed in on accuracy to suggest that negative reporting on Trump was manipulated:

> The LameStream Media has gone totally CRAZY! They write whatever they want, seldom have sources (even though they say they do), never do "fact

checking" anymore, and are only looking for the "kill." They take good news and make it bad. They are now beyond Fake, they are Corrupt.[28]

As Trump faced impeachment investigations in fall 2019, he continued to connect journalists with Democrats as a collective opposition:

> The Radical Left Dems and LameStream Media are just trying to make it hard for Republicans and me to win in 2020. The new Impeachment Hoax is already turning against them![29]

This tweet also indicates Trump's pivoting toward his re-election campaign, when Trump positioned himself as running against not just a Democratic opponent, but what he characterized as biased journalists. Because Trump was already in power, he again needed to elevate the press as an adversary with power on par with his as both president and the symbolic head of the Republican Party.

No matter the label, Trump treated journalists as a unified political actor using its considerable power to stop him. This language has two effects: First, it treats journalists as a unitary, organized adversary. This line of attack implants and reiterates the notion that journalists are joined together in their active detestation of Trump. Second, it collapses animus toward Trump with animus toward "the people." The entire nation, and not just Trump, is represented as the victim of journalists' attacks. Once defined this way, journalists striving to stay out of the story could not help but be pulled into it. They are unable to fall back on professional detachment as a defense and are drawn into the political arena that they seek to cover from a distance. From this perspective, the underlying meaning of the preceding messages is not that any particular story was wrong or should have been told from a different angle. Instead, this discourse conveys a more fundamental message that the accounts that journalists produce should not be seen as truthful or legitimate. He is seeking to undermine the production of journalistic factuality at its roots.

Sparring with Journalists: Trump's Press-Bashing Performance

With less than two week before the 2020 election, Donald Trump ventured out of the conservative news spaces to which he had become accustomed in order to appear on CBS's venerable *60 Minutes* program in an interview with Lesley Stahl. Word had leaked days earlier that Trump had walked off during the interview, which heightened attention ahead of the broadcast. Trump officials preemptively attributed his actions to Stahl's biased questions.[30] Trump directly criticized Stahl in a series of tweets, including, "Watch her constant interruptions & anger. Compare my full, flowing and 'magnificently brilliant' answers to their Q's."[31] Even before it aired, the narrative of the interview had settled into Trump versus Stahl—and, by extension, all political journalists.

The interview began with Stahl asking, "Are you ready for some tough questions?" and Trump responding "You're gonna be fair" and complaining that Joe Biden had not been challenged.[32] Stahl continued to press Trump during the interview, challenging him on his claims about his economic record and the current state of the coronavirus pandemic. Trump and Stahl sparred across political issues, with the topic shifting back to news coverage. Trump complained that journalists ignored scandals involving Biden while also bringing up debunked conspiracy theories. Stahl pushed back, citing the lack of evidence for Trump's claims. When she argued that presidents should be subject to difficult questions, Trump responded by saying, "That's no way to talk." After the interview was interrupted briefly, Trump said as he stood and walked off, "I think we have enough of an interview here, Hope [Hicks]. Okay? That's enough. Let's go. Let's go. Let's go meet for two seconds, okay? Thanks. I'll see you in a little while. Thanks." Trump did not return and instead Vice President Mike Pence sat for a scheduled interview.

The interview made for dramatic television, but assessments fell predictably according to political allegiances. For Trump supporters, Stahl's combative tone and her challenging of Trump provided evidence of journalistic bias, particularly among elite journalists. For Trump's critics, Stahl gave a masterclass in holding the president to account and not letting him make false statements. What got lost in the aftermath was the substance of the disputes. Ultimately the skirmish between them became a matter of political performance, with the authority of Trump buoyed by his refusal to sit through an interview and the authority of Stahl boosted by her toughness. Both sides benefited—but everyone lost.

Trump's clashes with journalists speak to his general approach of pulling no punches, but they also augment his frequent characterizations of journalists as enemies. They demonstrate Trump standing up against his journalistic opponents, often in ways that strengthen the symbolic nature of these performances by bringing attention to forms of news stories rather than their content. Although Trump engaged in skirmishes with many journalists, the sections that follow take up two examples. The first concerns how Trump regularly insulted journalists of color, often by invoking racist stereotypes around intelligence and obedience. The second focuses on a public dispute between Trump and CNN reporter Jim Acosta in 2018. Both illustrate how Trump's fights with reporters reverberated with his image of standing up to a journalistic enemy.

Targeting Journalists of Color

Trump rarely spares any journalist from his ire, except those within conservative media channels, and the preceding sections looked at these attacks at a general level. However, Trump engaged in a particular pattern of specifically calling out journalists of color as unintelligent or unruly. In doing so, Trump activates deep-seated stereotypes that African Americans face regarding intelligence, which have become ingrained in social settings like education.[33] The perniciousness of this stereotype is a cultural artifact of racism and efforts of the white majority to allege its superiority through the assumption of minority deficiency. When Trump invokes the intelligence of African American journalists, he is connecting to this mythology in a way that activates racist sentiments among his supporters.

None of these attacks are unprecedented. Trump has repeatedly made racist statements or taken racist positions, from his discriminatory policies as a landlord to his role in pushing the "birther" conspiracy around Barack Obama, and from his stereotypes of Muslims and Mexicans during the campaign to his statements as president.[34] In addition to journalists, Trump has also attacked a number of African American politicians using racist stereotypes, also often around intelligence.[35] All of this provides context for his attacks on Black journalists, and we talk about how journalists confronted this racism in greater depth in Chapter 5.

CNN anchor Don Lemon, a high-profile African American journalist who has vocally labeled Trump a racist, has been a particular target for Trump. Trump singled out Lemon as a target in his Twitter tirades, calling him "dumb" or "dumbest" at least eight times. For example, Trump pushed back on a *New York Times* story alleging his habit of watching copious amounts of television news by specifically insulting Lemon's intelligence despite Lemon's lack of relationship to the story:

> Another false story, this time in the Failing @nytimes, that I watch 4-8 hours of television a day - Wrong! Also, I seldom, if ever, watch CNN or MSNBC, both of which I consider Fake News. I never watch Don Lemon, who I once called the "dumbest man on television!" Bad Reporting.[36]

Trump also commented on Lemon's intelligence in a separate tweet about CNN's ratings that again had nothing particular to do with Lemon's specific ratings:

> Wow! CNN Ratings are WAY DOWN, record lows. People are getting tired of so many Fake Stories and Anti-Trump lies. Chris Cuomo was rewarded for lowest morning ratings with a prime time spot - which is failing badly and not helping the dumbest man on television, Don Lemon![37]

Fellow CNN anchor Chris Cuomo, who is white, was not similarly insulted for his intelligence.

Trump has also attacked Lemon more directly for his reporting, including for Lemon's interview with NBA star LeBron James in which James criticized Trump for his divisiveness. In a tweet, Trump insulted the intelligence of both Lemon and James (while showing support for Michael Jordan):

> Lebron James was just interviewed by the dumbest man on television, Don Lemon. He made Lebron look smart, which isn't easy to do. I like Mike![38]

The tweet became news because it was targeting two African American males, but also because Trump had only recently attacked US Representative Maxine Waters of California as possessing a "very low I.Q."[39] Trump subsequently rejected claims that he had a pattern of engaging in racial stereotypes around intelligence while simultaneously attacking Lemon's intelligence. After Lemon invoked Trump's racist rhetoric during a debate of Democratic presidential candidates, Trump tweeted:

> CNN's Don Lemon, the dumbest man on television, insinuated last night while asking a debate "question" that I was a racist, when in fact I am "the

least racist person in the world." Perhaps someone should explain to Don that he is supposed to be neutral, unbiased & fair.[40]

Trump's attacks on Lemon have unfolded over years, but they coalesce in a focus on denigrating Lemon for intelligence rather than pointing to opinion differences or reportorial skill. Trump even quoted himself in an April 2020 tweet labeling Lemon as "Don Lemon, the 'dumbest man on television.' "[41] Taken together, these tweets promote racist stereotypes that resonate with a significant portion of the population that shares these prejudices. Doing so conflates Trump's frequent efforts to delegitimize journalism with racist rhetoric, both of which serve his appeal to a populism rooted in white ethnocentrism.

Trump also came under fire for attacking women journalists of color using the same stereotypes. During a single week in November 2018, Trump insulted three female African American journalists. He dismissed a question by CNN's Abby Phillip as "stupid" and told her, "You ask a lot of stupid questions." In a different press gaggle, he said of American Urban Radio reporter April Ryan: "You talk about someone who's a loser. She doesn't know what the hell she's doing," and called her "very nasty." At a press conference, he responded to PBS *NewsHour* correspondent Yamiche Alcindor's question about Trump and white nationalism as "a racist question" while publicly berating her in front of the White House press corps for being disrespectful.[42] The notion that Alcindor, as a Black woman, needed to show public respect for Trump, a white man, directly connects to the social enforcement of racial hierarchies that plagues US history. The series of attacks brought the issue to public attention, and drew special condemnation from the National Association of Black Journalists.[43]

Trump continued to critique journalists of color throughout his presidency. When CBS News White House correspondent Weijia Jiang asked Trump a question about Covid fatalities at a press conference in May 2020, he responded by telling her, "Maybe that's a question you should ask China."[44] When Jiang followed up about why he made the comment to her specifically, he called it "a nasty question" and then abruptly left the briefing. At a rally a month before the 2020 election, Trump referred to MSNBC anchor Ali Velshi getting hit by rubber bullets fired by police as "the most beautiful thing" and equated it to the appropriate exercise of law and order by police.[45] Velshi was covering protests in Minneapolis after the murder of George Floyd when police began attacking reporters. He was among many journalists that the police targeted.[46]

It can be difficult to disentangle these instances from the mass of denigration that Trump aimed at the press as a presidential candidate and then as president. The attention that journalists of color received from Trump was tangled up in his constant targeting of journalists, including his frequent use of amorphous collectivizing identifiers like "fake news," "corrupt news," and "lamestream" media. Nonetheless, special attention is owed to his targeting of journalists of color because they connect back to the white nationalist elements of his populist rhetoric. They point to the erosion of decency and a rejection of diversity. This is heightened in an era of tribalism in which journalists of color are doubly written off as biased. Any suggestion of journalistic professionalism falls away with the racist assumption that because they are not white, they cannot cover issues involving race objectively. For Trump, journalists of color become one more enemy to be combated and vanquished.

Trump versus Acosta

Trump singled out many news organizations as president, but CNN was an especially prominent target in Trump's tweets and rallies. It became a go-to for accusations of liberal bias and collusion with the Democratic Party, despite CNN's penchant for pundit-driven, both-sides-based coverage. CNN also competes with the Fox News Channel, a regular vehicle that Trump used to communicate outside of traditional news channels. Already, this chapter and the previous one contain many examples of Trump berating the network and its journalists. One notable clash that deserves attention involved Trump and CNN White House correspondent Jim Acosta. Acosta comports himself in the tradition of other White House correspondents with an adversarial questioning style designed to be overtly challenging rather than deferentially eliciting information.[47] This combativeness is itself a type of performance used to signal journalists' independence from their sources—in this case, the president of the United States. Trump, with his own predisposition toward combativeness, is able to transform his interactions with the press into another opportunity to castigate journalists. Doing so transforms press conferences into a space of conflict that feeds both journalists' desire to show independence and Trump's arguments that he is the victim of journalistic hostility. Finally, Acosta's Cuban American roots and Latinx last name connects to the deeper nativist themes present in Trump's populist rhetoric.

Trump and Acosta first clashed at a press conference on May 31, 2016, shortly after Trump secured enough delegates to be assured the Republican nomination and after press-bashing became a more pertinent part of his campaign rhetoric. When Acosta went to ask a question, Trump responded sarcastically: "I've watched you on television, you're a real beauty."[48] At a press conference on January 11, 2017, following the election, Trump attacked CNN for reporting on a BuzzFeed news story alleging connections between the Trump campaign and the Russian government. When Acosta tried to interject and ask a question, Trump brushed him off by telling him, "Your organization is terrible" and then added, "You are fake news."[49] Trump was sworn into office later that month, and Acosta remained a visible member of the White House press corps.

Things boiled over at a press conference at the White House on November 7, 2018. This was the day after the midterm elections in which Democrats made historic gains to retake a majority in the House of Representatives in an election largely interpreted as a referendum against Trump. Following the custom of his predecessors, Trump took questions from the press. He began by touting Republican Senate victories and explaining away Democratic victories through a populist amalgamation of elites that included the Democratic Party, the wealthy, journalists, and the ambiguous category of "special interests" that suggests a mixture of labor unions and nonprofit organizations: "We did this in spite of a very dramatic fundraising disadvantage driven by Democrats' wealthy donors and special interests, and very hostile media coverage, to put it mildly."[50] Trump went on to defend his record before turning it over to questions.

Eventually Trump called on Acosta, who adopted an adversarial style of questioning common among the White House press corps: "Thank you, Mr. President. I wanted to challenge you on one of the statements that you made in the tail end of the campaign in the midterms, that this . . . ," at which point Trump interrupted with "Here we go." Acosta pushed Trump on his characterization of Central American migrants as an "invasion" headed to the United States, which Trump continued to assert. After a back-and-forth, Trump told Acosta: "I think you should—honestly, I think you should let me run the country, you run CNN." Acosta persisted with another question, further angering Trump, who responded, "That's enough. Put down the mic." During the exchange, a White House intern tried to remove the microphone from Acosta. Acosta resisted by pulling his arm away and telling her, "Pardon me, ma'am." When Acosta didn't stop, Trump, visibly upset, said: "I'll tell you what: CNN should be ashamed of itself having you working for them. You are a rude, terrible person. You shouldn't be working for CNN." Off-mic, Acosta confronted the president over the threats CNN had received as a result of Trump's constant criticism. Trump responded by telling Acosta, "When you report fake news, which CNN does a lot, you are the enemy of the people." The exchange became the most prominent moment of the press conference, eclipsing any other statements that the president made about the midterm elections or policy prerogatives in the second half of his term.

Later that day, Acosta had his press pass confiscated by the Secret Service, effectively ending his ability to report from the White House. The White House justified the action by pointing to Acosta's treatment of the intern that had tried to take back the microphone. This was supported by a controversial video created by a frequent contributor to the right-wing conspiracy site InfoWars that seemed to show Acosta physically striking the White House intern who had tried to remove the microphone from his hand. Press Secretary Sarah Sanders distributed the video as evidence supporting Acosta's ban, but the video had been doctored to make the exchange look more violent.[51] Sanders's circulation of and support for the video drew complaints from other journalists, including the White House News Photographers Association.

The banishment of Acosta resonated within the White House correspondent community. Just two days later, during a press gaggle held next to a waiting helicopter, Trump was asked about his treatment of Acosta: "Mr. President, how long are you going to leave Jim Acosta in the penalty box?"[52] This was the language of sports, positioning Trump as referee and suggesting that Acosta had been given a temporary suspension for some infraction, rather than a more serious question of press censorship. Trump answered the question by condemning Acosta's reportorial style:

> I think Jim Acosta is a very unprofessional man. He does this with everybody. He gets paid to do that. You know, he gets paid to burst in. He's a very unprofessional guy. Whether it was me or Ronald Reagan or anybody else, he would have done the same thing. Look, I don't think he's a smart person, but he's got a loud voice.

A reporter followed up to ask if the ban was permanent. Trump answered:

And as far as I'm concerned, I haven't made that decision. But it could be others also. When you're in the White House—this is a very sacred place to me. This is a very special place. You have to treat the White House with respect. You have to treat the presidency with respect. If you've ever seen him dealing with Sarah Huckabee Sanders, it's a disgrace.

The gathered reporters stayed on the topic of Acosta by referring to the doctored video that gave an impression of Acosta's physical aggressiveness when a White House employee tried to strip him of the microphone. Trump rebutted claims of alteration:

Nobody manipulated it. Give me a break. See, that's just dishonest reporting. All that is, is a close-up. See, that's just—that is just dishonest reporting. I watched that; I heard that last night. They made it close up. They showed it up close up. And he was not nice to that young woman. I don't hold him for that because it wasn't overly, you know, horrible. But it was— but all that was—when you say "doctored," you're a dishonest guy. Because it wasn't doctored. They gave a close-up view. That's not doctoring.

This attention to Acosta during the informal gaggle rather than other issues reveals the concern that other White House correspondents had with the story, but their questioning only gave Trump space to reiterate his own criticisms without adding new information.

Trump also attacked Acosta in an interview with the *Daily Caller*, a conservative news site.[53] When asked about Acosta, Trump spoke at length about the situation, calling Acosta "a grandstander" who is "bad for the country" because he is disrespectful of the presidency. Trump pivoted from Acosta to again call journalists "the enemy of the people":

You know, when I say that the fake news is the enemy of the people, it really is. A lot of the animosity that we have in our country is because of fake news. They're so angry at the news. They get it. You guys are at my rallies all the time, you see the anger when I mention the words "fake news" and they turn around [to look at the journalists in the press pen].

Trump then dismissed the importance of press freedom as a factor in his banning Acosta:

Is it freedom of the press when somebody comes in and starts screaming questions and won't sit down after having answered a couple of them?

The interview provided an example of Trump using partisan media channels friendly to him to attack traditional media channels (which, in the interview, included ABC, CBS, NBC, and the *New York Times*). For Trump, Acosta served both as an egregious example and as a metonym symbolizing other news outlets. The latter was made possible through Trump's repeated attacks described earlier in the chapter. Acosta became just one more example in a self-serving narrative of a powerful press corps intent on defeating Trump.

As Acosta's ban lingered, CNN responded with a lawsuit against Trump and other administration figures. *CNN v. Trump* was filed on November 13, 2018, with famed media law lawyer Theodore Boutrous as counsel. The network sought the immediate restitution of Acosta's credentials on the grounds that he had been denied due process. The case was dropped less than a week later on November 19 after the White House agreed to reinstate Acosta, staving off a potentially high-profile trial.

The seeming feud between Trump and Acosta spilled out beyond the White House. Writing in the *Columbia Journalism Review*, Nina Berman noted how Acosta became a fixture at Trump rallies. Like other journalists covering Trump's speeches, Acosta was sequestered in the press pen. These cordoned spaces provided some security to the journalists, but they did so by increasing their visibility to the rally attendees. We have already discussed Trump's use of journalists as props at his rallies. Acosta, with his visibility from challenging Trump, became a particular target for the crowds. Berman described the scene:

> For the Trump audience, demeaning Acosta is a bonding experience. He is both an enemy and a selfie trophy. I saw a father directing his young daughter to walk by the press cage and take a photograph of Acosta with her phone. When she did, he put his arm around her in affirmation. For Acosta, the experience appears harrowing. The CNN anchor comes across as gentle and unassuming in person, but clearly the attention from Trump's supporters is exhausting, mystifying and no doubt distressing as he could be seen working with security guards on either side of him.[54]

Acosta's presence mattered. In the act of covering Trump, he himself was on display. For Acosta, this was physically perilous but professionally reassuring.

After returning from his ban, Acosta resumed his style of confronting Trump. For example, at a February 15, 2019, press conference, Trump took the controversial step of declaring a national emergency in order to divert military funds to the building of a border wall.[55] The wall had been a consistent campaign promise of Trump's, and an enduring symbol of his hardline anti-immigrant policies that fed into his nativist populism. Given the spurious nature of the emergency designation, the press conference was contentious in tone. At one point, Trump called on Acosta, who confronted Trump:

> Let me just ask you this: What do you say to your critics who say that you are creating a national emergency, that you're concocting a national emergency here in order to get your wall because you couldn't get it through other ways?[56]

The question was a familiar one that had been at the forefront of political conversation preceding the announcement, but Trump responded by arguing with Acosta that the emergency was indeed real. As before, they both sparred over facts, with the exchange becoming increasingly heated. Trump then attacked Acosta more directly for asking "a very political question," stating: "You're CNN. You're fake news. You have an agenda. The numbers that you gave are wrong. Take a look at our federal prison population. See how many of them, percentage-wise, are illegal aliens. Just see. Go ahead and see. It's a fake question." That Trump's use of statistics was misleading at best is beside the point.[57] The encounter did not result in any new information. Instead, it served a performative function. Confronted with data contradicting the foundation of his declaration, Trump berated Acosta as a way of berating CNN, which, for Trump and his supporters, symbolized pernicious media bias broadly. The supposed agenda of Acosta was expanded more broadly to journalists everywhere working against Trump. A disagreement over factual details, which theoretically could be adjudicated, turned into accusations of deeply held bias that could not be verified. The argument that Acosta, in asking a legitimate question, was doing so out of a political agenda makes the disagreement over facts disappear, aiding Trump's political cause.

Meanwhile, the reinstated Acosta also gains from this confrontation. His questioning becomes not just a means of gathering information, but a symbolic display of journalistic independence in the face of Trump's press-bashing. Acosta literally and symbolically stands up to the president of the

United States. The action then becomes part of the story, with Acosta doubly serving as a journalist and a news source, symbolizing not only by CNN but other news outlets as well. This performance aims to underscore the authority of the press, but it does so in a way that does not alter the basic political situation. Trump persisted in pushing a policy that was driven by political identity rather than any actual justified need, regardless of the flimsy arguments he put forth to support his plan. Public opinion remained unchanged. Acosta stayed on in his role, and on August 5, 2020, Trump tweeted, "Jim Acosta is a Fake reporter!"[58]

We are left to conclude that the appearance of confrontation is more important than the substance of it. As president, Trump retained massive power, both practically and normatively, to alter policy. Journalists lack a corresponding check on such power when their confrontational performances fail. They persist in raising questions, challenging claims, and exposing holes in reasoning, but they do not alter the outcome. Thus while we support the right of journalists, Acosta included, to confront the power of the president and loudly condemn efforts to exclude or demonize reporters, we are simultaneously left to question what difference it made in this instance. Did Trump inoculate himself against reporters to the point where he was impervious to their challenges? If so, was the ado around Acosta an empty performance of journalistic autonomy? These are the difficult questions we must ask when we examine how journalists have confronted contemporary demagoguery in a polarized media environment rife with deep mistrust of journalists.

Conservative Media as Agitator of and Amplifier for Trump's Attacks on Journalists

The Trump presidency, as we have shown in this chapter, was largely a battle over grievances and grudges against perceived foes. Perhaps nowhere is this more evident than in Trump's ceaseless invocation of the "enemy" and "fake news" labels for journalists, which served both to undermine faith in the press generally—ensuring his supporters would not take seriously the evidence-based investigations that news media dug up throughout his term—and to create performative showcases against journalists in a way that would draw attention away from more substantive evaluations of his administration's policies. As a former reality television producer, Trump deftly drew journalists into his made-for-TV presidency as an unwitting bad guy—inflating the importance of the press as an existential enemy with tremendous power, even as he waged war against that foe on behalf of "the people," the real Americans, from episode to episode and season to season, always the triumphant hero. But these attacks on journalists were not simply the stuff of tweets and rallies, nor were they reflective of Trump's personal predilections alone. Rather, they were aided by and reflective of a conservative media system that preceded Trump and will long outlive him. The final section of this chapter considers the impact of conservative media—as an infrastructural arrangement of media amplification occurring through a vast network of television shows and social media surrogates, and as a cultural arrangement with a long history of go-to tropes and tendencies, including ones that situate the press as a something of an "enemy" to American conservatives.

To illustrate this point, let's return briefly to how Trump developed his most potent line of attack against journalists. Beyond Twitter and his rallies, Trump also used conservative media as a ready platform to label journalists as enemies of the people. In an interview on the Fox News Channel's *Hannity*, he was not subtle in defending his use of the phrase. After suggesting vaguely that journalists concoct controversy through unnamed sources, Trump said that the news "really is the enemy of the people. It's fake news, but it's the enemy of the people, more importantly."[59] He made a similar argument a few months later again on the Fox News Channel while appearing on Laura Ingraham's show, *The Ingraham Angle*.[60] As a specific example of why the enemy title was deserved, he cited a lack of accurate coverage concerning the size of the attendance at his political rallies. This was in keeping with his tendency to isolate what he considers personal slights against him as evidence of bias—a bias not just against him, but part of a larger prejudice against "the people," never more evident than when the news media were involved.

Importantly, then, Trump's presidential clashes with the press—from his enemy tweets to his mano-a-mano escalation with Acosta—did not occur in a vacuum. They did not fall from the sky, nor did they fall on deaf ears. They drew from and simultaneously reinforced a much broader, more enduring drumbeat of discontent with journalists that has animated American conservatives for the second half of the twentieth century.[61] Much of that discontent rests on the belief that mainstream news media are irredeemably biased against (or at least willingly ignorant of) the lived experiences and interests of Republicans generally and the Christian right specifically. When Trump rages against the press, he is tapping a well of conservative grievances about perceived media mistreatment, accumulated over decades and perpetuated by the likes of talk-radio hosts such as Rush Limbaugh, advocacy groups such as Accuracy in Media and the Media Research Center, the editorial pages of *National Review*, the *Weekly Standard*, and the *Wall Street Journal*, and, of course, the Fox News Channel, the most visible and influential expression of right-wing frustration with perceived left-wing journalistic bias.[62]

Conservative News Cultures

Animus toward the press has been a key organizing force behind the development of what A. J. Bauer and Anthony Nadler call "conservative news cultures." This refers to the ensemble of actors, networks, ideas, and familiar modes of media production and circulation that have come to define the modern conservative movement and have "helped cultivate an attachment to conservatism as a social identity."[63] In many respects, contemporary conservative news cultures represent an allergic reaction to mainstream news cultures—a collectively expressed, if loosely coordinated, form of pushback against perceived failings and blind spots in traditional journalism. Seen one way, these conservative news cultures can be imagined as part of the broader media culture that we described earlier, just another constellation in the expanding universe of media choices, within and beyond the realm of what passes for "news." Yet, from another view, conservative news cultures seem to be a world apart, differentiated from other "news cultures," to use Stuart Allan's phrase,[64] by virtue of their distinct partisan flavor and ideological commitments.

Conservative news cultures are more than simply the institutionalization of right-leaning news sources. Rather, they are defined just as much by the dialectical relationship that is developed between media producers and media audiences—a shared set of cultural understandings and forms of meaning-making that move back and forth among creators, consumers, and modes of circulation. This co-constitution, Bauer and Nadler note, is evident in the way that news, whether conservative or not in its orientation, "varies according to the words and actions of newsmakers, according to the judgments of particular reporters and outlets, according to cultural and political economic structures of circulation, and according to the myriad interpretive frameworks employed by audiences."[65] Mutual reinforcement is the essence of what makes (conservative) media work.

Conservative news cultures, though regrettably neglected in journalism studies,[66] have long afforded right-leaning Americans a sympathetic space for their political thought, particularly with the emergence of a populist brand of conservatism that first blossomed on commercial talk radio in the late 1980s and 1990s and then took fuller shape in the early 2000s with the surging success of Fox News on cable television and the *Drudge Report* and *Townhall* online.[67] Indeed, in a nod to how conservative news institutions contribute to shaping broader developments of media culture, including the struggle over journalistic relevance, Bauer and Nadler point to the outsized impact of the *Drudge Report*: "The enormous popularity and influence of [the site] . . . cannot be separated from the decline of professional journalism's hegemony, the burgeoning of online citizen journalism, and the powerful dynamics of online attention that favor sites establishing prominence early in the development of a digital genre."[68] Since the early days of the internet and throughout its expansion, conservative "news entrepreneurs"—such as Michelle Malkin, Andrew Breitbart, and Ben Shapiro—have proven adept in proactively adopting emerging media technologies, from blogs to podcasts to YouTube.[69] As Jen Schradie has shown, the rise of online forms of political mobilization, far from leveling the playing field between haves and have-nots, benefited more powerful, entrenched, hierarchical interests, and has, in particular, been a boon to conservative activists and causes more so than progressive ones.[70]

Between the continued impact of right-wing talk radio and Fox News as well as the proliferation and popularity of right-wing digital offerings, the cross-platform reach and impact of conservative news helped enable Trump's rise and also allowed him and his supporters to find solace in something of an alternative media universe.[71] As Bauer and Nadler note, "The vast power of conservative news cultures to affect the circulation and norms of political discourse could not be rendered more starkly" than it has been in recent years.[72] For example, consider the state of affairs on Facebook, where, in 2020, right-wing influencers such as Shapiro were by far the most dominant shapers of political discussion, their articles consistently among the top ten best-performing links posted by US Facebook pages. "The reason right-wing content performs so well on Facebook is no mystery," wrote the *New York Times'* Kevin Roose, who tracks partisan fare on the social network. "The platform is designed to amplify emotionally resonant posts, and conservative commentators are skilled at turning passionate grievances into powerful algorithm fodder.["73] Roose may accentuate the technology's influence, but clearly a sizable audience interested in this content exists.

Beyond merely amping up the scope and spread of right-leaning sources, however, conservative news cultures served an especially crucial function in supporting Trump's salvos. They both provided fodder for Trump's attacks against his foes and, in the way they reposted and repeated his messaging, lent an amplified visibility and a reverberating sense of legitimacy to his claims—including quantitative measures of popularity in the form of likes and shares as Trump's messaging circulated within right-wing media networks and in wider public discourse. It is a process of reinforcement that is so familiar that it almost went without notice during the Trump presidency, as described in this dispatch from August 2020:

> Most days, Donald J. Trump tunes in to *Fox & Friends*, a cable talk show whose sometimes conspiratorial news judgment is often reflected in the president's trademark early morning tweets. Those tweets are themselves treated as news—the controversial ones covered breathlessly by mainstream political reporters across mediums. The president's supporters like and re-tweet his posts, spreading their content among likeminded and followers across platforms, while his detractors retweet with snarky rejoinders. Often rejoinder tweets themselves go viral, giving quaternary life to bits and pieces of news originating in the judgment of Fox News reporters, editors, and commentators.[74]

These conservative news cultures thus acted as information subsidies for Trump "pre-publication" and as promoters for him "post-publication." Like public relations agencies seeking to get news coverage for their client, they would feed the president a continuous stream of material, which in turn he would monitor by tuning in to his favorite Fox News hosts or the more stridently right-wing stations Newsmax or One America News, scrolling his Twitter feed for things to retweet (such as memes or links from supporters), or asking aides, as he was known to do, for printouts of his preferred right-wing websites (such as *Breitbart* and the *Daily Caller*).[75] At the same time, this expanding pro-Trump network of actors served to echo and extend the availability and influence of Trump's talking points—or, what he chose to "publish," as it were, from what was on offer to him in an information environment they helped create.[76]

"Safe Spaces" for Protection against Journalists—and Platforms from Which to Fight Back

Conservative news cultures have served as a friendly enclave for Trump—as well as his supporters—to retreat to in order to avoid being challenged by journalists working elsewhere in the media environment. The CNN journalist Brain Stelter,[77] one of the most consistent chroniclers of this phenomenon through his *Reliable Sources* newsletter,[78] noted how the president was "self-isolating at his safe space" to avoid difficult questions as he began to face mounting criticism for his administration's handling of the unfolding coronavirus pandemic in late March 2020.[79] Some six months later, amid a persistent pandemic and as the president himself was recovering from his own bout with Covid-19, the *New York Times* noted, "At the most politically and physically vulnerable point of his presidency, Mr. Trump has retreated to his safe space: conservative media programs, where he can rely on warm, ego-boosting chats with supporters like Maria Bartiromo, Sean Hannity, Rush Limbaugh and Mark Levin."[80] Indeed, by the late stages of the 2020 election campaign, Trump had in his time in the White House granted more than one hundred interviews to Fox News programs, compared to only a handful to the other major networks.[81]

It could be argued that such extreme friendly media isolation was not good political strategy, walling off Trump, as it did, from a larger audience of potentially persuadable voters available via mainstream networks. Nevertheless, it fit comfortably within the larger framework that Trump had assembled over the course of his presidency. He had come to trust, in effect, that he did not need to directly address the broader media audience convened by the legacy press to convey his message and win elections. Perhaps he imagined that the press, shrinking in size and increasingly decentered in the larger media culture, would unwittingly amplify his tweet-sized communiqués anyway—which, in fact, it did, often allowing Trump's tweets to set the media agenda.[82] Or, perhaps the self-reinforcing conservative media ecosystem would accomplish enough of that amplification work for him. Regardless, the outcome was the same: Trump tapped a ready-to-go network of right-wing media enablers that would effectively insulate him from the criticism he so hates, keep his base in a state of constant vigilance and anxiety, and present him all the cultural and informational resources necessary to take the fight directly to journalists themselves—the dreaded "enemy of the people."

Ultimately, Trump's base-only political strategy failed. He lost to Joe Biden by seven million votes and an Electoral College margin of 306 to 232. But the scope and persistent influence of the conservative media infrastructure, one that so assiduously cultivated and reinforced Trump's grievances against journalists and other "radical Left" enemies, became even more visibly apparent in the months after the November 2020 election. Following several days of uncertainty after some state races were too close to call on election night, the legacy press—from national newspapers to all the major broadcast and cable television networks, including Fox News—all made it clear by November 7: Biden had won and Trump's presidency was over. But Trump, who for months had signaled he would treat any results that did not go in his favor as "rigged," claimed on Twitter that same day, "I WON THIS ELECTION, BY A LOT!" That tweet would end up being the third-most popular of some sixteen thousand tweets he posted while president.[83] His campaign to "stop the steal"—to achieve something of a self-coup by overturning the election results in his favor—was on, and right-wing media allies were ready. Even as some news-side Fox News journalists pushed back against claims about election fraud, citing the complete lack of evidence, the network's opinion hosts and commentators were eager to sow doubt and confusion. "We don't know how many votes were stolen on Tuesday night," Tucker Carlson said on his popular evening show in the week after the election. "We don't know anything about the software that many say was rigged. We don't know. We ought to find out."[84]

The same pattern of amplifying Trump's election denialism—even giving oxygen to the most wackadoodle conspiracy theories—played out across talk-radio shows by the likes of Limbaugh and Levin, right-wing news sites like Breitbart, and upstarts like the fringe Newsmax TV, which saw its ratings soar as conservatives looked for a more assertively pro-Trump alternative to Fox News.[85] It wasn't just pundits, of course. Republican elected officials at many levels accepted the "big lie" that Trump had won the election because it was politically expedient to do so.[86] Even as dozens of lawsuits failed to offer evidence of fraud and were thrown out by state and federal judges around the country, the GOP enterprise—from its politicians to its media surrogates to its fervently pro-Trump base—descended deeper into the "stolen election" narrative, one that both readily tapped into and was fueled by the frenzied conspiracies of the QAnon movement, with its notions that the US government is controlled by a global cannibalistic cabal of Satan-worshipping pedophiles.[87] Behind much of the anger about supposed electoral corruption that occupied many of Trump's tweets and his allies' airtime for weeks after the election was a recurring theme that had animated this conservative news ecosystem for years: the notion that journalists, like the Democrats and dreaded "deep state" elites, were part of a vast conspiracy. As CNN's Stelter described it in the days after the election:

> From [radio host] Mark Levin to [Senator] Ted Cruz, one of the Trump-might-have-won crowd's main themes is that the major [television] networks hastily called the election for Biden. It's a farcical claim since we all waited five days to know the outcome and since the networks simply report on the results of the vote count. But the claim is sticking, nonetheless, and it is stoking right-wing rage against the media. Sean Hannity put up a graphic on Monday night that said "THEY HATE YOU," referring to the media and the tech platforms. That's been the takeaway from his show for years, but he rarely says it so bluntly. Subtext is becoming text all over the place right now.[88]

These persistent and unfounded claims of election fraud foretold the deadly events that transpired on January 6, 2021. For weeks, Trump and his supporters anticipated a massive gathering in Washington as a show of force to protest the certification of the election results affirming Biden's victory as president-elect. "Big protest in D.C. on January 6th," Trump tweeted on December 19, in one of several tweets promoting the day. "Be there, will be wild!"[89] Such prompting led to tens of thousands supporters pouring into the nation's capital. In a rally speech outside the White House, Trump fulminated against the "fake" news media and the "fake" election, as if they were two sides of the same coin.[90] He told his supporters to fight, and so thousands of them did—marching on the Capitol, breaching security barriers, breaking windows, trashing congressional offices, and assaulting police in an insurrection that will long remain part of political memory. Summing up the scene, *Washington Post* columnist Max Boot wrote:

> Five people died during the storming of the Capitol, and it could have been a whole lot worse. The attackers chanting "Hang Mike Pence" came within a minute of finding the vice president. Federal prosecutors allege that a retired Air Force officer who was carrying zip-tie handcuffs wanted to "kidnap, restrain, perhaps try, perhaps execute members of the U.S. government." Police officers interviewed by *The Post* described a "medieval

battle scene" with rioters "battering the officers with metal pipes peeled from scaffolding and a pole with an American flag attached."[91]

Yet, within days of the shocking attack, many of the same high-profile actors in conservative media who had fanned the flames of "stop the steal" had already begun to whitewash events. Even as the story grew in the following days, a corresponding effort to make the story go away commenced across pro-Trump media figures. As CNN reported, "Far-right personalities are trying to minimize the Capitol attack and divert blame away from President Trump. There are even some strands of full-fledged 1/6 denialism, something akin to the 9/11 'truther' movement that has festered on the internet for nearly 20 years."[92] Within hours of the assault on the Capitol, right-wing pundits, without any evidence, began blaming Antifa, and the charge gained particular traction after Fox News' Ingraham said the attackers "were likely not all Trump supporters" and her guests speculated about Antifa's possible role.[93] The far-right cable channel One America News labeled the attack an "incident," as if it were an innocent misunderstanding.[94] Republican politicians, as noted in the case of Rubio above, were quick to shift the blame elsewhere, including by suggesting that the press bore some responsibility for being politically divisive.

Outside the conservative bubble, however, several critics assigned complicity to the merchants of misinformation in right-wing media—most prominently, the Fox News Channel,[95] the "beating heart" of the right-wing media body.[96] "There is a whole infrastructure of incitement that will remain intact even after Trump leaves office," Boot argued in the Washington Post. "Just as we do with foreign terrorist groups, so with domestic terrorists: We need to shut down the influencers who radicalize people and set them on the path toward violence and sedition." Washington Post media critic Margaret Sullivan—who also wasn't shy about criticizing journalists for their failings in covering the Trump administration—also singled out Fox News for its unique role in sustaining and amplifying Trump's falsehoods:

> Day after day, hour after hour, Fox gave its viewers something that looked like news or commentary but far too often lacked sufficient adherence to a necessary ingredient: truth. Birtherism. The caravan invasion. Covid denialism. Rampant election fraud. All of these found a comfortable home at Fox. In the Trump era, the network . . . was his best friend and promoter. So to put it bluntly: The mob that stormed and desecrated the Capitol on

Wednesday could not have existed in a country that hadn't been radicalized by the likes of Sean Hannity, Tucker Carlson and Laura Ingraham, and swayed by biased news coverage.[97]

While the nature, causes, and consequences of right-wing radicalization will be a point of debate for many years after the 2021 attack on the Capitol, what remains clear is that the central tenets of Trump's approach to journalism—casting journalists as perpetual enemies of the people while creating an alternative reality—cannot be sustained by a single individual alone. It is an institutional accomplishment. It relies on the support of many actors, large and small, profiteers and provocateurs, all organized around a shared goal of perpetuating a narrative while ignoring information that undermines this narrative. This requires a media culture expansive enough to allow for such partisan isolation to flourish.

Conclusion: Why Trump's Attacks Matter

A single chapter can only capture a sample of the total public vitriol Trump directed at the press during his presidency. Yet even this snapshot is overwhelming and exhausting. Moving from these specific insults back to the big picture, we are left with two questions: When the president engages in such vehement attacks, what effect does this have on journalists' ability to assert that they provide truthful accounts to their audiences? And what does it mean when these attacks have become so normalized? Even as the analysis in this chapter tries to identify nuances and patterns, Trump's constant bashing of the press eventually blurs together into a mass of invective. Moreover, the unpleasantness of these messages makes them repulsive to anyone who is not an ardent supporter. That does not make them unimportant. The previous chapter introduced Trump's press-bashing as a form of political performance where the repetition of messages matters as much—if not more than—the content of the messages. It is a reaffirmation of core beliefs, or a type of creed, that helps hold together a community through its opposition to journalistic elites. From this perspective, the escalation of Trump's anti-press rhetoric deserves attention for how it alters the basic tenets of journalism's relationship with political power.

Trump's hostility toward journalists may be unlikely to persuade opponents, but it does resonate with political conservatives who have long shared a belief that most national journalists are against them and their party. Evidence for the widespread effectiveness of Trump's message is difficult because these are issues of belief and interpretation with long histories, but public opinion surveys do bear out a crude representation of such feelings. A July 2019 survey by *The Hill* and HarrisX found that a third of the population agreed that the press could better be classified as an "enemy of the people" than as an "important part of democracy."[98] Predictability, this was a partisan response, with 51% of self-identified Republicans preferring the enemy language. A Quinnipiac University survey from May 2019 reported nearly identical numbers, with 49% of Republicans agreeing with the enemy label.[99] On the one hand, these surveys indicate that a very large swath of the public agrees with Trump. Yet a problem with these surveys is that they tend to dichotomize responses instead of allowing for nuanced reactions. Respondents are forced to select between extreme positions—journalists as angels or as demons. In addition, they do not distinguish between different kinds of news media, but treat all journalists as a mass. Those frustrated with journalism have their concerns channeled into extreme positions, and these positions are fed back to the public as representing public opinion. In doing so, they normalize Trump's enemy rhetoric as a widespread position on journalism, which then may feed back into people's expectations. In this way, these constant attacks do matter in that they reaffirm a totalizing position that extends beyond the critique of an individual story, journalist, or outlet. They feed a narrative of anti-press sentiment.

Trump's attacks on the press are notable for how they subvert expectations from the literature on news sourcing. Certainly, the relationship between journalists and their sources has been a complicated one precisely because it cannot be reduced to merely cooperation or conflict. Herbert Gans compares the source-journalist relationship to both a tug-of-war and a coordinated dance.[100] That these positions are both correct requires careful consideration of how they fit together. At a functional level, journalists and sources form a mutual dependence on one another to achieve their goals.[101] News sources, from those in positions of power to those seeking to attain such power, need the publicity afforded by the news. But the relationship is antagonistic for the same reasons. Sources encounter risk when they rely on journalists because they lack control over the news product. Certainly the Trump administration operated within this dynamic as it promoted its policy agenda. Journalists continued to press Trump for information when they could, and administration officials engaged in interviews with journalists—on and off the record.

But Trump encased this exchange within a broader prism of journalistic conspiracy, imbuing all news coverage with the suggestion of partisan taint.

In attacking journalists as he did, Trump was able to take advantage of the convergence of three structural conditions: journalism's neutrality norms, embedded discourses of press bias, and a media culture that increasingly decenters journalists. There is no shortage of criticism of Trump within news discourse, whether in response to his attacks on journalists or more broadly about his policy agenda and his personal behavior. However, because the presidency is accorded such a degree of political and symbolic power, he continued to be covered as a legitimate news source, often through an objective lens. No matter how vicious his attacks, he remained a powerful and legitimate source because of his position. Trump also benefited from the long-standing claims of liberal media bias such that he would draw on them to activate this sentiment in his followers. Even if this approach alienates a broad segment of the population, it simultaneously rallies others to his side. Trump channeled this long history of liberal bias claims into a populist perspective that amplified journalists' elitism as much as their political opinion. By also according journalists with political power as either the oppositional party or as working in tandem with Democrats, journalists became entrenched as an enemy. This strategy constructs an us-versus-them dynamic, but Trump's divisiveness remained a political asset rather than a liability when he was able to marshal the bare minimum of support to attain power.[102] Finally, Trump benefited from a media culture marked by audience fragmentation and an expansion of channels outside the confines of traditional mass-media outlets. The benefits of this fragmentation were most visible in his use of Twitter to reach voters and shape media coverage, as the many examples we have cited show. But Trump consolidated the messaging around him in the period when he ended daily briefings by the press secretary, such that he alone dominated White House communication. Meanwhile, he utilized conservative media channels to advance his attacks on the press.

Given this confluence, Trump's focus on vilifying journalists is not about trying to spin news frames. It goes deeper to strike at the epistemological foundations of news reporting.[103] This resulted in a blanket rejection of news narratives through the frequency of attacks, the severity of the charges he made against reporters, and the ambiguity of who these enemies were. Furthermore, Trump's attacks were remarkable in how they were absorbed into the larger news discourse such that they came to color all news reporting on Trump. All of this points to the ways in which Trump waged an epistemic battle against journalism's institutional knowledge structures. And the degree to which journalistic norms of detachment constrained journalists' abilities to respond only served Trump's interests. Trump has shown that political gain can be had in engaging in divisive politics that exploit racist and nationalist tendencies, in maligning journalists while drawing on partisan media networks for support, and in disregarding democratic norms—all of which point to deep-seated trends that will persist for some time. He also exploited journalists' inability to respond and their penchant for the controversial and sensational. Taken together, this all signals continued antagonism commensurate with authoritarian governance. Accusations that the press is the enemy invite violence toward journalists and the need to turn to politicians for protection from this enemy. In what may be a harbinger of things to come, the Committee to Protect Journalists recorded 110 arrests of reporters in the United States in 2020, compared to just 9 in 2019. In addition, more than 300 journalists were assaulted, mostly by police.[104] This is a recipe for democratic dysfunction.

While Trump may have derived a short-term political advantage from his frequent press-bashing, the long-term effects are more difficult to discern. The examples in this chapter point to a wider crisis of relevance for journalism. What makes the issue of relevance more difficult is that journalists have few means of enforcing their authority outside of appealing to norms that support their work. These norms have been built in a way that position journalists as central to democratic governance while detached from the messiness of power. But this position has long been eroded as larger swaths of the public find fault with journalism. Journalists continue to function as if the past rules governing how news works in society—that is, how sources ought to act and how audiences ought to respond—remain largely in place. The examples in this chapter make us not so sure. Trump has found political success in attacking journalists at the level of their legitimacy rather than at the level of their facticity. Others will surely follow in this strategy. In response, journalists have begun to ask why this has become the case and what they can do about it, which we now turn to in the remaining chapters.

4

The Press Fights Back

Reclaiming a Story of Relevance for the Press

In early August 2018, the *Boston Globe* put out the call. It would be a single day—August 16—in which dozens of news organizations across the country might band together in solidarity in a loud response against President Trump's attacks on the press. The editors had had enough: they viewed Trump as deliberately undermining a major pillar of US democracy with his "fake news" assaults. By August 14, some 200 newspapers said they would join the cause. Two days later, it was 411. And by the end of August, more than 600 had chimed in. The hashtag #FreePress and #NotTheEnemy peppered social-media platforms. In California, the *San Diego Union-Tribune* built an entire site dedicated to explaining journalism.[1] In Tennessee, the six Gannett newspapers joined to craft a single editorial. For Nancy Acrum, editorial editor at the *Miami Herald*, the decision to participate was a no-brainer: "This is what we do," she told the Poynter Institute.[2] Student presses, radio journalists, tiny community papers, and behemoths such as the *New York Times* raised their editorial voices with one common message: *We are not the enemy*. And in doing so, they went beyond just chiding Trump in their fight to reclaim power over what we call journalism's "grand narrative"; they were seeking to reclaim relevance.

The previous chapters chronicled how Trump pushed to the fore longstanding narratives of journalists as power-hungry, unscrupulous, or pushers of an exclusive, elite-centric worldview. This strategy is savvy in how it undercuts the dominant messaging from the mainstream press, which suggests that journalists' accounts cannot be trusted or even that they perpetuate lies via "fake news." This direct, intentional, and ongoing campaign has stated explicitly, loudly, and to mass publics what had been a steady undercurrent of discontent about journalism for the better part of a century. Journalists have always been skeptical of the motives of their sources, and animosity between the press and politicians is by no means novel. But the

News After Trump. Matt Carlson, Sue Robinson, and Seth C. Lewis, Oxford University Press. © Oxford University Press 2021. DOI: 10.1093/oso/9780197550342.003.0005

degree of enmity underlying Trump's attacks signaled a greater schism. Accordingly, Trump's style of attack evoked an existential crisis for the press.

The journalistic story has never been without its contradictions, as we will make clear in this chapter, and the profession and its actors have always worked under great stress in the United States, as journalists have in all countries.[3] What has emerged, though, is a narrative in which journalists are victims in serving the public: they toil for long hours for often little pay, encounter hostile and recalcitrant sources, comb through endless documents, and even risk their personal safety to report complex issues to the public. Studies of news industry trends show that journalists face ample challenges in meeting the needs of the populace or democracy, as their newsrooms shrink and their ranks dwindle.[4] This is a popular narrative that accentuates journalism's instrumental role in America's democratic way of life—this idealized picture of who journalists are and what they do. It has gained authority over time as journalists seek jurisdiction over the nation's flow of information.[5]

On the other hand, people increasingly accept a counternarrative: journalists are not to be trusted because they place their own aggrandizement above truth, work to promote some kind of (usually liberal) agenda, do not accurately account for facts, and are corrupted by advertisers and political elites.[6] Meanwhile, digital platforms such as Twitter and partisan media sites offer right-wing populists channels to further demonize the press as untrustworthy. Surveys of news audiences show widespread dismay with the work of journalists.[7] We saw the disastrous effects of this on January 6, 2021, when thousands of Trump supporters stormed the Capitol in Washington, DC, as Congress attempted to certify the electoral votes showing that Joe Biden would be the next president of the United States. This act of political violence was simultaneously an assault on journalism. Videos from that day captured the intense vitriol these insurgents felt about the press as they screamed at reporters for being traitors to their country, attacked at least nine of them, and broke their equipment. Journalists found themselves in physical danger as the hours of mayhem wore on. Protesters scrawled messages like "Murder the Media" on Capitol doors.[8]

What possible response can journalists have to this kind of attack when it comes from the presidency and an unknown portion of the US population? How can journalists turn back this tidal wave of malevolence to productively explain their role in public life? The August 2018 coordinated effort in newspaper editorials was one of the first of its kind in the United States.

It represented an effort of solidarity rarely seen among such competitive, commercial entities. Amid the wrangling over journalism's future accelerated by the rise of Trump, these editorials provide an entry point for better recognizing how, for many people, journalism's preferred narrative has become toxic; for evaluating, from the journalists' perspective, the impact of an expanded media culture; and for assessing what journalists are trying to do about that loss of control over who and what they are. Through these editorials, journalists reacted to the strong headwinds buffeting the profession by heralding a golden age of mainstream press reporting, celebrating the founding principles of democracy, and recommitting to traditional practices of objectivity while tirelessly uncovering wrongdoing. They called upon particular symbols, including Watergate and the First Amendment, to support these claims. They situated their brands as important community guides, stakeholders, and even family and friends. This was a call to the public and a yearning for audiences to recognize newspapers' importance, even as their circulations dwindle. Through all of it was a dogged commitment to a specific moral voice that connects journalism with democracy, as the "good guys" who fight evil, meant to appeal to an assumed shared moral code about Americans' sense of righteousness for freedom of the press and against tyranny.

But it is not enough for journalists to remind citizens of their presence and reassert their normative role as watchdogs. We argue that any effective response to contemporary cultural and epistemic conditions requires that journalists confront their own shortcomings. Journalists need a deeper appreciation for how the story of US journalism has too often excluded important stakeholders and systematically misrepresented groups of people. Journalists cannot return to their core arguments as if nothing has changed. Instead, a new narrative is needed, beginning with a willingness to ask why public trust has so dwindled. They need to acknowledge how structural inequalities prohibit many, especially those in typically marginalized communities, from finding a place in the vision of American democracy conveyed in news accounts. And they need to develop new methods of telling and sharing stories that are more expansive, incorporating other kinds of value systems—ones not so centered on grand binaries of good and evil, and which also appreciate alternative perspectives about what it means to be an American. Of course we support journalists fighting back against an onslaught of mostly partisan critique aimed at invalidating legitimate news, but we also view this moment as an important opportunity to move from a defensive stance to one focused on inclusive community-building.[9]

In this chapter, we examine the newspaper editorials themselves and the industry trade-press response as reflexive discourse about the role of journalists in society. In doing so, we offer insight into the battle for the story of journalism, at a time when populist movements—under the guise of being for the people and against political elites and broken institutions—attack the legitimacy of journalism. We first consider how grand narratives allow institutions to perpetuate singular value systems that inevitably privilege certain approaches and perspectives, and how these narratives legitimate institutions as authorities—logistically, politically, morally, and otherwise. In particular, we consider how grand narratives can be involved in building institutional trust, but also examine how those institutions have too often overlooked essential stakeholders and thereby consolidated power in the hands of too few. We then recount how certain depictions of the press contribute to its authority by framing journalists as purveyors of democracy— the press-as-hero archetype. Of course, an alternative story of distrust competes with this grand narrative, and we spend some time documenting how the press-as-villain caricature has come to dominate current political discourse. This lays the ground for examining how the six hundred-plus editorials defending journalism that ran in August 2018 formed an effort to reclaim journalism's narrative and retain its relevance. In examining these editorials, as well as publishers who opted out or who criticized the effort, we reveal the rhetorical links between authority, truth, and power that play off each other in this discourse. In these stories, we see journalists wrestling with the tension between their detached, objective voice and their innate closeness to communities, seeking the right moral voice—one that will not betray their foundational *raison d'être* while being more attractive to an increasingly diverse public. The press does not quite succeed at navigating this tension. Ultimately, these counterattacks begin to shift the narrative toward a more personalized, customized storyline that might be more amenable and attractive to citizens today. While on the surface this episode may appear as a unifying moment for journalism, a closer look reveals a deep fracturing within the industry as news outlets engage in epistemic struggles over what journalism is, what it should look like, and who produces truthful accounts. Furthermore, the January 6, 2021, attacks indicate a much more fundamental task ahead for mainstream journalists, one that is less about the press itself than about producing a shared sense of democracy as a foundational value for the United States. The events of the 2021 insurgency revealed that what is more dangerous than the distrust of the press is the complete rejection of any shared set of facts—an essential element to self-governing and a shared sense of community.

Grand Narratives

To explore the grand narrative of journalism, a first step is to explain how we use the term "grand narrative." Many definitions exist, but generally it refers to an overall story or series of stories that convey a dominant value system and exist to explain life's phenomena. We derive this definition from theorists who think of grand narratives as similar to myths but distinct from mere story. These theorists believe that through storytelling we construct meaning about the world around us and form connections. And they suggest that grand narratives create and perpetuate worldviews that contain a system of knowledge that guide us.[10] In these grand narratives—just like in myth or any kind of complete narrative—we find heroes and villains, dominating frames and themes, motivations and overarching morals. An example of a grand narrative at the social level—and one frequently reproduced through news accounts—is the American Dream. The mythology of the American Dream might lead to accentuating how a new business owner overcomes obstacles to achieve success, or how an immigrant fleeing turmoil elsewhere flourished in the United States. In both examples, the message is clear: if you work hard, you shall reap rewards.[11] This dream typically is reinforced via quotes from the Declaration of Independence, "The New Colossus" poem affixed to the Statue of Liberty, or some other national emblem. Such grand narratives are durable in the face of contradictory information. Despite ample evidence that social mobility in the United States has declined in recent decades, that class distinctions have hardened, and that systemic racism shapes individual opportunities, the mythology of the American Dream persists as a way of imagining and ordering the world around us.[12]

As an analytical tool, the notion of a grand narrative invokes two seemingly contradictory positions. On the one hand, grand narratives achieve a level of reification, where they seem to endure as a common set of rules and expectations that dictate how people act in the world. They have a moral weight, as they are viewed as perpetual, constantly reproduced, and solidified, such that altering the fundamentals of the narrative appears difficult if not impossible. Grand narratives are resilient. From this perspective, grand narratives operate as "sociopolitical forces in our interconnected world," and these stories support institutions that structure the way we live.[13] Institutions make use of these grand narratives. As a result, "Having been given a narrative framework, the audience simply knows—without being told—what is likely to happen and what actions they are supposed to take."[14] Journalism, as a political and social institution,[15] reproduces grand narratives in myriad framing decisions that shape how news stories order the world for people. This includes how the news distills complex political problems into binaries, highlights the competition between different "sides" of an issue, and privileges powerful institutions when crises and tragedies hit. Thus, this view of grand narratives suggests that we navigate the world through the stories we have. "I can only answer the question 'what am I to do?' if I can answer the prior question, 'of what story or stories do I find myself a part'?" suggested the poet Alasdair MacIntyre.[16]

Yet grand narratives, at their core, are not free-floating entities but socially constructed ones. They are continuously enacted through discursive agents who promulgate and shape them. This view corresponds to Anthony Giddens's argument that actors within a structure have agency to improve or undermine the structure at hand—including the grand narrative.[17] Indeed, the very notion of a grand narrative has sprung up alongside its critique, particularly through postmodernism. Jean-François Lyotard coined "grand narrative" and "metanarrative" in his 1979 book *The Postmodern Condition* to argue that societies were moving away from such all-encompassing narratives.[18] Institutions have always relied on grand narratives to achieve a level of authority for acting within particular jurisdictions. But as trust in institutions has fallen in recent decades,[19] the cohesive ideas traditionally relied on to help us find order amid chaos have also fragmented. As postmodernists have asserted, grand narratives cannot be static things; they become fragile as societal conditions evolve, shifting the relative importance or diminishing the impact of social institutions.[20] In this view, grand narratives are doomed because of the ongoing splintering of shared beliefs.

We approach the concept of grand narratives from both directions. We recognize that shared identities emerge through the stories that get told, and that specific narratives unite people across space and time. People look to these grand narratives to establish both inspiration and prohibitions around acceptable behavior. But we also recognize the mutability of grand narratives as discursive constructs, and we are attuned to the question of power—that is, who speaks for the grand narrative (and why), and how others are denied this position of authority. Particularly as we examine journalism in its response to Trump as an agent and as a symbol, both of these dimensions of grand narratives need attention.

The Grand Narrative of the Press over Time

During the colonial period and in the wake of the Revolutionary War, the founders made it clear the press would be an integral part of making a democracy work, enshrined in the US Constitution's declaration in the First Amendment that "Congress shall make no law . . . abridging the freedom . . . of the press."[21] Early on, even before the establishment of the United States, Americans hoped the press would provide a check on the government, using truth as a major weapon. Or at least this is the mythology that has endured. In actuality, an elite-oriented partisan press ruled, often serving as mouthpieces for the politicians in power.[22] If this is the case, how did this mythology develop, and whose interests has it served? Journalistic practice has always been accompanied by narratives that legitimate the news, give it a history, and place it within the larger story of American democracy. James W. Carey lamented how an optimistic framing of journalism as a constant march toward improvement obscures the cultural dynamics of journalism in any time and place.[23] Nevertheless, this section recounts the broad strokes through which a triumphant history of American journalism has been written.

The grand narrative of journalism that predominates today can be traced to developments a little more than a century ago. In the early twentieth century, in response to pro-democracy reforms of the Progressive Era, the American press underwent an important transition, with journalists eschewing the sensationalism of the nineteenth century for an emerging mode that stressed individualism and rationality over partisanship and emotionality. This coincided with journalists' growing efforts to steer their occupation toward becoming a profession with generally accepted norms, ethics, and standards—and the story of a press as central to democracy went along with these changes.[24] Trade press organizations such as the Society of Professional Journalists began popping up, often in association with new journalism schools attached to universities.[25] This epistemic shift accompanied an economic one, too: as news audiences swelled, advertising dollars followed. For newspapers in that period, a nonpartisan orientation was an effective way to reach more people.[26]

The grand narrative of journalism is supported both by a normative language and through a referencing to key events and figures. An example of how a grand narrative about truth, watchdogging, and intrepidness slowly took hold was the 1947 Hutchins Commission. It formalized this grand narrative in a report that chastised the press for not living up to its own storyline.[27] In the report, the commissioners—a mix of academics and publishers—peppered the rhetoric with the word "freedom" (e.g., "freedom of the press means freedom of and freedom for"), reminded journalists that they had an obligation to society (e.g., "it must be accountable to society for meeting the public need and for maintaining the rights of citizens and the almost forgotten rights of speakers who have no press"), and declared that the press's role was about "making a contribution to the maintenance and development of a free society."[28] And, by 1959, journalist Douglass Cater's *The Fourth Branch of Government* popularized a notion of the press as a check on the other three branches of government because of its watchdog-reporting role, one dedicated to the health of the republic and its notions of democracy.[29]

The apotheosis of the narrative that the press is a powerful profession entrusted with holding leaders to account came with the Watergate scandal and the resignation of President Richard Nixon.[30] Over time, the story of Watergate has crystallized into a narrative starring *Washington Post* reporters Bob Woodward and Carl Bernstein as dogged reporters single-handedly defending democracy. This was helped along by their best-selling memoir *All the President's Men* and the 1976 movie by the same name. Mark Feldstein recounts how Woodward and Bernstein's publisher described the plot of the book as the story of how "two young reporters . . . smashed the Watergate scandal wide open," and Warner Brothers summarized the movie as "the story of the two young reporters who cracked the Watergate conspiracy" and "solved the greatest detective story in American history."[31] Matthew Ehrlich and Joe Saltzman point to the symbolism of having actors Robert Redford and Dustin Hoffman always standing in the light, with government buildings always in shadows.[32] In its cinematography, the movie "graphically portrays the David-versus-Goliath odds against the two reporters by showing them as mere specks against the Washington landscape or inside the Library of Congress."[33] In many ways, this press-centric retelling of Watergate leaves out the crucial work of many in the judicial and legislative branches. But this has not halted its importance for journalism's self-identity, providing a point of pride that would continue to serve as a guiding mythology for journalists who came into the industry many years after the scandal. It retains its symbolic importance as journalists draw on its inspiration to counter attacks on their industry.[34]

The resilience of the grand narrative is also apparent in moments when it seemed threatened. In the face of scandals—such as the fabrications of Janet Cooke at the *Washington Post* in the 1980s or Jayson Blair at the *New York Times* in the 2000s—mainstream news organizations have engaged in the ritual of "paradigm repair" to isolate potentially foundational threats as the work of lone actors while propping up the overall institution.[35] Dan Berkowitz positions paradigm repair as a "professional ritual" for reporters that does double duty for the press and the public.[36] The protection of professional ideology in no small part rests on the restoration of journalism's grand narrative. When questions about journalistic performance arise, journalists mount a defense by calling on the tenets of the narrative: independence from faction, adherence to verifiable facts, distance from sources, and veneration to codified principles. By publicly reiterating the norms of the profession, journalists insulate themselves from the wayward soul who has sullied journalism in some way. Following the ways of the institution preserves the assertion that the resulting news stories are "correct."[37] Failure to follow the ways of the institution means banishment from the industry and no longer fitting into the grand narrative except as a symbol of deviancy.[38] This system may be effective for policing journalism, but it inhibits a more sustained reflexivity among journalists and the public about why failures in journalistic performance occur and what could make journalism better.

The journalistic community often explicitly reaffirms its own social role, such as when journalists are reflexive during times of remembering, such as anniversaries of major news events or the deaths of prominent figures. Barbie Zelizer's classic work catalogs how journalists have used the anniversary of US president John F. Kennedy's assassination to perpetuate an image of themselves as the established and rightful storytellers of the event.[39] Zelizer notes that journalists—much like politicians and historians—"use constructions of reality to mold external events into preferred forms."[40] Thus, over time the story of Kennedy's assassination has downplayed the confusion or mistakes made during the event for a version that puts journalists in the center of the story. This narrativizing that positions journalists as prominent actors within the stories they cover has persisted through the decades. For example, journalists revisiting the devastation of Hurricane Katrina constantly reminded audiences of their presence in New Orleans during that devastating Category 5 hurricane and its aftermath.[41] They connected their authority to their presence in the space of the story.

Although these illustrations situate journalists as the primary definers of the profession's grand narrative, pop culture plays an essential role as well.[42] In particular, fictional depictions often represent journalists as American heroes when the (usually white male) reporters uncover scandal and protect democracy against the evils of repression and abuses of institutional power. Prominent examples—for example, *All the President's Men, His Girl Friday, Citizen Kane, Good Night and Good Luck, The Newsroom, The Paper, Spotlight,* and *The Post*—may portray journalists as less than perfect and the news-making process as hectic and messy, but they generally support a heroic vision of the journalist.[43] Even in negative depictions of the press, journalists are portrayed as persistent, resourceful, and idealistic.[44] Given that the mythology of the grand narrative depends on the idea of defending truth, it is fitting that Superman and his alias of reporter Clark Kent can each act as a "tireless fighter for truth and justice" and "the American way."[45] These pop culture depictions of journalists draw on and reinforce the grand narrative, feeding off its cultural scripts and assumptions while also supporting a heroic vision of journalists and their social role.

This section has cited several prominent examples of how journalism's grand narrative is maintained and restored through discourse that connects the past to the present and imagines a continuation of journalistic authority into the future. That these stories matter beyond the journalists directly connected to them demonstrates how journalism's grand narrative contributes to a shared professional identity, in spite of a lack of professional licensing and intense competition between reporters and across news organizations.[46] While we want to be careful not to overstate the cohesiveness of journalism, these stories do matter for how they come to reside not only within the mythology of the profession but also within the larger cultural mythology as a whole. And they became particularly useful for journalists seeking to fire back at Trump after being subjected to years of press-bashing.

Who Tells the Stories of America?

As a knowledge-producing institution, journalists have long promoted a grand narrative that places their work as central to society and indispensable to democratic life. Journalists' bid for relevance cannot be read purely by looking at news texts, but instead requires attending to how the news is rendered discursively as deserving of its special status and privilege. For journalists, this has meant the perpetuating of "Grand Virtues,"[47] such as that democracy represents the common good and institutions are benevolent—a particular morality that is bounded and inflexible. We do not question the earnestness of these expressions or suggest they are a ruse. On the contrary, these narratives as they are framed in news stories are built into the very fabric of how we think of ourselves as Americans. Our interest in this book is to point to how modern journalistic practices exist alongside a set of narratives that justify and legitimate the practices of these institutions, including the press as an institution. We need to continuously ask who creates and encourages these narratives and for what purpose, and what their implications are for how society and culture are constructed. But we also need to be clear that these narratives exist within a particular social context and that these fundamental assumptions about what it is to be an American are being challenged—as the next section attests.

If we revisit Trump's (and others') persistent attacks on journalism discussed in the earlier chapters through the lens of journalism's grand narrative, we can see his attempts to rewrite the story of journalism in America. His press-bashing seldom homed in on specific quibbles but rather aimed at journalism as a broad, amorphous, and powerful entity that was antithetical to his presidency and, by extension, the United States and its people. As we have cataloged throughout the pages of this book, Trump regularly declared the *New York Times*, *Washington Post*, CNN, and any number of mainstream, legacy news outlets to be "fake news" and damaging to the health of the United States. And these attacks appear to resonate with a large swath of the nation: 45% of respondents in a fall 2017 Gallup / Knight Foundation poll said they no longer trusted the news media, and their reasoning had to do with journalists' supposed "fake news," "bias," and "alternative facts."[48] Similar numbers have been reported for countries across the world as well.[49]

Yet, even with such vocal press-bashing, we caution against giving too much credit to Trump for this situation. The groundwork of an antagonistic metadiscourse about the press had already been laid. The conditions in which journalism's relevance has come to be questioned have a long history and deserve attention to better set up a discussion of the August 2018 editorials. If we examine journalism as one communicative form within the broader space of mediated communication, it helps us to see the contingency of journalism as a knowledge-producing institution in this larger context. But we also see how the boundaries of journalistic professionalism have fractured and weakened both internally and externally, complicating efforts by journalists to maintain or defend the authoritative power of the press. It is hard, and perhaps impossible, for journalists to rebuild trust between the news and the public in such an environment by retreating to their usual processes, as if nothing has changed. But pushing forward in new directions is also fraught. For journalists facing these problems, there are no easy solutions.

Editorials as a Coordinated Story of Relevance

Journalists have struggled with how to respond to the rise of right-wing populism, Trump, and a wave of anti-journalism sentiment. But this has not stopped them from responding. There are many isolated examples of journalists asserting their social role, such as in February 2017, when the *Washington Post* began affixing its new slogan, "Democracy Dies in Darkness," atop its print front page and online banners. In this part of the chapter, however, we highlight a uniquely large, coordinated response: more than six hundred newspaper editorials that ran in August 2018 to push back against the frequency and ferocity of Trump's verbal volleys against the press. As we will see in the next chapter, this show of solidarity portended deeper discussions among journalists grappling with how to remain true to their professional identity while also acknowledging the changing value systems around information and what it means to be a "good" journalist. As metadiscursive artifacts, these editorials represent an effort by journalists to use their privileged position within the media culture to argue for their continued relevance by reiterating their own position within the media culture and positioning how others ought to act toward journalism. While much of the normative language employed will sound familiar, the existence of these editorials speaks to a growing acknowledgment that journalists are engaged in a larger struggle over the relevance of journalism as a knowledge-producing system.

The initiative to get newspapers to collectively editorialize about the virtues of journalism began on August 10, 2018, when the *Boston Globe* issued an invitation to news publisher associations:

The *Globe* proposes to publish an editorial on Aug. 16 on the dangers of the administration's assault on the press and asks others to commit to publishing their own editorials on the same date. Publications, whatever their politics, could make a powerful statement by standing together in the common defense of their profession and the vital role it plays in government for and by the people.[50]

The *Globe*'s invitation posits a particular outcome—a mass of editorials—and a particular tone—a normative register built on top of democratic ideals. At first only a few dozen newspapers signaled their intention to participate, but ultimately more than six hundred news organizations joined in on August 16 and in the following week. These news outlets spanned the country and ranged in size from a tiny one-person operation to student journalists to all the major newspaper chains. They used short prose (such as the *Deseret News* merely writing "Ditto") and longer philosophical approaches extolling the role of journalism. Even some Canadian outlets participated. Taken together, the extent of the editorials magnified a perception that the press was speaking in a unified voice, standing up to Trump's "enemy of the people" accusations in an aggregate, loud, and insistent dissent. This rare outpouring of solidarity from hundreds of news organizations who pride themselves on their independence was an unprecedented symbolic action in defense of a free press.

While the overall mass of editorials offered up a collective rallying cry, the editorials themselves employed a wide variety of messaging strategies, from a grand-narrative approach positioning the press as essential in a democracy to the much more personal, relational technique of situating journalists as part of the community. Some news organizations adopted a defensive tone as they worked to separate themselves from national news organizations. In looking across the editorials, we explore these strategies to reclaim the narrative, and we situate them within an epistemic tension between whether journalists should maintain an objective, detached position or whether they should approach the audience from within, as a member of the community. As part of this response, publishers and editors amplified journalism's grand narrative and also committed themselves to their own narrative role—one organized around grand virtues of democracy and public watchdogging as well as a more localized vision that positioned them as advocates of community values and unifiers of publics.

The Press as Defenders of Democracy

Across the editorials, the most prevalent claims positioned the press in the United States as representing a Fourth Estate. The editorials mobilized the US Constitution and evoked as evidence the founding fathers, especially Thomas Jefferson's famous words about newspapers being more important than the government. As a collective response, the editorials presented a unified argument that the news media acted within the functioning of democracy as part of a system of checks and balances. These democratic normative arguments formed the basis of an often explicitly invoked challenge to Trump's attack on democracy. This included countering Trump's declaration that the news media were the enemy of the people by going on the offensive against Trump himself, trying to turn the phrase around to be against him. When the Vermont's *Barre-Montpelier Times Argus* argued, "We are the enemy. It's true. We say that with no hesitation. If you abuse power, we are the enemy," it attempted to co-opt Trump's line of attack and reinforce its indispensability for democracy.[51] Many editorials set up an "us versus them" frame to introduce a pugnacious aspect to the storyline. Instead of merely being a "watchdog" in this version of the narrative, journalists were fighters against a specific leader. As one small paper asked, "Do you know what Hugo Chavez, Mao Zedong, Joseph Stalin and Donald Trump have in common? They have all characterized independent media sources as 'enemies' of their countries, in attempts to undermine free speech and consolidate the power of the press among their own supporters."[52] Another newspaper directly articulated the grand narrative: "Those dictators tell their people only what the government wants them to know. That's not the American way."[53] These editorials attempt to evolve the narrative focus and switch up the villain. Trump is called "narcissistic and sociopathic" and depicted as someone who "cannot . . . act in the best interest of the country."[54]

Just as the grand narrative tells a tale about keeping those in power accountable, it also praises episodes when the system is seen as working as it should. Many of the editorials recalled the mythology of the Watergate reporting to evoke the collective memory of a time period in which journalists were regarded as heroes. A McClatchy editorial that ran in dozens of newspapers repeatedly compared Trump to Nixon: "Like Nixon, Trump still pines for the kind of coverage his behavior makes impossible. But his place in history will be far less mixed than Nixon's if he continues to menace James Madison's best work."[55] Similarly, the *Philadelphia Tribune* opined: "Many elected officials, from small-town mayors to presidents, are not fond of the media, whose job it is to hold them accountable. It was known that in private, President Nixon was very critical of the media covering the White House, especially the Watergate scandal."[56] And the *Albuquerque Journal* listed the big press victories in the United States, from the 1971 Pentagon Papers publications that shifted public opinion of the Vietnam War to the 1996 exposés of big tobacco companies' lies around smoking health risks.[57] This nostalgia for the so-called golden era of the press is meant to bolster this institutional authority of journalists as the ones with jurisdiction over facts as watchdogs and trusted intermediaries. Over and over we saw these claims of their institutional importance: "Today, *The Jefferson Chronicle* joins with news publications across the United States—both print and digital—in *The Boston Globe* initiative conceived to garner support in preserving the sanctity, dignity, and safety of our nation's free press—the very cornerstone of our democratic republic."[58] Editorials that aligned their missions with the US Constitution could then pivot to the defense of journalism as the defense of the country. The *Daily Messenger* of Canandaigua, New York, went even further to equate the death of soldiers with the protection of press freedom while lamenting the sharp declines in news-media trust among the public: "Especially scary, these poll results . . . indicate a complete lack of understanding that freedom of speech and freedom of the press is a right—one of the many rights that many brave American soldiers have fought and died to defend."[59] This insistence on the institution of the press as an essential mechanism of a working democracy formed the basis of an argument meant to rebuild trust.

Journalists as Neighbors

Another strategy nurtured a different kind of trust-building based on the shared location between journalists and their audiences. In overt and subtle ways, these editorials pivoted their arguments for authority away from a detached voice and toward an embodied one. This was common among smaller newspapers, but it was not limited to them. For example, a *USA Today* editor wrote himself into his defense of journalism: "First, let me tell you a little about me. . . . I live the American Dream. My family fled communist Cuba in the early 1960s. My family rarely talked about their pain, except to say it was better to die free than slaves to a dictatorship. I was 17 months old when we arrived in Florida."[60] In telling his backstory, the editor inserts himself into a very powerful grand narrative: that of the American Dream. He works through his biography before mounting a defense of the investigative journalism performed by *USA Today* as serving the public. This narrative then personalizes reporting within one the largest news organizations in the United States. This editorial appeared in many local Gannett newspapers—the parent company of *USA Today*—even though the editor is spatially removed from these newspapers. Nonetheless, this language of connection was meant to create feelings of trust among individual community members, to form a shared *symbolic* space as Americans.

More often, shared *geographic* space was accentuated. Newspaper editors and publishers outside of major metropolitan areas like New York and Washington reminded readers and viewers that their coverage focused on the communities in which they live. Instead of pointing to significant political stories—like Watergate—and First Amendment norms, they called attention to news stories of children's soccer games or how they provided much-needed information about societal problems such as the opioid-addiction crisis. The *Pueblo Chieftain* broke down the gap between the newspaper's journalists and its audience: "We are your neighbors. We are people who live and work in the same towns as you. Like you, we send our children to local schools. We struggle to pay our bills. We shop in local businesses."[61] Its employees, the paper asserted, represent regular people. A South Dakota *Rapid City Journal* editorial provided another example of this effort to eliminate distance by calling attention to the biographies of its journalists:

Journalists are hardly "the enemy of the people." Candace DenOuden was raised on a family farm near Avon in eastern South Dakota where her parents still live. She went to a Christian college in Indiana, is a 10-time aunt, a godmother, a 4-H alum, a volunteer and church choir member. These *Rapid City Journal* newsroom staffers are among those the president of the United States likes to call "the enemy of the people," a charge that has rippled across the nation in a bid to undermine free speech and demonize those who aim to hold government accountable, report the news, and cover events and sports in their communities. We are not, however, the enemy of the people; rather, we are the people. Just like in every other workplace, the *Journal* has parents, grandparents, aunts, uncles, veterans, volunteers, homeowners, renters, care-givers, outdoors sports enthusiasts, sports fans and taxpayers who like our friends, family and neighbors have a stake in the future.[62]

Such local-minded editorials identified individual reporters, talked about their own lives in the community, and told their own backstories as a way to highlight connections, both symbolic and literal.

Other editorials worked to accentuate how their journalists were part of the fabric of the community, as in this editorial by the Oregon *Hillsboro Tribune*:

> Our publisher is a mother of a recent Forest Grove High School graduate. One of our newspaper editors is active in the Forest Grove Daybreak Rotary Club. Another is a regular at Hondo Dog Park, near his home in Hillsboro. Our sports editor can often be found at the Forest Hills Golf Course. Our features editor grew up in Vernonia. Our staff photographer has children in Hillsboro schools. Our advertising director hunts and fishes in the wilderness of western Washington County. Our office manager is a longtime Forest Grove resident who knows seemingly everyone west of Cornelius-Scheffin Road. When we go to work, we are working on behalf of a community that we care deeply about—because we are all a part of it.[63]

Here reporters are connected to local businesses and organizations, schools and neighborhoods, and families of the town. They want citizens to understand that not only are reporters part of the fabric of the community, but they also part of its support system, like the police or librarians. In some editorials, the journalists presented the reporters themselves as being part of that safety net. The Allentown, Pennsylvania-based *Morning Call* followed this path:

> *Morning Call* journalists have written dozens of stories in a years-long series on how opioid addiction is destroying families. Three reporters—Pamela Lehman, Carol Thompson and Laurie Mason Schroeder—took their involvement to the next level. They trained to administer Narcan, which can save the life of an overdose victim. "As often as we interview people suffering from the disease of addiction, I worry that it's only a matter of time before I'm present when someone overdoses," Mason Schroeder wrote. "At least now, I'll be ready to help." An "enemy of the people"?[64]

These editorials equated journalists as town residents, taxpayers, parents, and "regular" citizens who hold dear (assumed) universal values such as altruism and goodwill toward fellow humans. We can see a shifting away from the normative mode of distanced objectivity. Instead they present an emergent morality centered on individual concern for a fellow human.

In creating an "us" that placed local reporters within their communities, many of the editorials purposefully distanced themselves from the "them" of the metro and national legacy organizations such as CNN and the *New York Times*. In highlighting difference rather than sameness, these editorials echoed critiques that elite journalists are biased or out-of-touch. "To be clear, some of the fault for perceptions of bias in the media lies with outlets that have blurred the lines between which content is news and which is opinion," wrote the *Anchorage Daily News*.[65] Several editorials explicitly called out these national, more institutional organizations as the purveyors of "fake news." The *Albuquerque Journal's* editorial mostly hewed to the normative language of news as central to democracy in its attacks on Trump, referencing the Pentagon Papers, Watergate, and a slew of other famous news stories. But it also positioned elite journalists as part of the problem:

> Yes, there are some media outlets—big and small, liberal and conservative—that have stretched the bounds of objectivity in the age of Trump. CNN appears intent on tearing President Trump down no matter the issue, while Fox News has taken on the role of being the president's defender-in-chief. And a *New York Times* columnist acknowledged during the 2016 presidential election that there were new rules for covering Trump.[66]

The editorial went on to defend journalistic independence and facticity as essential, which served as a further critique of cable news and national newspapers.

Local editorials drawing a distinction from national news organizations painted themselves instead as the ones who *really* cared about the local community and who *really* had the facts, at least locally. For example, an editor at InDepthNH.org—a nonprofit investigative news site based in New Hampshire—admitted that "sometimes the good guys and the bad guys aren't so easy to tell apart. . . . Even more appalling, some who call themselves journalists have an agenda, sometimes an ax to grind." It takes in-depth local knowledge to be able to sort out the various actors, and this is best carried out by local journalists, this line of thinking goes. For these local news organizations, the "view from nowhere"[67] is replaced by an emphatic view from somewhere that is presented not as a form of bias but as a corrective to potential bias.

An emphasis on connection to place and a rejection of journalistic distance indicates a fracturing of journalism's grand narrative. To the extent that this grand narrative depends upon a unified front within the journalistic community, these fissures point to the need for more nuance in understanding the dynamics of local news.[68] What emerges in the narrative of journalism is the development of alternative storylines that overlap considerably, but also diverge in key ways. Perhaps what is most starkly illustrated in the editorials of local news organizations is the contrast between journalistic authority based on an institutional notion of the press as central-yet-distant (which has been advanced in this book) and journalistic trust based on the shared social spaces and experiences of individual journalists and their audiences. Trust moves from a generalized idea entrenched over time as part of a normative understanding to a social trust that must be continually rebuilt and enacted. It locates trust not only in institutions, but in people. Journalists' identities as professionals become explicitly aligned with their personal identities as residents of the places they cover.

Even while accentuating place, these editorials unite with others in stoking fear of Trump's rhetoric as authoritarian by arguing that democracy is in jeopardy and alleging that their communities would be made vulnerable to corruption without a healthy and free press.[69] "All who value the free exchange of information should think long and hard about what America, Washington and Spokane might look like without watchdog journalists," warned the *Spokesman-Review* as it identified national and local ramifications.[70] They try to evoke feelings of warmth and friendship by declaring their love for their towns and their belonging.[71] These are savvy strategies that cannot be separated from the incessant economic challenges faced by local news.

The Resisters

While the *Boston Globe* was able to motivate hundreds of newspapers to editorialize on behalf of journalism, not all news organizations joined—though for different reasons. The *Los Angeles Times* notably argued that the editorials played into Trump's contention that the news media were colluding against him: "The president himself already treats the media as a cabal . . . suggesting over and over that we're in cahoots to do damage to the country."[72] The editorials only served as evidence for Trump that journalists were indeed trying to stop him. Instead of joining in, the *Times* touted its "independence" from other news organizations. Similarly, the *San Francisco Chronicle* editorial page editor also weighed the independence of the newspaper as more important than joining the other newspapers: "Our editorial page will continue to speak out against this president's war on the free press. Our silence on Thursday is testament to our commitment to do it in our own way, on our own timetable."[73]

As predicted by the *Los Angeles Times*, Trump promptly responded via tweet to label the editorial collaboration as "collusion" while reiterating his commitment to "Freedom of the Press":

> There is nothing that I would want more for our Country than true FREEDOM OF THE PRESS. The fact is that the Press is FREE to write and say anything it wants, but much of what it says is FAKE NEWS, pushing a political agenda or just plain trying to hurt people. HONESTY WINS![74]

Trump responded as he had all along—by accusing journalists, with only ambiguous and vague evidence, of conspiring against him. His argument is not as nuanced as the editorials he combats, but his messaging clearly strikes at the core legitimacy of journalists. Where the editorials assert motivations of grandeur having to do with nurturing democracy or giving people information they need, Trump spun the story, characterizing their "real" intentions as "pushing an agenda or just plain trying to hurt people." In this response, Trump continued undermining the authority of the journalists in order to elevate himself as a trusted authority. Trump's message is powerful because it draws on a history of people being told not to trust the news. It recasts the editorials as only confirming the news media's bias against him and his populist ideals.

Conclusion: A Missed Opportunity to Demonstrate Journalism's Relevance

When Trump and his supporters committed to a narrative depicting the mainstream press as "fake news" and "enemies of the people," they tapped into resentment and disdain that had been festering for generations. They did so to construct a discursive attack aimed at undercutting the authority of journalistic accounts. As the previous chapters showed, press-bashing was not a marginal activity; rather, it was central to Trump's campaigning and governing, with the assaults amplified through conservative media, digital platforms, and even within traditional news reporting. This anti-journalism rhetoric becomes effective when political polarization and selective exposure entrench confirming viewpoints. When the narrative becomes about the press as the enemy, the heroes are those who stand up to conniving reporters and call out fake news. Journalists get cast as the villains in this story, as one more group of elites working against the interests of the people.

When faced with accusations about their lack of trustworthiness, their ulterior motives, and their relevance in the contemporary media culture, journalists understandably have responded by falling back on their own grand narrative for support—one that has sustained their claims to legitimacy for a century. These joint editorials are one form of overt counterattack that journalists are able to control at a time that feels chaotic for news professionals. The editorial response served a dual purpose: it reiterated a narrative of America as a democracy protected by strong institutions that provide checks on each other and also restated the essential role that journalists play in this democratic system. But the substance of the message that journalists sent using the August 2018 editorials was two-pronged: aside from aligning themselves with the traditional norms of journalists as detached, objective agents of democracy, they simultaneously positioned journalists as a part of the community fabric. In this rhetorical work, they aligned themselves with enduring values in people's lives—freedom from faction, a desire for truths, a feeling of community belonging—in a bid to renew bonds of trust with their audiences. In the variety of editorial stances that emerged in 2018, we see an internal struggle over the relevance of mechanisms for public knowledge even as journalists took this opportunity to unveil the backstage work they do to access truths via their community relations. They utilized a number of strategies discussed in this chapter to do this, including emotion, hoping to build a more affective kind of trust with their readers.[75]

Yet in shifting this moral voice, they failed to acknowledge past wrongs within their own communities—such as harms from longstanding media stereotypes and journalists' support for a status quo that left out marginalized groups. They failed to commit to being better for all of their constituents. As such, journalists harnessed nostalgia for the golden age of the media as an institutional Fourth Estate and also as a member of communities, a neighbor, and a friend. And, indeed, the magnitude of the coordinated response was extraordinary. Yet, in the end, the editorials—even in aggregate—did little to stem the tide against the mainstream press. They made little difference, and the press-bashing continued in earnest.

We believe the collective effort was a missed opportunity for the journalistic community to more carefully examine the conditions that have led to this moment. Strikingly, not a single editorial we found engaged with the deeper roots of the erosion of trust and the conditions that have imperiled the relevance of journalism. Reflecting on journalism under Trump, media critic Michael Massing wrote that news organizations "have shown some serious weaknesses, including bias, insularity, groupthink, and condescension, which have provided ammunition to Trump and his supporters as they seek to discredit the press."[76] The introspection necessary for confronting such criticism was absent in these editorials, where journalists privileged the preservation of their professional autonomy as paramount. This strategy no longer works, especially given the epistemic diversity on offer in an increasingly complex media culture. Any journalistic response needs to confront more substantively the *reasons* these grievances—be them from anti-elitist, right-wing populists or from marginalized communities—have been so successful in sowing distrust. The very idea of buying into a grand narrative that props up the establishment without reflecting on the underlying trust issues in the broader culture risks being branded as naive and quaint at best, ignorant and irrelevant at worst. Journalism's grand narrative needs to be scrutinized for the ways in which it enables elite-centric, myopic, and episodic reporting in place of pursuing the systemic problems that actually matter much more.

In these messages to the world, news outlets missed an opportunity to turn their lens inward and address the discontent that Trump has so effectively tapped into. The editorials, without exception, were cheerleading and unequivocal in praising journalism's positive roles in people's lives, communities, and democracy. Little critical, detached analysis appeared, and we suggest that this was a mistake. How might the narrative shift if it reflected a more introspective press, if it spoke of lessons learned and pathways forward to mending cultural fissures? Perhaps a more complex and multidimensional storyline would be received more widely, opening a pathway toward rebuilding trust through reconciliation. Primarily, journalists need to engage with a proactive, collective, pro-democratic mission to remind people how fragile our republic is and find ways to build bridges and reconnect through a shared set of facts. That is, no doubt, a challenging proposition, an intractable complication that suggests we are way beyond simply reminding people that journalists are community members too.

When antagonistic metadiscourse circulates, it influences how citizens think about journalism as well as how they approach news, but especially how we determine what is true collectively. Given how this antagonism strikes at the heart of journalistic authority, journalists need to first acknowledge these discourses for what they are: the continuation of a partisan-driven counternarrative that has been going on for years. Editorials alone will not be sufficient. Rather, journalists need to counteract anti-journalist discourse through a variety of venues, focusing on different kinds of trust and different elements important to their communities, by being critical of their own practices, and by finding ways to reconnect with millions of Americans who believe in an alternate, false world of intentional misinformation. Yes, journalists need to advocate for the value they bring in a much more convincing manner. It is imperative that they foremost admit when they have contributed negatively to public discourse. Though none of these actions directly "reclaim" the grand narrative, they implicitly move toward a rethinking of what the grand narrative should be to build trust anew around a shared commitment to democracy. We are not sure how much clearer the message could be for mainstream journalists as we watched insurgents attack the Capitol on January 6, 2021. This violent act demonstrated the ultimate effects of a polarized political and media culture of competing information. "You're all friggin' fake news," screamed a protestor at an ABC News reporter as she stood outside the Capitol. "You are all pieces of shit. You're traitors to America." These domestic terrorists chanted "Stop the steal" as they brandished weapons, beat police with poles bearing Confederate flags, and carried zip ties in case they took hostages.[77] Such moments challenge journalists to reckon with their own practices and their place in society. In the next chapter, we examine how journalists struggled with how to cover Trump's lies and racist statements. In the conclusion chapter, we go further in presenting a vision of what journalism could become, particularly if journalists learns from their past failings and develop a new approach built around a more inclusive, realistic, and authentic moral voice.

5

Journalistic Moralities

Confronting Trump's Lies and Racism

Donald Trump's first lie as president pertained to his first moments as president. Despite demonstrable evidence that the crowd attending Trump's inauguration had been smaller than Barack Obama's in 2009, Trump and his staff insisted on the opposite, claiming that many more thousands of people attended his inauguration on January 20, 2017, on the West Front of the US Capitol in Washington, DC. Five days later, during his first prime-time network television interview, with ABC News's David Muir, Trump brought up the crowd size to again lie about it: "I had a massive amount of people here. [The news media] were showing pictures that were very unflattering, as unflattering—from certain angles—that were taken early and lots of other things. I'll show you a picture later if you'd like of a massive crowd." When the pictures did not support the lie, Trump intervened in the editing of the inauguration photographs to make the crowd look larger.[1] He then blamed journalistic bias for reporting that went against this narrative. A lie about crowd size might seem petty or odd, but in retrospect it established an immediate pattern. By his final day as president, Trump had made over thirty thousand false or misleading statements, according to the *Washington Post*.[2] That's more than twenty lies a day on average, although the *Post* noted an upward trend over time. The sheer number of lies is startling, but before dismissing this as typical political spin, the inauguration example shows the degree to which Trump is willing to say things that are demonstrably not true, even when contradictory evidence is freely available.

Trump's racist remarks are not as frequent as his lies, but they may be even more glaring.[3] To offer just a few examples: On July 14, 2019, Trump singled out four Democratic members of Congress—all women of color—as being "from countries whose governments are a complete and total catastrophe" and asked, "Why don't they go back and help fix the totally broken and crime infested places from which they came."[4] A year later, Trump retweeted a

News After Trump. Matt Carlson, Sue Robinson, and Seth C. Lewis, Oxford University Press. © Oxford University Press 2021. DOI: 10.1093/oso/9780197550342.003.0006

video of one of his supporters yelling "White power!"[5] He took down the video, but never apologized for amplifying its message of white superiority.

Trump's lies and his refusal to denounce racism culminated in an angry mob attacking the Capitol four years after that 2016 inauguration day, convinced by Trump that the 2020 election had been rigged and democracy needed saving. It was perhaps Trump's ultimate lie, and one that demonstrated how dangerous false information worlds could be. Many of the attackers bore explicit symbols of white supremacy as they waved Confederate flags, donned T-shirts with racist and anti-Semitic statements, and hurled racist epithets at Black police officers.[6] Visible among the attackers were members of the Proud Boys, a far-right group with a history of violence and white supremacy.[7] Ultimately, the mob that stormed the Capitol attributed their assault as doing Trump's bidding to take back their country after Trump told them: "Something is wrong here, something is really wrong . . . if you don't fight like hell, you're not going to have a country anymore."[8] They listened and they acted.

Trump's persistent fabrications and blatantly racist remarks have posed a quagmire to journalists. Underneath practical questions of how to report such statements lies a series of fundamental questions: Is it the role of the press to call out the president for lies and racism, even if it gives the appearance of taking sides? What, exactly, is a lie? How do we know if a statement is racist? And racist to whom? These are questions of morality, and, as such, entail a subjective determination that journalists regularly declare to be outside the professional jurisdiction of day-to-day reporting. From the view of what we call the standard model of journalism, being a moral judge is the antithesis of being balanced and objective. It requires making assumptions about motivations and intentions that cannot be verified, and therefore, are not necessarily rooted in fact. But this is the position journalists found themselves in when they reported on Trump.

This chapter explores how journalists struggle with what their role should be. James Ettema and Theodore Glasser dubbed journalists the "custodians of public conscience"[9] during the twentieth century, and the mainstream press has undertaken this role through a professional approach built around the idea of objectivity. However, in the present era of polarized politics and a fractured media culture in which the relevance of traditional journalistic institutions is faltering, we must ask: how do journalists grapple with the demands of objectivity, their changing functions in a democracy, their problematic legacy of excluding non-white and non-male voices, and their moral obligations in the face of direct attacks on their authority? In the process of answering these questions, journalists display much hand-wringing over what journalistic professionalism demands today, as we saw in the previous chapter. A salient concern is whether their ability to communicate accurate portrayals has succumbed to a procedural notion of objectivity that allows for the normalization of lies and racism in the name of seeking balance by reporters. That is, journalists do not need to sanction lies and racism for them to spread this language through their reporting.

However, the capacity for journalists to frame cultural and social values is questionable at best in this political and media culture. Journalists wrestle with their own power as they also find themselves cast as actors within the larger political story of the moment. This is a role that journalists have played before, but always with awkwardness and trepidation given their predilection for being central-yet-distant. For many, journalists are often made out to be the bad guys, the ones with questionable or at least unrelatable morals. Trump and other right-wing populists argue that the kinds of moralities on display in mainstream news stories and espoused by journalists do not resonate with the authentic majority of non-elites, or worse, that these moralities are merely facades, masking a liberal, elitist, exclusionary mindset. The vocal attacks chronicled in the preceding chapters expose a fundamental symbolic weakening of the press and its effectiveness as a moral guide—and thus its relevance for people. As journalists face the prospect of their diminished role within political discourse and the media culture, we need to then ask, Who emerges as the moral influencers in this environment? And what should journalists do to retain or augment this role as a custodian of conscience?

To scrutinize all of this, we must first appreciate the myriad dimensions of morality. We also should consider the history of the press's power to weave moral truth as well as how journalists have brandished that power (or not) in the face of politicians' blatant obfuscations and prevarications to serve as custodians of conscience. In being forced out of their comfort zones, journalists have had to confront larger questions of whether objectivity, even in its modified state, retains its epistemic power or whether a stronger moral stance better fits the contemporary political and media context. This questioning emerged somewhat in the August 2018 editorials examined previously, as journalists began to question their moral obligations in a hostile environment marked by concerns over their relevance. This chapter takes up how journalists have addressed issues of morality, first by examining the difficult conversations around how to properly cover Trump's lies and racism and then through interviews with journalists about how they understand their work. Ultimately, what we see is a significant rejection of objectivity-as-distance and growing calls for journalists to be more assertive in making judgments. This shift has not been without its detractors, some of whom might consider such measures by journalists to be political acts. But we prefer the term "democratic acts," in the vein of Stephen Ward's call for democratically engaged journalists.[10] As we hinted at in the previous chapter, journalists must move away from their focus on saving their industry and turn their attention to protecting democracy at all costs. And to do this, journalists must pivot and become intentional moral actors.

The Murkiness of Journalistic Morality

The topic of morality occupies a vast literature such that even providing a definition of the term is fraught. However, we can make a distinction between morality as a descriptive term and as a normative term associated with moral theory.[11] We are more interested in the former in that it refers to an accepted and shared set of codes that transcends any one individual and governs or guides a community into a way of being. Morals are the social judgments drawn from shared conceptualizations of right and wrong and that give rise to what may be (or may not be) considered ethical behavior. Lies in particular are immoral, for example, because they fail to allow true relationships to happen, fail to allow someone to react authentically, and fail to show the necessary respect for a fellow human, according to Kant.[12] Our approach, then, is decidedly about the practical implications of addressing questions of morality, rather than taking up morals as abstractions.

Discussions of journalism with morality may at first seem an odd fit, or even as contradictory.[13] But morality can be translated into journalism by asking about the purpose of news in society. What is the good, after all, that journalism brings to the public? This question belies an easy answer, but contemporary journalism has landed on the provision of facts as its aim. How such facticity can be arrived at in the messy world of contending forces, contradictory information, and endless perspectives is the familiar emphasis on a professional lens that dictates standards of appropriate actions. According to the standard model of journalism in the United States, objectivity—however battered—has long provided a spiritual core for approaching the epistemic task of revealing the world to news audiences. It asks reporters to compartmentalize their own viewpoints and biases to the best of their abilities in a rigorous accounting of facts.[14] This combination of professionalism and objectivity results in the routinization of news conventions. Journalism's epistemic strategies include "quoting" people, to convince consumers that these specific words were said by this specific person; naming people, to provide accountability for their words through source attribution; and explicitly verifying information, such as by citing a report or database from some credible agent or by providing eyewitness accounts. Quoting notably offloads responsibility, shifting it from journalists reporting statements to the officials who make them.[15] Overall, this standard model of reporting has dominated the journalistic imagination in the United States for generations now,[16] and has been criticized for many reasons, including for what Jay Rosen has called "the view from nowhere"—a term he borrowed from philosopher Thomas Nagel.[17]

And yet it would be a mistake to equate journalists' epistemic commitment to objectivity with moral indifference. When Herbert Gans enumerates the ideologies of news, he is really identifying the dominant and persistent morals shared by reporters.[18] This is decidedly not a neutral position, but a worldview reflective of a predominantly white, well-educated, older audience and expressed through "enduring values" ranging from responsible capitalism (e.g., that you can make money but not be too greedy in doing so) to altruistic democracy (e.g., that a democratic form of government is desirable as long as it is propped up by notions of a common good and shared values that move beyond the individual). These values reside within the built-in assumptions that structure news coverage and implicitly guide reporters in choosing stories, finding credible sources, selecting a frame, and so on. News then identifies what Gans calls a "moral disorder" to be rooted out for the sake of the larger public.[19] Thus, journalists use conventions, narratives, and frames to convey these mores. In aggregate, these reflect and maintain a dominant value system that then affects such practices as source selection.

The role of morality in journalism has been most fully explored in the work of James Ettema and Theodore Glasser on investigative journalism, who coined the term we mentioned earlier of journalists as "custodians of conscience." As a subdomain within journalism, investigative journalism sits uneasily between the conventional neutral news account and more subjective forms of advocacy journalism. In this way, investigative journalism's moral underpinnings conflict with the broader journalistic desire to refrain from making moral judgments.[20] Ettema and Glasser's research shows the elaborate strategies that emerge to quell this conflict, including the use of irony to make implicit pronouncements. But they are quick to point out that all news stories entail narratives that make clear what is good and what is bad: "Reality does not provide a storylike account. What does provide such an account is an essentially moral vision of events. Indeed, it is the moral force of a story that provides the semblance of reality."[21] Morality is not anathematic to news, but very much a part of how it is structured.[22]

Investigative journalists evade the explicit invocation of a moral language by going to great lengths to position moral judgments within the confines of professionalism. Ettema and Glasser dub this process "the objectification of moral standards":

> By steadfastly maintaining that their judgments concern not "right and wrong but important and unimportant" and that their procedures "simply bring something to light," these reporters claim that their reporting involves no exercise of conscience but only application of empirical method—and that their finished reports are not moral discourse but simply information.[23]

When journalists then seek to foment moral outrage as a basis for pursuing a certain story, they tap into deeply held collective values that all communities supposedly hold dear, such as industriousness, justice, and democracy. Furthermore, the protocols of objectivity provide journalists with a means to freely structure facts into a story that resonates, as Ettema and Glasser note, with moral judgment: "We maintain that any attempt to gain truly important knowledge of human affairs—knowledge of individual innocence and guilt or institutional malfeasance and responsibility, for example—is built on a foundation of facts that have been called into existence, given structure and made meaningful by values."[24]

Invoking morality exposes the contradictions that exist within the epistemology of news as practiced in the United States over the past century. While the news communicates narratives of good or bad and right or wrong, professional norms inhibit journalists from making explicit reference to the basic shared moralities that enable one to call out overtly immoral behavior. Journalists avoiding bold statements resort to ventriloquizing their judgments through sources, adopting an ironic voice to imply judgment, or adopting false equivalencies to counter outright lies or racism.

A persistent issue remains that the journalistic protocols set up to maintain objectivity, such as using government-supplied evidence, put journalists in a position where they are continuously wary of losing their access to these sources. Reporters maintain a symbiotic relationship with political officials wherein both reporters and officials gain from the relationship.[25] This results in a complicated quid pro quo that privileges those credentialed by formal institutions as powerful actors—overall disproportionately white, male, and older than the population as a whole—as being credible and authoritative. Historical examples abound, including journalists' acquiescence to the unfounded claims of Senator Joe McCarthy during the Red Scare of the 1950s.[26] But such acquiescence is much more mundane, as journalists' work routines, value systems, and general etiquette have long prevented them from calling out presidential lying.[27] Famed reporter Carl Bernstein, writing in 1976 about his Watergate reporting, lamented how journalists pulled their punches: "Natural caution, fear of offending the powerful, anxiety about seeming irresponsible—all these reinforced the national media's desire to serve as a bulwark of legitimacy and stability."[28] How journalists interact with elite sources indicates journalism's competing values of creating an account of what their sources say and holding these sources to account for what is said, in the absence of an equally powerful countersource to rely on for including conflict.

Much of the consternation over allotting elite sources too much power concerns the ability of the latter to perpetuate lies or spin unchecked to the public. But another murky area is the degree to which journalists have a moral obligation to provide inclusive and complex representation of the publics they cover. Ample journalism scholarship has documented how news coverage frequently either lacks diversity or falls into stereotyping that turns complicated issues and individuals into one-dimensional caricatures of non-white, non-educated, non-heterosexual, non-Christian, non-American groups.[29] How journalists represent disadvantaged groups in the news becomes a moral issue when these reports are laden with built-in assumptions. Linda Steiner and Silvio Waisbord's research on news coverage of Baltimore—where Black residents comprised 63.7% of the population in the 2010 census—shows that race plays out in the geographical descriptions offered by journalists, "with the spaces of Black people marked as unsafe and unhealthy, and thus the people who live there as dangerous."[30] News accounts about minority populations are not neutral or merely informational; rather, they figure into larger discourses about morality.

When journalists lack an ability to render moral judgments, an overreliance on public officials and government institutions threatens to perpetuate problematic power dynamics by falling back on social structures assumed to be benevolent and good. This is exacerbated by journalism's traditional emphasis on itself as independent from faction and removed from power—a norm of distance-keeping that retains particular prominence among news values. But this has had the side effect of dampening journalism's moral force, creating huge chasms of distrust over the years in many different kinds of communities, including among African Americans and rural working-class people.

In sum, introducing morality as a keyword for thinking about journalism complicates how news is understood. The news is never *not* moral. Rather, morality asserts itself through the epistemic conventions of news. Expressed through conventions, this morality fades into the background, but it all comes to a head in discussions of how to cover Trump and leaders like him seeking to claim moral authority for all.

Debating the Moral Response

The lens of morality helps us understand the dilemmas that journalists face in covering officials who intentionally spread lies and hate to sow discontent and divide people. Using Trump as an example of how this division plays out in public discourse, this book has described press-bashing as a type of political performance meant to heighten political power while simultaneously discrediting mainstream journalism. In this part of the book, we are documenting and critically analyzing journalists' responses. In the previous chapter, we considered how journalists looked to the underlying normative paradigm for a defense. We found that they drew on the long and venerable "grand narrative" of journalism, though some fissures in the storyline appeared and the response could have been more introspective. In this chapter, we detail and explain how journalists responded to the kinds of falsehoods and racist statements that Trump repeatedly made as a candidate and as president, and how this upset the entrenched reportorial patterns regarding how to cover political elites via a specific kind of moral voice. Ultimately, these debates are not about how to cover a single individual, but a larger wrestling over what journalism ought to be doing in response to a changing media culture and a politically polarized landscape.

Journalists have always struggled with how their commitment to objectivity affects their ability to pronounce what is true and what is not. But in this environment the pitfalls of objectivity create dissension and division in journalists' collective response that are much deeper than just disagreements regarding how to respond to the peculiarities of Trump. As we analyze this public debate, we show how the professional commitment to objectivity is grounded in a desire to provide factual information as stringently as possible, but that as a moral stance its failures are clear in heightening distrust among the public and creating voids that become entry points for other, self-interested moral agents.

When Should a Falsehood Be Called a "Lie"?

Given the number, scale, and ubiquity of his lies, Trump is unprecedented in contemporary politics. Trump's lies as president numbered in the tens of thousands, on some days coming in the dozens.[31] Of the Trump claims investigated by PolitiFact, only about 14% were deemed "true" or even "mostly true," while half were rated "false" or "pants on fire."[32] As a result, fact-checking sites such as FactCheck.org, PolitiFact, and the *Washington Post*'s fact checker offer abundant online archives of problematic statements. Fact checkers struggled to keep pace with Trump. In just a five-day span in 2020, FactCheck.org ran the following articles: "Trump's False Claim on Coronavirus Harm," "Trump's Misguided Tweet Seeking Wallace Apology for Noose 'Hoax,'" "Trump's Baseless Attacks on Times, Post Reporting on Russia Probe," and "Trump's False Military Equipment Claim."[33] Certainly, all presidents utilize the symbolic power of their office to spin narratives to their advantage.[34] But the sheer number of falsehoods generated by Trump tips into something different—a nonchalance about truth and verifiable facts that is overwhelming when looked at in its totality.

The lies themselves range from meaningless vanity, such as the inauguration attendance numbers discussed at the top of this chapter, to such grave falsehoods as accusing Google of manipulating millions of votes for Hillary Clinton.[35] Although some statements could be excused as interpretations of ambiguous facts or the cherry-picking of particular information, many of Trump's lies are easily discredited through available evidence, or completely lack evidence. In these cases, journalists had to contemplate how to cover statements from the president—which are often treated as newsworthy and authoritative because they come from the president—when the statements are not true.

It would be unfair to accuse journalists of not paying attention to Trump's lies. In 2017, the *New York Times'* opinion section published a comprehensive interactive list of "Trump's Lies," complete with color-coded calendars and a graph showing public distrust in Trump.[36] Fact-checking sites buzzed with thorough dissections of Trump's falsehoods from the campaign to his last days in office. News accounts of Trump's speeches—including significant events like the annual State of the Union address—came accompanied by fact checks. News organizations even worked on developing fact-checking in real-time using automated journalism tools.[37] Labeling journalists as stenographers would be an oversimplification that elides this meticulous body of work. Our attention focuses on the more mundane reportorial decisions that journalists make in deciding on story frames, fashioning headlines, selecting quotations, and, of course, struggling with the duality of balancing the newsworthiness of what the president says with his penchant for lying. Susan Keith and Leslie-Jean Thornton provide a typology of the approaches that journalists have taken with reporting on Trump's outright lies, including

> "stenographic objectivity," in which journalists simply reported what Trump asserted, with little further explanation; what we call "comparative objectivity," in which Trump's assertions were reported in conjunction with information challenging them; and what we call "interrogative objectivity," in which journalists overtly questioned the truth of the assertions, making that questioning the point of the article. A fourth type of response, which we call "evaluative subjectivity," appeared in opinion sections, but emphasized reporting techniques to cast the counterfactual statements as lies.[38]

The variety of approaches indicated a lack of a fixed convention for dealing with Trump when he would deviate from the discursive norms of his predecessors. Keith and Thornton note that journalists struggled with questions of intention versus confusion or even delusion when figuring out how to cover the president.

Trump's lies became an issue immediately after he became president. Trump's deceptiveness had been noted throughout a campaign that many had expected he would lose. When he became president, expectations of deference to the presidency clashed with Trump's determination to continue lying in ways easily disproved. Less than a week after the inauguration, media critic Mathew Ingram asked in *Fortune*, "Is it ever appropriate to use the word 'lie' in such circumstances?"[39] This question connected to concerns that reporters abet the president in his duplicity when they repeat his false claims. Writing in the *Atlantic,* Derek Thompson made the case that news coverage itself was the problem when it provided a medium for lies to spread: "The traditional news media are thoroughly infected by the Trump virus. It is not only spreading the disease of the president's lies, but also suffering from a demise in public trust—at least among one half of the electorate."[40] To Thompson and others, journalists were culpable for amplifying lies through normal journalistic routines.

Yet journalists differed in what it meant to engage Trump's lying. Much of the discussion involved distinctions around language usage and the unknowability of intention. Writing about these discussions in the *Columbia Journalism Review,* Pete Vernon noted "the debate over when to use the L-word is nuanced. Trump provides [a] steady stream of untrue statements, but are all of them lies?"[41] The Associated Press standards editor expressed apprehension around the use of "lie" as too interior-focused and favored instead sticking to the exteriority of facts: "We feel it's better to say what the facts are, say what the person said and let the audience make the decision whether or not it's an intentional lie."[42] *New York Times* editor Dean Baquet did not rule out the "lie" label in all cases, but he argued for restricting its usage:

> The word "lie" is very powerful. For one thing, it assumes that someone knew the statement was false. Another reason to use the word judiciously is that our readers could end up focusing more on our use of the word than on what was said. And using "lie" repeatedly could feed the mistaken notion that we're taking political sides. That's not our role.

Others called for more nuance in classifying just what types of falsehoods were being uttered. CNN's Brian Stelter—a vocal critic of Trump's deceptiveness—argued for this approach on his *Reliable Sources* program: "We need to distinguish between a deflection, an exaggeration and a straight-up lie."[43] Contrary to this early opposition to using "lie," *Washington Post* media reporter Paul Farhi noted that by 2019 news outlets had grown bolder in appending the word to Trump in their headlines. Farhi included examples of its usage in descriptive ways—for example, "President Trump Lies to Troops about Pay Raise"—and in evaluative ways—for example, "It's True: Trump Is Lying More, and He's Doing It on Purpose."[44]

Given that Trump's lies number in the thousands, it is hard to pinpoint any one lie or set of lies as illustrative of the overall pattern. But Trump's lies during the early months of the 2020 Covid-19 outbreak in the United States are among the most pernicious for a variety of reasons. First, they involve scientific evidence that makes false statements easy to disprove. Even with ambiguity about what was known and unknown, epidemiological patterns were clearly available. Second, a virus outbreak is not itself a political issue, even if how it is handled is deeply political. The point here is that discourse cannot alter the basic facts of the spreading virus. The final reason concerns the extreme consequences that misinformation from elected officials have during a pandemic. Indeed, as many countries in the world were able to bring the coronavirus relatively under control in 2020, the United States struggled, resulting in a disproportionately high death toll.[45] It has been speculated that a better response from Trump would have saved many more lives.[46]

The White House began holding daily press briefings in March 2020 featuring either Trump or Vice President Mike Pence, and joined by other government officials. Because the White House had previously abandoned the practice of press briefings, these Covid-oriented events became a way of consolidating government messaging and dispersing the latest findings. But they also became a vehicle for Trump to lie about the severity of the virus and suggest treatments that were medically dangerous.[47] The lies became so numerous that the *Atlantic* started a stand-alone feature on Trump's coronavirus lies.[48] Trump would pepper his press conference with insults toward the journalists who were there to cover them, which echoed his earlier behavior.[49] This included his practice of insulting journalists of color when he told African American CNN reporter Yamiche Alcindor, "Be nice. Don't be threatening."[50]

Whether it was responsible or irresponsible to cover the briefings live became a point of contention within journalism, with many journalists urging their colleagues to stop. In an opinion column titled "Stop Airing Trump's Briefings!" *New York Times* columnist Charles Blow accused the press of continuing its now long-standing practice of giving too much attention to Trump. Blow put it bluntly: "Let me be clear: Under no circumstance should these briefings be carried live. Doing so is a mistake bordering on journalistic malpractice. Everything a president does or says should be documented but airing all of it, unfiltered, is lazy and irresponsible."[51] Similarly, Jay Rosen argued that it had become far too dangerous to cover Trump live. He advocated for "exiting from the normal system for covering presidents—which

Trump himself exited long ago by using the microphone we have handed him to spread thousands of false claims, even as he undermines trust in the presidency and the press."[52] Rosen articulated a number of strategies for covering Trump that would be less credulous and more focused on his actions. *Vox*'s Matthew Yglesias challenged any notion that the reporters present could temper Trump with their questions, and instead compared the press conference to a rally: "You can't stop the president from holding rallies and lying, or even from streaming those lies live to a slice of the public. But there's no reason to cover them as if they are legitimate policy briefings, and it's a dangerous delusion to believe that asking tough questions on camera can undo the harm of misinformation."[53]

Against this call to limit Trump's access to live television, *New York* magazine's Olivia Nuzzi argued the opposite to better expose Trump's deficiencies: "When we extract his words in clips or quotes in news articles, when we divorce them from their rambling context to place them in the context of the real world, and his real record, we are also helping him articulate a semicoherent worldview and ideology when there usually isn't one."[54] Nuzzi's comments bring to light the journalistic processes that act as their own kind of disinfectant to remove the more egregious discourse from public scrutiny by filtering Trump into pre-existing models of what news coverage of a presidential press conference ought to look like. Eventually, Trump's regular press conferences receded, even as the virus continued to strike across the country.

Even as journalists grew bolder in identifying Trump's lies, the core conundrum remained: presidents, by virtue of being presidents, make news with their statements; they possess great symbolic and administrative power that justifies constant coverage. Journalists devote ample resources to covering the presidency, and the beat of White House correspondent is among the most prestigious in journalism. Yet Trump's constant lying upended this dynamic, putting journalists in the position of judging whether to communicate Trump's falsehoods as newsworthy statements, ignore them so as not to assist with spreading them, or call them out as lies. This was made more complicated with an expansive media culture that gave Trump other vehicles for spreading lies—chief among them his use of Twitter. Journalists responded by expanding their fact-checking apparatus. This move is about maintaining relevance through a strategy of restoring the sanctity of facticity.[55] But doing so evades questions of morality by instead presenting facts as external and verifiable "things" in the world. This reflects journalism's rationality bias: if only the news audience had the facts, it would detect lies and hold liars accountable. But the present political context and media culture hamper this idealistic vision. Questions of journalistic relevance arise in the face of constant press-bashing and doubts about journalism's position of speaking from nowhere. This has resulted in further considerations of just what journalism should look like, which we examine in what follows.

When the President Says Racist Things

Trump's racist statements did not number in the tens of thousands like his lies, but they were at times startling in their flagrance and impact. From accusations about Mexicans at his 2015 campaign launch, to his calling white supremacists "very fine people" after the 2017 Charlottesville events, to the summer 2019 tweet telling four congresswomen of color to "go back" to where they came from, to telling Capitol attackers, "I love you," in January 2021, there is a clear pattern. An *Atlantic* article titled "An Oral History of Trump's Bigotry"[56] tracks decades of racist incidents and remarks. The timeline includes a 1973 Justice Department lawsuit against the Trump Management Company that showed Trump and his father routinely discriminated against Black and Brown tenants; Trump's use of full-page advertisements in New York City newspapers in 1989 to call for the death penalty for five Black and Latino teenagers falsely accused and convicted of raping a jogger; and his 2011 "birther" conspiracy claims that Barack Obama was not born in the United States. As with lies, journalists struggled with what language to use, when to condemn, and how to balance professional practices with a broader sense of morality.

For the purposes of this chapter, racism is defined as "an attitude consisting of a tendency to respond negatively toward a racioethnic group."[57] As the authors of this book, we feel comfortable using the term "racist" to describe Trump's statements. But it is also important to examine Trump's racist statements within their political context: Trump's political ascension follows Obama's historic election in 2008 (and re-election in 2012) as the first African American president and the attendant discussion of whether the United States had entered a post-racial stage in which overt racism had become a relic of the past. Yet this post-racial mythology has always overstated progress by overlooking the extent to which structural racism exists.[58] Perhaps this is best illustrated by a refusal among many Trump supporters to acknowledge anything wrong about Trump's statements. In 2019, 91% of Republicans surveyed did not think of Trump as racist.[59] Instead, Trump's backers largely ignored his statements, denied any racial implications, or defended Trump's claims on the grounds that he was actually arguing against reverse racism. The latter connects to the politics of identity reviewed in Chapter 1. Trump's ability to tap racial resentment was built into his populist messaging quite explicitly.[60] As Jessica Grant Schafer argues, Trump and his supporters think of "political incorrectness" as being a positive, refreshing stance. Moreover, Grant argues that racist statements are denied as such when they are "situated in the neoliberal white racial frame" and "become a signifier in current politics as a means through which backstage, or overt, racism and bigotry can be communicated with an illusion of subtlety by white citizens in the public frontstage of social media and political discourse."[61] Trump, by making racist statements that he then denies are racist, voiced what many Americans *really* feel. The question put in front of journalists was whether to connect the public, front-stage discourse with its true, racist backstage sentiment. In other words, should they call out the innate racism directly?

News organizations struggled with how to cover the increasing frequency of racist displays once Trump took office. For those journalists committed to a vision of objectivity as privileging facticity over evaluation, it was enough to provide ample, verified evidence and allow people to decide for themselves. Racist statements were not ignored, but not labeled so bluntly. For others, calling out Trump's racist remarks for what they were was a top priority. These journalists sought to maintain their relevance by connecting to a broader moral framework that clearly abhors racist statements. This tension forced the press to question its long-held protocols, particularly those that allowed reporters to distance themselves from controversy by using he-said/she-said sourcing practices. CNN's Brian Stelter raised this issue in his defense of journalistic judgment: "He said/she said is a tried and true journalistic technique, of course, but it is insufficient at a time like this. If telling Democratic congresswomen to 'go back and help fix the totally broken and crime infested places from which they came' isn't racist, what is?"[62] Stelter, as we will see subsequently, has been a consistent advocate for covering Trump in a way that is more grounded in critique, with care not to unquestionably convey Trump's lies or racist statements to the public. But the issue played out in debates across newsrooms.

Two examples help make clear how news organizations struggled to balance a commitment to professional practice with appeals to basic morality. The first involves internal strife at Reuters over how to label Trump's racist comments. As an international wire service that serves many news organizations, Reuters does not have a strong voice of its own. It is hemmed in by this position, which makes it more reluctant to call out racism so openly. Yet *Washington Post* media columnist Erik Wemple wrote about what he called a "brawl" within the wire service following reporting on Trump's racist rebuke of the four congresswomen of color.[63] Reuters editorial policy forbids the use of "racist," but journalists reporting on Trump's attacks used "racist comments" with the quotation marks referencing a House resolution condemning Trump's remarks.[64] As reporters sought to use more stark language, their superiors clamped down on phrasings like "racially charged" and "racist comments." Wemple reported the compromise of "widely criticized as racist" as accepted by the organization. When he reached out for comment, Reuters provided the following statement:

> As a global news organization operating independently in 166 countries, Reuters is committed to sharing accurate, unbiased information upon which people can make the most informed, intelligent decisions. Our coverage is providing all the information, background and context to enable users to determine for themselves whether President Trump's recent tweets were racist.

This position echoes those above in offloading judgments related to morality to the audience. Wemple rebuked Reuters for its unwillingness to condemn racist language while also pointing to the equivocating nature of the approach it took: "Reuters's troubles highlight the realities of deploying adjectives: Doing so always triggers some level of judgment, deduction and analysis. Don't abandon that exercise just because its outcome speaks ill of the president of the United States." Wemple is making this statement from the position of a columnist sanctioned to offer opinions. Reuters situates itself at the opposite extreme of presenting news as a commodity, and therefore locates its legitimacy in the ethos of facticity. Furthermore, Reuters and others seemed reluctant to air these internal debates in public, worried that the indecision would make them look less authoritative on this moral ground.[65] And, finally, Reuters' position assumes that people are rational in their political judgments and that they share a common moral outrage toward racism so that it does not need to be labeled as morally wrong. The stance also assumes that most people know what racism looks like and rejects the notion that it is the journalist's job to tell them.

A second example of how discussions of race played out in newsrooms takes us outside of Trump to probe the question of how journalists amplify—or even normalize—racist ideas when they give space to racist viewpoints. Does this create a false equivalency, or does it fall in line with the objectivity tenets of professional journalism? These issues were front and center when National Public Radio interviewed Jason Kessler, the white supremacist organizer of the 2017 "Unite the Right" rally in Charlottesville that turned deadly. Kessler appeared on NPR's *Morning Edition* on August 10, 2018—a year after the Charlottesville rally and two days before a second rally in front of the White House. Host Noel King prefaced the seven-minute interview with a warning—"full disclosure: some of what you're about to hear is racist and offensive"—before asking Kessler about his beliefs.[66] The interview was at times polite and at times contentious, with King somewhat challenging Kessler. But the interview nevertheless gave Kessler a public, legitimized platform for espousing his racist ideas.

The interview prompted instant outrage from journalists inside and outside of NPR. Karen Attiah, the "Global Opinions" editor for the *Washington Post*, blasted the interview for its failure to push back more forcibly against Kessler: "When it comes to handling racist and white-supremacist subjects, the job of a responsible media outlet does not end at simply letting figures like Kessler speak unchallenged, in the name of neutrality and balance." Attiah acknowledged there is news value in interviewing such public figures, but called for "aggressively countering racist lies and propaganda with facts and truth."[67] The watchdog group Media Matters for America called the interview "a gift to white supremacists."[68] Other critics echoed these sentiments.[69]

Internally, NPR public editor Elizabeth Jensen weighed in with a column detailing the step-by-step decision-making that went into the interview.[70] NPR made transparent the due diligence it did before inviting Kessler on the show, asking listeners and having newsroom-wide discussions about the interview. After exploring the production aspects, Jensen concluded:

> NPR's audience is vast; it is still overwhelmingly white. Part of how one heard it may depend on how closely one has followed this story and whether one experiences that type of prejudice. There is no right answer here for everyone. I do think Kessler's racism and general illogic came through, even in the absence of the more aggressive pushback some critics wanted, and NPR listeners are smart enough to hear that. NPR has decided it will air these interviews. I am on the fence about whether they are necessary. But if

NPR is going to go that route, it needs to strengthen its practices for a more responsible execution.

Jensen tried to locate a position between offloading moral judgment to the audience and asking NPR journalists to do more to make the deplorability of racist ideas clear. Meanwhile, Noel King defended the interview on Twitter by noting the backgrounds of those producing the segment: "I'm a biracial woman. Our Executive Producer is a Black woman. I understand you didn't like this interview; I understand why, but Morning Edition is a notably diverse team who thought long and hard before airing this."[71] King's position fit with others in the organization who defended talking to a racist as an important act of journalism aiming to make sense of the racist marches in Charlottesville and Washington. Here, NPR defended itself by claiming that even the Black and Brown people on staff felt the interview with the racist would fall in line with their missions as journalists. In this discursive work, we see how entrenched the professional identity of the journalist is, trumping even that of personal identity for these producers.

For journalists, calling something a lie remains easier than calling something or someone racist. With falsehoods, journalists marshal evidence and can rate statements as ranging from the misleading twisting of facts to outright fabrications. But applying the label of racist has a higher threshold—something may be partly true, but being partly racist is still being racist. Calling out racism then requires more journalistic agency to make the judgment. Journalists express discomfort at such pronouncements with their moral character, but the Reuters and NPR examples demonstrate that there is also discomfort at ignoring these pronouncements. The concern is about amplifying racist messages in the process of reporting them. This is not a small issue, given the prominent role of race in the governing and election strategy of Trump.[72] Journalists calling out the president's racist language cannot assume that they occupy a unified cultural position in which Trump is one side and everyone else is on the other. Trump had copious supporters who welcomed racist sentiments, and racial resentment is baked into political identity, as we discussed in Chapter 1. This gets us back to the larger question of how journalists should approach their balance of professionalism and an appeal to morality.

What Should Journalists Do? A Shifting Moral Voice

The debates around covering Trump's lies and racist statements connect to deeper issues than just how to cover Trump as an individual. Journalists wrestling with coverage choices are forced into the position of having to reflect on what the news should look like. This discussion is not free-floating. Rather, it is inscribed in the shifting contextual conditions of the media culture—one in which journalists are increasingly decentralized within the cacophonous landscape of public discourse. This section presents two different positions that have been articulated in response to Trump: a facts-first defense grounded on the existing principles of news and a morality-centric vision from journalists critical of objectivity norms.

Facticity's Defenders

The first position is one focused on facticity. Journalists produce facts, and they do so according to set procedures that have emerged through the professionalization of the field. Careful adherence to practice is paramount for legitimating news accounts. This position has many adherents, but this section will focus on how it has been articulated by two of the most prominent journalists in the United States: *New York Times* executive editor Dean Baquet and *Washington Post* executive editor Martin Baron (who stepped down from the role when he retired in 2021). As heads of two of the most powerful and well-resourced news organizations, Baquet and Baron would compete to break news stories, particularly with regard to political elites in Washington. But they are also friends after having risen through the news ranks at the same time.[73] As journalistic elites, they are often invited to make public remarks about the state of journalism, and each has a long track record of statements about what news ought to be. They recognize that their positions grant them this discursive space, but also make them targets of critique. As the *Columbia Journalism Review* put it, "Clearly, however, a fresh wind is shaking the philosophical and representational foundations of the US news industry as a whole, and Baquet and Baron—as two of the industry's most central pillars—are feeling the vibrations more than most."[74] In this way, they are not only powerful journalistic actors, but also powerful symbols of the standard model of American journalism.

Baquet has argued that it is not the role of the journalist to act as society's moral judge. For example, in the aftermath of controversy over an August 2019 *New York Times* headline that read "Trump Urges Unity vs. Racism,"[75] the paper came under fire for not adopting a stronger voice against Trump's racist statements. Baquet credited the poor headline to a bad choice made by the copy desk before engaging a broader discussion of the journalistic direction of the *Times*. In an interview with CNN, Baquet worried that more explicit judgments would harm rather than expand the newspaper's independence: "Our role is not to be the leader of the resistance. . . . Inevitably the resistance in America wins. Inevitably the people outside power gain power again. And at that point, what are you? You're just a chump of the people who won. Our role is to hold everybody who has power to account."[76] In this view, journalistic judgments are political rather than moral—or at least are seen that way. Baquet defended the *Times*'s reporting on Trump and blamed a "generational divide" in the newsroom in which younger journalists were more vocal about the need for more activist-oriented reporting.

Baquet addressed concerns over objectivity raised by younger journalists in the *Times* newsroom in another interview in June 2020 in the aftermath of nationwide protests following the police murder of George Floyd in Minneapolis. Baquet acknowledged his own path as a Black journalist coming up in the South, and recognized that the concerns about diversity at the *Times* from Black and Brown journalists in the newsrooms were more about substance than merely diversity percentages. But Baquet also saw his own responsibility as maintaining the core of the *Times* brand. He noted: "I have to protect the place. I have to make it better but also sometimes resist the things that they want to change."[77] While somewhat vague in what this means, Baquet differentiates his vision for the *Times* against a more aggressive or activist slant preferred by others in the newsroom. This has been a public struggle.[78]

Baron has echoed much of the same sentiment as Baquet in defending the record of the *Washington Post* in reporting on Trump. Even as the newspaper added the slogan of "Democracy Dies in the Darkness" a month after Trump's inauguration in 2017, Baron resisted a more activist style of news for the *Post*. One of the more lengthy explanations of Baron's vision of journalism can be found in the Reuters Memorial Lecture he presented at the University of Oxford in early 2018, a year into Trump's presidency.[79] Baron reflected on the question of journalism's relevance in this particular moment given shifts in the media and political context of journalism: "I do think we must recognize that something profound has changed in our profession. Journalism may not work as it did in the past. Our work's anticipated impact may not materialize. The public may not process information as it did previously." This was a frank admission that the news industry operated in a difficult environment that journalists could not ignore. Baron's answer lay in a commitment to facticity: "At *The Post*, we take inspiration from the principles that were articulated for our organization in 1935. They begin as follows: 'The first mission of a newspaper is to tell the truth as nearly as the truth may be ascertained.' Judging from digital traffic, a surge in subscriptions and reader comments, much of the public believes we are doing just that." Indeed, the *Post* has risen in prominence since Amazon founder Jeff Bezos purchased the newspaper in 2013, provided it with more resources, and pushed it to strengthen its digital operations to extend its reach. Baron reacted to Trump's attacks on the newspaper through an insistence on sticking to fact-centric reporting: "Amid an unrelenting assault from the most powerful person on earth, the answer for us is clear: Just do our job. Do it honestly, honorably, seriously, fairly, accurately, and also unflinchingly." To Baron, professionalism provides the clearest path forward and facticity conquers demagoguery.

As the Trump presidency continued on, Baron's message was quite consistent. For example, in a graduation message to Harvard's class of 2020, Baron deepened his commitment to stringent facticity in the face of the coronavirus spread: "Only a few months ago, I would have settled for emphasizing that our democracy depends on facts and truth, and it surely does. . . . But now, as we can plainly see, it is more elemental than that. Facts and truth are matters of life and death. Misinformation, disinformation, delusions, and deceit can kill."[80] Baron alluded to Trump's pattern of health misinformation and his continued denial of the severity of the virus. As Trump flooded the public with bad information, Baron positioned the *Post* as a beacon for trusted information. His focus remained on information above all. But his vision has received pushback from journalists of color in his newsroom, leading to division about what the voice of the *Post* ought to be in the face of growing attention to systemic racism in American society—including within newsrooms.[81]

It would be a mistake to see Baquet and Baron—and others who agree with them—as rejecting any moral stance for journalists. They envision the moral ground of journalism accountability through the provision of verified facts. For them, journalism's moral ground is to avoid direct accusations and declarations that can be construed as biased in order to provide an antidote to the self-interest of political elites and institutions. Trump's lies and racism are treated as political acts that must be treated as such journalistically. To do anything else would be to deny their moral, professionalized obligation to the truth. They are facticity's defenders, elevating the journalistic fact above all. But this singular, inflexible moral code assumes that Americans agree on what a credible fact looks like and that they will accept news reporting as valid and accurate. This is a big assumption at a time when attacks on the relevance of mainstream journalism have been so persistent and widespread.

Morality's Defenders

In his history of journalistic objectivity in the United States, Michael Schudson notes that just as the ideal achieved its hegemonic status, it was assailed as unworkable.[82] Alternatives have always been floated, as attacks on a rigid conception of objectivity are easy to mount.[83] Rather than pile onto a century of critique in any abstract sense, we assert that criticisms of objectivity need to be contextualized as speaking from a particular time and place. Qualms about objectivity are about specific failures endemic to actual epistemic situations, not just philosophical musings about the uncertainty of knowing. It is from this position that we examine how objectivity again came to be assailed in response to Trump and his allies. This was not a marginal conversation taking place among academics and the alternative press at the fringes of journalism, but one emerging from a growing contingent of mainstream, traditionally minded journalists who responded to Trump by arguing for a new era of journalism.

Some of the most forceful voices in this conversation have been media critics. Traditionally, media critics have been accused of being overly constrained by professional norms so as to stave off more radical criticism.[84] Typically, media critics have patrolled the boundaries of journalism through opinion columns and cable talk shows—calling out violations of accepted practices and celebrating particular journalists as exemplars of the profession. But recently these critics have stepped forward as a source of moral authority within the profession. And, their brand of morality goes beyond merely sticking to information as presented to instead call out lies and explicit racism.

Brian Stelter, the media commentator for CNN, emerged as a particularly strident critic of the press for its failure to consistently call out Trump.

In a 2018 interview with the *Columbia Journalism Review*, Stelter summed up his main focus as the attacks on journalists from the Trump administration: "The coordinated campaign against journalism—what I would call anti-journalism—is a theme that I've been trying to track and cover and write about. . . . It obviously didn't start with President Trump; it dates back decades. He just poured a huge amount of gasoline on the already burning fire."[85] Not content to focus only on journalists, Stelter used his program to connect Trump's lies with warnings of "creeping authoritarianism" and "democratic backsliding."[86] In this way, Stelter's role as a moral authority provides further evidence of the degree to which journalists have become part of the political stories that they tell. Stelter blurs—or even erases—the boundaries between media critique and political news. For example, in June 2020, Stelter engaged in a heated debate with Trump legal adviser Jenna Ellis over a particularly bad showing for Trump in a recent CNN poll. The debate spilled over beyond questions of how the news media use polls to larger questions about lying and the Trump administration.[87]

For his critiques of Trump and conservative media, Stelter has become a favorite target of the Right. Ordinarily, it would seem unusual for a media critic to be exposed to such political vitriol, but Stelter's focus on lies and racism by Trump and his allies places him in a position to be attacked. Fox News, which is the subject of a critical book by Stelter,[88] has consistently jabbed at him. Headlines about Stelter appearing on the Fox News site include the following:

CNN's Brian Stelter widely ridiculed after blaming tech issues for bizarre anti-Trump segment

CNN's Brian Stelter lampooned on social media over documentary announcement

CNN's Brian Stelter's apparent hesitance to cover Tara Reade's Biden accusations raises eyebrows

CNN's "Reliable Sources" with Brian Stelter hits rock bottom in key demo[89]

These stories use the familiar attack format of elevating accusations into facts. Even Trump insulted Stelter directly on Twitter: "@brianstelter is just a poor man's lapdog for AT&T!"[90] Trump's comment aimed at three entities: AT&T as a media conglomerate, CNN as a cable network, and Stelter as a journalist.[91] This pushback against Stelter again shows how media criticism has shifted from an internal gaze at news to part of the larger political discourse dealing with questions of what's true and who should be believed.

Looking inward, Stelter has chided journalists for uncritical reporting as he pushes them toward a position of cultural leadership based on morality. Stelter made this argument in a commentary that appeared on the CNN site and on his program: "Morality is not partisan. Decency is not exclusive to any one political party. People can disagree about what's immoral and what's indecent, but it is important to have the conversation. And journalists can help lead the way."[92] Here, Stelter anoints journalists as facilitators for public moralizing. On his program, Stelter argued for a shift from prioritizing facticity to carving out space for morality: "In part, our role is to keep collecting facts. All the facts so citizens can make up their own minds. But I think it's also our role to stand up for decency and morality especially if others won't."[93] He is suggesting that journalists go beyond being mere facilitators of the conversation about morality to become moral arbiters themselves. Yet Stelter acknowledged the barriers for this type of thinking within the journalistic community: "I think sometimes the media has a hard time talking about morality, talking about issues of ethics. You know, it's not in our language the way that law, basic things like law are." We quibble with Stelter on this point; as we saw in the previous chapter, when journalists invoke the grand narratives of the profession, they call forth a core moral system with many in-built moral assumptions. By situating discussions of journalism within this moral language, Stelter is playing an active role in pushing journalists to assess their normative grounds.

Similar to Stelter, *Washington Post* media critic Margaret Sullivan has also engaged journalistic practice at a fundamental, moral level during the Trump presidency.[94] Sullivan had served as the public editor for the *New York Times* and came to the *Post* in May 2016 during the presidential campaign. She has consistently asserted that a failure to call out lies and racism both explicitly and frequently risks eroding journalists' authority as a democratic moral guide. In a column headlined "Tiptoeing around Trump's Racism Is a Betrayal of Journalistic Truth-Telling," Sullivan argued: "When confronted with racism and lying, we can't run and hide . . . in the name of neutrality and impartiality. To do that is a dereliction of duty."[95] Sullivan describes the label of racism not as the product of journalistic judgment, but as an accurate reflection of what was said—all part of journalism's goal of "telling the truth as plainly and directly as possible." This argument positions the calling out of lies and racism within the moral ground of facticity—a stance we also agree with. Nonetheless, Sullivan's concerns about the press are largely about relevance. In comparing reporting on Richard Nixon with that on Trump, Sullivan argued that journalism has always relied on other institutions: "By itself, journalism—no matter how proficient or how brave—can't save us from political corruption at the highest level. It never could."[96] For Sullivan, journalists could not count on their reporting by itself being enough; it requires the intervention of an external authority capable of enacting change.

Other media critics also supported efforts to make morality a more salient quality of news reporting. *New York Times* TV critic James Poniewozik wrote:

> A real problem is that politics in Trump's era has taken on a moral dimension that news outlets either aren't equipped to cover, or think it's their duty to avoid. And if they avoid it, they avoid their job, which is to accurately represent to their audience what's happening.[97]

For Poniewozik, like Sullivan, journalistic morality is not a matter of moral judgment but of a need for journalists to engage in moral claims to adequately describe the actions of Trump and his administration. Barriers to this approach are well entrenched, as *Baltimore Sun* media critic David Zurawik posited:

> Many of us in the press shy away from talk of morality and moral behavior because we think it will make us seem biased in some way. But with an amoral president—and Trump certainly fills that bill—a moral framework is necessary to remind citizens of how craven some actions of this president truly are. Without that moral context, I fear his craven, cruel and hateful words and acts will become normalized.[98]

Journalists had become distressed and fed up, and when copious fact-checking and investigative reporting did not seem to get results, these critics turned deeper to a moral core as providing the grounds for admonishing Trump.

These critics point to a deep dissatisfaction, either with how Trump is covered or with what happens to this coverage once it emerges. Many of these suggestions are predicated on the extraordinariness of Trump in the face of the lies and racist statements reviewed earlier, but they also connect with larger questions of what journalism ought to look like as media and political worlds continue to shift. This forward-looking perspective moves these discussions past Trump to consider how journalists can rethink the very basis of their authority. In many ways, the January 6, 2021, attack on the Capitol served as a trigger for more explicit efforts to counter what *New York Times* columnist Nicholas Kristof called "an ecosystem of mass delusion spread by Fox News and many Republicans."[99] To many media watchers and journalists, the 2021 insurrection was the ultimate example of the direct consequence of this battle over factual information. Our final point is that when these critics bring up morality, it is not a radical viewpoint. They are not abandoning journalism as it is and hawking something new. Rather, they are reorienting the voice of journalism—a topic we take up in the final chapter.

The Conflicted View of Journalists

The voices quoted in this chapter—from big-name newspaper editors to media critics tasked with constantly commenting on the press—have gained prominence in the public discourse around journalism. These are elite journalists who, through their positions, speak for a big segment of mainstream journalism. But the question remains how widespread these sentiments are throughout the profession. Through in-depth interviews, focus groups, and surveys conducted with reporters and editors throughout the United States during 2019 and 2020,[100] we heard these tensions articulated over and over again as journalists recounted ethical and other concerns about their coverage of Trump's lies and racism. Journalists admit to being conflicted when their actions are often not able to match what they wanted them to be. The majority of these reporters—who hail from small to mid-sized newsrooms and were evenly distributed geographically—emphatically do not consider themselves "custodians of conscience" in the Ettema and Glasser vein. To consider themselves as such would be contrary to what they see as their primary mission: to relay accurate, relevant information in the vein of the standard model of journalism. People who are not journalists, they said, have to be their own conscience. But when pressed about their actual role in their communities, a majority of the journalists we spoke with believed that news outlets were in a unique and important position to help their communities better communicate across differences, for example, or to help their places develop solutions to societal problems. These contradictions were articulated in a number of ways:

- Even though only a handful of news outlets publish their ethics policies or make ethical statements on relevant stories, almost all of them thought that it would be a good idea to do so and thought that they should do it.
- Even though a majority of the participating reporters thought that newsroom-wide social justice training would be a great idea, only a tiny fraction had ever done any.
- Even though a majority of reporters thought that building bridges in their communities to help resolve political polarization on issues ranging from gun control to abortion was something they could and should be doing morally, very few had ever actually taken any steps to do so, such as hosting community forums.

But a striking factor emerged as well: journalists feel as if citizens believe them to be indifferent to morality, or even villainously immoral. That perception has deflated them—from small-town reporter to mid-sized publisher to national political reporter. The quagmire is this: the moral obligation to call out lies and racism contributes to the rampant distrust among certain audiences in certain places. Again and again in focus groups, interviews, and surveys, the journalists identified this situation as a significant challenge (after, of course, lack of time and resources). One journalist lamented that "stories that are factually based are labeled as fake news." Another reporter said, "People have become suspicious. ... [S]ome make assumptions about how I am doing my job or why." The interviews elaborated how in this environment calling out lies and racism becomes a problematic responsibility that can contribute to distrust. "Basically, people don't understand what really motivates us," a journalist said, adding: "They often think we are just in it for the power or influence or to write a salacious story." As a result, some of these reporters—especially those covering politics and those who were high profile in our sample—told us about a constant stream of vitriol. One reporter indicated being "less inclined to work with my audience or take tips from readers if I feel like they are being rude to me and dismissive of what I'm currently doing." Another added, "As for trust, I sometimes feel hopeless that people will trust us to give them factual, unbiased information. It seems like people more and more are simply seeking information that confirms what they already believe, instead of seeking a diversity of information to truly educate themselves. I am not sure how we overcome this complete lack of trust in experts."

Morality, then, is caught up in a conception of truth and trust as being a transaction with "factual, unbiased information." These reactions affect the way the reporters behave morally, with many closing themselves off and declining to make themselves vulnerable to the "engagement" that audiences might bring in order to focus on uncovering truths. In other words, some of the rank-and-file journalists we spoke with found it wrong to engage with such audiences because it distracted them from their main mission, and so they found themselves less willing to engage with anyone at all. Accordingly, their moralities center on the content—making sure it is accurate, being transparent about sourcing, triple-checking facts. Consider this comment from one of the survey participants: "We like to point to our sources when we can online (research, studies, etc.) to show where we are getting the information we use in stories. We've also in the past made a video explaining how an investigative story was reported, to show the steps. And I try to highlight (through social media) that we have actual working humans in the newsroom and we're here to listen if the audience wants to reach out." The reporter lays out the principles at work—accuracy, transparency—as ethical guidelines for her small newsroom in the Midwest as being centered on content. Audiences can "reach out" if they want, but for the most part this survey response highlights the chasm between journalists and community members.

And yet, throughout the responses and reflections of the journalists we spoke to, their words reveal a growing sense of purpose around community problems and polarization that seeps into how they think about their role. A female reporter at a large news outlet in the Northeast wrote in reply to an open-ended question about her function as a journalist:

> I want my journalism to lift up community-focused solutions to systemic problems. I think communities do not need journalists to come in and solve problems for them, but rather organize people to come together, connect, exchange information, and organize themselves to create actionable ways to change the things they think suck about their neighborhood or city. I want to also hold those in power accountable for perpetuating the problems that the communities are trying to solve.

Here again we sniff the grand narrative from Chapter 4, whereby journalists must "hold those in power accountable" even as the role is *not* to solve problems for communities. However, this comment hints at a proactiveness about these community problems that is not always present in journalistic rhetoric. Consider, by contrast, how accuracy, transparency, and evidence are situated in these interviews as the moral antidotes to lying and racism:

> I strive to present the best version of the truth I can find, regardless of my personal views and attitudes. I do not have bias and try to be as transparent as possible, Training, Honesty, and Integrity is the values I always hold onto [sic]. I always do my own work which means I do not accept notes, recordings, etc. from anyone else to write the story. My rule is to always conduct the interviews myself. That way I know what the source really said. I continue to build trust with my audiences through great reporting, public service journalism, and attentiveness to the reader/viewer needs.

This survey response from a (white, male) reporter at a tiny niche-oriented publication in the Northeast suggests that journalists—and perhaps only journalists—should be trusted as moral beings capable of communicating true accounts of events in the world. Their lack of bias, as this comment puts forth, elevates what they do into a value-free realm where truths are disseminated in a manner that is as unvarnished as possible. In these pontifications about morality around truth-telling, reporters position themselves as uniquely alone in this work.[101] From this evidence, it is clear that journalists feel caught between, on one hand, understanding that they need to be more active in their judgments and, on the other, lacking trust that community members will give them the benefit of the doubt regarding their political neutrality. Feeling untrusted, journalists tell us they fall back to norms and routines of the standard model of journalism to distinguish themselves and to preserve the sense of authority they have spent more than a century cultivating, brandishing objectivity as their main weapon. Although we can certainly understand this dilemma and the journalism that emerges from it, we must ask in this book: At what costs? Is objectivity still truly achieving what these journalists think they are offering? We do not believe so. The changing media culture demands new approaches to journalism, especially in regard to its roles in our communities and democracy.

Conclusion: Journalism's Moral Struggles

Despite its blemishes, objectivity has long remained a gold-standard moral code for journalists, forming a core part of their professional identity and remaining a talisman that separates professional journalists from people who traffic in information without the credentials or training to do so.[102] Objectivity suggests that intrepid reporters in their pursuit of the truth exercise their fact-finding in as balanced and as neutral a manner as possible. Or, as Dean Baquet described it, it is what happens when a reporter "gets on an airplane to pursue a story with an empty notebook, believing that he or she doesn't fully know what the story is, and is going to be open to what they hear."[103] That is, journalists are free from the subjectivity that might guide the rest of their life. The morality of the profession is preserved as objectivity, at least in its idealized form. As it is practiced now, though, objectivity no longer enables a moral voice in this environment—if it ever did. It can no longer be a guiding norm, at least as it has been practiced. Objectivity has devolved into an ethos of detachment, one that staves off vital questions about how journalists connect to audiences, how they communicate certain values in society, and how they contribute to conditions for social trust and understanding.

With his constant lies and his racism, Trump brought these issues to the fore. During Trump's four years in office, journalists were forced to confront a conflict between adhering to a well-established precedent of treating whatever the president says as newsworthy and actively judging his statements to be wanton falsehoods or bigoted speech. One key event came in March 2020 when CNN and MSNBC refused to carry live Trump's misleading and meandering press conferences on the coronavirus situation.[104] Following the 2020 election, it became clear that a sea change was taking place when the three major television news networks—ABC, CBS, and NBC—collectively cut away from Trump's unfounded rants alleging that the election had been rigged. *NBC Nightly News* anchor Lester Holt explicitly articulated this decision because of Trump's falsehoods: "We have to interrupt here, because the president made a number of false statements, including the notion that there has been fraudulent voting." Referring to the president's claims, Holt added, "There has been no evidence of that."[105] These actions indicate a slow cohesiveness forming around privileging a moral stance of protecting democracy and a rejection that journalists merely stand apart from powerful sources to act as witnesses.

Yet these actions, while potentially a positive step for journalism, often fail to reach the people who believe Trump and who have abandoned mainstream news. Journalists may consider such cutaways and recriminations to be a brave step, but Trump supporters might see them as an affront—as another rejection of themselves, of their values and their worldviews. This viewpoint has been primed by the drumbeat of invective directed at journalists by Trump and others, including extreme claims that journalists are the enemy of the people. When journalists make a show of turning away from the elected officials who conservatives believe represent them, news media come to be considered irrelevant if not outrightly undemocratic, furthering a spiral of distrust. We are not suggesting that it was wrong for journalists to cut away from dangerous lies. They did the right thing. But we are suggesting this is precisely the kind of complicated terrain that journalists find themselves in as they attempt to more assertively protect democracy.

As we contemplate all of this, we need to position Trump not as the cause of the moral questioning within journalism, but as a symbol of larger shifts taking place. The journalist's role has been to make order out of chaos in the world. But news stories have never been reducible to the transmission of facts.[106] The news has always been about creating narratives, usually from a centrist position, that prompt citizens to trust in the American Dream, government institutions, democracy, and the values of working hard and living modestly. Regardless of Trump, fewer and fewer people are able to attain the American Dream, crushed by global changes in labor markets, widespread industrial layoffs, skyrocketing costs for higher education, jobs replaced by technology, and fiscal policies favoring the well-off at the expense of the rest. As a result of these forces, as well as a broader decaying of social ties and community fabric,[107] trust in our institutions and democracy has declined. Meanwhile, journalism's centrist position has come under fire for upholding as unproblematic what are in practice problematic institutions that have privileged powerful actors while working against whole groups of people.

All of this means that the authority granted to the press to be the neutral arbiters of information is disintegrating. As journalist Jeffrey C. Billman wrote: "The bigger problem is that this erosion of trust will outlive Trump's administration. This is a business built on a premise of integrity; for newspapers to work, the communities we serve have to believe that we're not making shit up for fun and profit."[108] The knee-jerk reaction that journalists should double down on objectivity, that accurate reporting speaks for itself, and that detractors can be ignored is no longer tenable in this environment. Journalists should take the threat of their irrelevance among many different publics seriously and question how their moral norms around truths and informed governing are faltering. How to confront this situation and rebuild journalism as a trusted, relevant institution providing shared knowledge is daunting. It is only through reimagining what (and whom) journalism is for—and especially how it can be more firmly connected to a democracy that incorporates the millions who were still supporting Trump after years of lies and even after the 2021 attack on the Capitol and subsequent impeachment—that we can move toward this future.

Conclusion
What Relevant Journalism Looks Like
Developing a Moral Voice

In a January 2019 article provocatively titled "Does Journalism Have a Future?," *New Yorker* staff writer and Harvard historian Jill Lepore painted a nightmarish picture: "Journalism, as a field, is as addled as an addict, gaunt, wasted, and twitchy, its pockets as empty as its nights are sleepless."[1] The article surveys the long decline of print newspapers, the rise of digital news organizations operating outside of traditional norms, and the flood of social media content that overtakes news discourse. Lepore's account is stark, but by no means alone. The past decade has been rife with authors questioning the very relevance of journalism, even if they have not always used that term specifically.[2] To return to a question we posed at the beginning of the book, What happens when journalism doesn't seem to work anymore? What happens when its effectiveness and its practices are so under fire? At the most extreme, we have seen how flows of false information helped trigger the January 6, 2021, insurrection at the US Capitol, followed by a startling advisory bulletin by the Department of Homeland Security connecting enhanced warnings of domestic terrorism to the spread of "false narratives" through digital media.[3] But in more mundane ways, continuing doubts about conventional news reporting hamper the ability of journalists to provide shared stories to a broad public.[4] What is needed is a concerted effort, first, to take the question of relevance seriously and, second, to consider a path forward toward restoring relevance—not for the sake of journalistic relevance on its own, but one forged in the spirit of improving our cultural and democratic bonds.

Throughout the book, we have used the term "relevance" not in an isolated, evaluative sense but rather in a structural sense of journalism as one communicative form competing for epistemic and cultural authority among many other actors. The use of relevance shifts the frame of reference from a journalism-centric view primarily looking at the world through the eyes of journalists and privileging journalistic epistemologies and norms to looking

News After Trump. Matt Carlson, Sue Robinson, and Seth C. Lewis, Oxford University Press. © Oxford University Press 2021. DOI: 10.1093/oso/9780197550342.003.0007

at journalism as just one part of a larger media culture. Journalism cannot be adequately understood as a cultural practice if it is confined to some sort of analytical island of its own. Even the variety of forms housed in the term "journalism" belies a coherent set of agreed-upon practices. As a response, we have used the concept of *media culture* to encapsulate the wide range of material forms, practices, and beliefs associated with different media content. This larger framework helps us recognize how journalism exists alongside so many other forms while also accommodating the boundaries of journalism—its peripheries—as more fluid than is often recognized.[5] Digital media allow for a wide array of other "news-like" actors and ideas to enter into the mediated political sphere. Even if news practices at the core of journalism haven't radically changed, the transformation of the media culture—with the arrival of digital media, social media, ubiquitous mobile devices, and the cultural expectations and norms associated with them—feeds back into journalism. This, in aggregate, upends the social as well as the technological contexts surrounding how news is made, how it moves about in the world, and how people receive and make sense of it.[6] Journalism is not impervious to these shifts, nor can it be properly understood apart from them. But we risk missing these larger developments in media culture if we are too inwardly focused on the journalistic community.

Even more broadly, the changing media culture needs to be connected to ongoing political shifts. For many Americans, one's sense of identity—an identity that, in an earlier time, may have been defined more by religion or family or community affiliation—is increasingly oriented around partisan, tribal politics. The alignment between political identity and social identity deepens partisan divides at a time when exclusionary populist politics have overtaken the Republican Party. Trump's use of populist rhetoric, elevated to a demagogic register, positioned him to be a savior standing up for an aggrieved silent majority of Americans who believed they were victims of a two-pronged assault led by non-whites or non-Christians from below and political, cultural, and media elites from above. What has emerged is affective political polarization with animosity creeping into everyday perceptions.[7]

Into this maelstrom steps a beleaguered news industry, struggling to survive financially in an attention economy that is vastly more competitive and more culturally fractured than anything previously imagined. While surveys show that declining public trust in the news has been decades in the making and has mostly been a bipartisan phenomenon, appraisals of press performance—like many things in life these days—have become increasingly polarized. Almost universally, respondents who identify as Republicans tell pollsters they distrust the news media,[8] bringing to fruition a generation-long effort by conservative politicians and pundits to attack the press in order to undermine its institutional legitimacy. The coalescing of all of these factors enabled Donald Trump, but they also pre-exist his presidency and remain in place after it finished. Thus, any discussion of journalism needs to look beyond the individual moment to address how we have arrived at this point—to this precipice, of sorts—where the question of journalism's relevance has become so prominent and the future of news as a feature of public accountability has become so uncertain.

In this final chapter, we consider questions of news norms—not only for journalists, but also for politicians, news sharers, and news consumers. We are living through a time of intense epistemic and cultural transformation. Fundamental notions of fact, truth, and reality are being contested as never before in recent memory. What exactly constitutes shared American values—around decency and democracy, equality and expression—are unsettled. Although these trends and tendencies have been building for decades, we have arrived, it seems, at an inflection point that will shape the future of public life in the United States and many other parts of the world. What's at stake, in this case, is how news about communities and public affairs takes shape, and to what effect: Will the journalistic status quo persist in the face of declining relevance? Or will journalism be reoriented—not just for new media but with new norms—to meet the challenge of a changed media culture?

There is, as we have explored so far, a strong impulse for journalists to respond to these uncertainties by doubling down on what seemed to work before: a standard model of detached objectivity that dominated the twentieth century of broadcast and print media and remains a core part of the American journalistic DNA. Instead of taking this path, we close this book by arguing for a different one more suited to our contemporary media culture and thus more likely to help journalism reclaim a sense of relevance. We label this direction the "moral voice" of journalism, marked by a clarified sense of purpose, a more realistic awareness of limitations, and a more transparent approach to practice. In a digital media world where information is abundant, attention is limited, and authenticity is essential, a moral-based model is a way to rediscover what journalism is actually *for* in the first place.

Competing for Attention, Learning
to Embrace Authenticity

Thinking about journalistic relevance within the larger media culture places greater emphasis on ways of thinking about media that are often overlooked in journalism studies. Moving outside of a focus on traditional journalism sheds light on how digital media facilitate an increase in the number of voices within the media culture. This is not about a struggle for power between professional journalists and so-called citizen journalists, as people once erroneously feared, but rather about looking holistically at the range of representational forms that are emerging. This expansion engenders narratives of hope. It celebrates digital witnessing with the ubiquity of camera-equipped smartphones that extends accountability beyond news reporting.[9] These technologies make possible forms of social activism that draw on the collective power of social media.[10] But these narratives of hope overlap with narratives of fear when the expansion of voices exposes coordinated efforts that are antisocial, rather than pro-social, in nature. Thorsten Quandt calls this "dark participation" to indicate how the same technologies that enable collectives to work for the public good can be utilized for public harm.[11] Prominent examples include the deliberate production and circulation of fake news,[12] the spread of conspiracy theories,[13] trolling,[14] and rampant harassment through racist and sexist language[15]—including heightened levels of such abuse targeted at journalists, both in person and online.[16] What is confusing is how the same mechanisms give rise to such disparate outcomes. For example, Twitter served as a platform for the #MeToo movement to call out widespread sexual harassment in 2017,[17] while at the same time it was used by trolls to sexually harass female gamers, developers, and media critics during the Gamergate controversy in 2014.[18] What all of this indicates is just how complicated the present media culture is, of which journalism is only one part.

The bigger challenge is being noticed at all in a world of seemingly infinite on-demand digital information. In a media culture where human attention is the one truly finite resource, there is ever-increasing competition across media sites and technology platforms for people's limited time and focused presence.[19] Digital technologies have transformed the landscape of media away from a well-defined state of discrete media (e.g., a printed newspaper or magazine or a television or radio broadcast) to one where media coexist side by side on digital devices—each media product potentially a tap or browser tab away from another. Social media further complicate traditional separations. In Twitter timelines and Facebook newsfeeds that algorithmically vary from user to user, media products—say, the *New York Times* and its bundle of the day's stories—are broken apart as discrete items and atomized links, even "flattened" by the design of social media platforms to look like links shared from virtually any other site. This complicates any sense of where media products begin or end, or what can easily be recognized as coming from a higher-quality or lower-quality media brand. Indeed, if people get their news from social media or search engines rather than going directly to a particular news site, they are less likely to recall the news brand they read.[20]

And that is assuming, of course, that people are following news at all. In the contemporary media culture, news is but one form of content competing for our attention among others in the same digital spaces—the *Washington Post* competing against influencers on Instagram, CNN against everything else more interesting on YouTube, and all of them against the galloping growth of video-game streaming on Twitch. All are vying for the accumulation of tiny amounts of advertising revenue or to collect monthly subscription fees. News becomes part of the interstitial moments of life[21] or gets sandwiched between other types of media: a social media timeline might include news of a tragedy followed by a friend sharing a funny dog video.[22] By acknowledging these challenges of attention, we can point toward a future of more proactive forms of journalism, including ones that seek to create innovative forms of value in people's lives. Among these could be news products that actually require less attention from consumers because they make better use of people's time by offering more straightforward, purposeful prose.[23]

A final element of our changed media culture that deserves special attention in order to reimagine the future of journalism is the concept of authenticity. In the hegemonic vision of journalistic content—the straight news story stripped of the reporter's opinion—the idea of authenticity does not seem to apply. The news takes the form of a professionalized discourse, with its epistemic authority associated with following procedures, not the individualized and personalized discursive qualities associated with authenticity. Yet authenticity as both an idealized representation and a type of everyday media performance has become a key feature of our media culture. YouTube is filled with amateur content that to some people is more believable precisely because it's stylized differently than staid news formats and because it emphasizes the relatability and accessibility of the creator.[24] Instagram influencers go to great lengths to be seen as "real" and yet not "too real."[25]

And reality television for decades has encouraged an ethic of being one's true self rather than a fabrication.[26] Clearly authenticity was evoked by Trump supporters who admired how he "says what he thinks," "tells it like it is," and "isn't concerned about being PC, but doing what is right."[27] However real or imagined authenticity may be, what remains true is that our media culture values greatly the perception and pursuit of authenticity. In a similar vein, scholars have begun to focus on matters of emotions as a way of understanding identity and culture through an "affective turn" that is evident across disciplines, including media studies[28] and journalism studies.[29] Examining the relevance of journalism within the contemporary media culture alerts us to the ways in which audiences confront the chasm between the value placed on authentic media content and journalism's emphasis on a social position of distance from its subjects. To what extent is news—in format and formality, in tone and style—out of step with the emerging expectations and cultural values underlying much of contemporary media content? This a question that needs to be asked if journalism is going to rebuild its relevance.

In all, these perspectives on digital media, attention, and authenticity indicate a need to recognize media culture as a big tent, a heterogenous space that demands to be understood in its totality.[30] It involves a number of media conglomerates (e.g., Comcast, the Walt Disney Company, and ViacomCBS) and powerful digital media companies (e.g., Alphabet, Facebook, and Apple) as well the actions of individuals who consume, share, and create content. Journalism remains one part of this media culture, much of it tied into conglomerates but also dependent on individuals for support. Economically, journalism has to exist within the gravitational forces that dictate digital media—many of which are quite anathematic to existing news cultures. And journalists fight for relevance daily in their bid to be listened to and to be considered authoritative and worthwhile speakers.

Just because we promote relevance as a framework for thinking about journalism doesn't mean that its relevance is necessarily assumed. Some may even feel that journalistic *irrelevance* is a positive development. It is not too much of a stretch to paint journalism as an anachronistic industrial and epistemic enterprise out of touch with the present—even irredeemably so. Nor is it difficult to condemn journalism for its lack of diversity or its deference to and support for power structures that benefit the few at the expense of the rest.

Our position is that we believe in the importance of institutional journalism and its epistemic social role in providing a common set of accounts about our communities. But we offer this support conditionally rather than blindly. As we have stated throughout this book, we have no interest in promoting the status quo ante, as if journalism's problems were not of its own making. We do not subscribe to the feeling that if only we could revert to a prior golden age, then all would be well. We are not advocating for Make Journalism Great Again. Journalists cannot fall back on normative defenses, asserting themselves to be pillars of democracy, without looking inward at how their practices fall short of these lofty ideals and without looking outward at how the media culture has shifted around news. If journalists are going to reclaim their relevance, it will not be because of some passive process of a pendulum naturally swinging back to traditional news forms, but through actively engaging in questions of what news can and should look like. Trump may be gone, but our concern is that, without some form of intervention from within, what we are witnessing is nothing less than the slow demise of journalism as a socially and culturally relevant institution. What we hope to accomplish through the framework of relevance is to instill a sense of the severity of this moment for the continued place of journalism and the need for a careful review of media structures within and beyond journalism.

The value of applying the notion of relevance to journalism is that it allows us to see journalistic practice as contested and malleable. Journalism is a type of knowledge practice aimed at producing an accurate accounting of happenings in the world, and, like all institutionalized knowledge practices, it is selective in how it decides what is a legitimate form or practice and what lies outside its epistemic boundaries. But, as we've shown throughout this book, journalism is beset on all sides—from external accusations that journalists are fundamentally dishonest to internal anxiety about norms and practices that seem increasingly unreliable and out of touch. What does getting to the end of the book tell us about the state of journalistic relevance? And how do we move forward? To answer these questions, we need to recognize that the question of relevance is about the present, but it is also about the future. And we can only consider a path forward by theorizing what journalism *should* be doing.

At this point in the book, we admit that we have provided much to be pessimistic about. In urging a shift in focus from Trump to the conditions that have given rise to and enabled Trump's presidency, we bring attention to a Pandora's box of issues that are unlikely to abate any time soon. We are concerned about a divisive, identity-based populist politics, one that has emerged most acutely with the Right but is evident to some extent on the Left as well, and which is based on an in-built critique of journalists as the elite other. This distrust runs deep, and is a powerful weapon wielded by politicians to signal their populist allegiance while inoculating against bad press. Trump's exit from the White House does not dissipate these feelings of animosity, which call into question the ability of the news to act as a legitimate form of communal discourse providing an account of the world to a wide public. We are concerned that the economics of journalism have become even more untenable in the wake of the Covid-19 pandemic, exacerbating a long-term trend that has hollowed out newsrooms, particularly at the local level. The decline in news corresponds with the continued rise of social media platforms that seem little interested in considering their social responsibility as public forums. And we are concerned that the journalistic community continues to be held back by a standardized normative defense, one that is more comfortable with espousing the tenets of objectivity than it is with confronting its own contributions to political turmoil, its failings at diversifying, and its replication of societal power imbalances. Combined, these are strong headwinds we face when thinking about the future of journalism.

And yet there are reasons for optimism. The chances that journalism will change in this moment are high because there *has to be* change. The status quo will not hold. Certainly, in every generation we can find public handwringing over the state of news, from the excesses of yellow journalism to the pronouncements of Walter Lippmann and John Dewey to the Hutchins Commission to concerns over twenty-four-hour cable news and the corporatization of newspapers. Given the social centrality of news and its claims of accurately representing the world, this is not surprising. But the present moment is one in which the current state of political fissures, dire news industry economics, expanded media culture, and fundamental questions about appropriate journalistic practices demand some larger reckoning. These conditions are such that shallow fixes do not seem adequate for the task. This moment is an opportunity to think more deeply about our present media culture because the future is so murky. But this can only happen if we broaden the frame of reference to think beyond journalism to consider how the news fits in the contemporary media culture.

Restoring Relevance by Reconsidering Norms

Plotting a path forward for news after Trump cannot begin with tinkering around the edges of news practices and suggesting a few changes here and there. Instead, it must start with examining what we expect from journalists by revisiting normative assumptions surrounding what is expected of citizens, politicians, and journalists. It is only from this foundational level that we can assess what needs to be changed and how it can be different. We have spent much time in this book laying out the growing irrelevance of mainstream journalism. This is in part because journalists continue to produce day-to-day news in mostly routine, unchanging patterns, even as the media and political environments and the way people encounter and engage information have transformed all around them. Yes, journalists have gone to lengths to adapt news to new technologies. But much less attention has been given to asking whether the tried-and-true norms of journalism—the unspoken assumptions, values, and expectations that guide how news is imagined and fashioned—are suited to our current media culture. To do this requires starting at the foundational level of journalistic norms.

The concept of a "norm," although a familiar idea within the social sciences as well as in everyday life, defies an accepted universal definition. To bring to mind a norm is to simultaneously invoke some relations between idealization, concrete behavior, and the expectations of social actors. Michael Schudson captures these elements through a definition of norms as "moral prescriptions for social behavior."[31] From this perspective, it is not the behavior itself that is at the root of the norm, but the suggestion of what *ought* to be. This ought-ness is legitimated through a moral component—a call to identify what is right from what is wrong, or what is acceptable from what is deviant. In this sense, norms do not pertain to behaviors as isolated or justified merely through repetition and familiarity, but as legitimated behavior, a notion that encompasses both action and the interpretive system that legitimates this action. In this light, norms "do not merely *describe* a way in which we in fact regulate our conduct. They make *claims* on us; they command, oblige, recommend, or guide. Or at least, when we invoke them, we make claims on one another."[32] Norms are not abstract ideals but consequential for action.

Norms have a dual existence. On the one hand, they are mutually understood and internalized by the relevant group as ideological guidance. Gary Alan Fine argues that "norms constitute a 'frame' within which individuals interpret a given situation and from which they then take direction for their responsibilities as actors in that domain."[33] This definition demonstrates the centrality of norms in creating a group identity based on shared interpretations.[34] But norms are also enforcement mechanisms. They shape and constrain practices, define the boundaries of communities, and provide criteria for judging action. The judgment that any behavior is correct or incorrect involves appealing to norms. Norms make possible the erection of boundaries and the position of certain behaviors as aberrant. In this way, norms require internal policing mechanisms that prevent normative pledges from coming unattached from their corresponding behaviors.

But norms are also not static or universal. To ask, "What should democracy look like?" is to survey the normative constellation of a particular time and place. The very asking of the question suggests a constellation constantly in motion. It also suggests that there is a continual, ongoing struggle to establish and maintain certain norms at the expense of others across a variety of cultural domains. And so it matters to understand how norms are determined, on whose terms, toward what ends, and so forth. Indeed, much of this book has been about questioning norms, pulling them out of the shadows, and placing them under the spotlight as artifacts rather than natural objects.

To push journalism forward, norms need to be evaluated for the moral assumptions they make surrounding citizen behaviors, political functioning, and journalistic practice. The preceding chapters chronicle renewed scrutiny of a wide range of normative expectations, including the communicative behaviors of Trump, the othering discourses of right-wing populism, and the reportorial strategies of journalists. When assembled together, they raise foundational questions about the normative assumptions underlying liberal democracy. Democratic governance is built on representing the aggregated interests of enfranchised citizens. These citizens provide the mandate for legitimate government through their actions as voters. Yet since the organization of the United States as a federal republic, both the enfranchisement and electoral responsibilities of the populace have expanded. Michael Schudson tracks the historical evolution of democratic culture in the United States, from the era of landed aristocracy to the raucous mass of party politics, and finally to the rational individualism of the twentieth century.[35] The historical portrait that emerges illustrates a key transition, from expectations about how one should behave as a citizen to the expectation that voters should become experts in political issues and candidates at all levels, from local officials to the president. As Schudson points out about the shift to the rational individualism model, "The cognitive demands on the American voter were extraordinary."[36]

Norms involving political behavior and norms involving journalism are closely linked. Consider the political idealization of the rational voter. This model legitimates a particular mode of information-based political behavior, which, by extension, legitimates a corresponding idealization of journalism as information transmission. News succeeds by supplying neutral information to be processed by rational voters. The main drawback of this model lies in the difficulty of identifying actual model citizens. Political scientists Christopher Achen and Larry Bartels put it bluntly: "The attentive, judicious, unprejudiced individuals attuned to the common good that populate the folk theory appear only too rarely in real life, and the barriers to erecting a satisfactory democratic theory on that foundation are formidable indeed."[37] A realist theory of democracy acknowledges that political decisions are driven by social identities, partisan allegiances, and reactions to changing circumstances. For many, politics are simply unimportant. This view is backed by consistent evidence of low levels of political knowledge.[38] Nonetheless, a belief that the possession of good facts leads to good decisions persists, with too little attention directed at the ways in which such facts are interpreted through social experience.[39]

The powerful influence of this normative model of a rational citizenry is visible in the paucity of theorizing around politics and emotionality. Even as emotions have been part of the discussion of politics at least since Aristotle, conventional ideas about democratic governance continue to presume rationality.[40] Paying attention to emotion as a driver of political behavior helps illuminate how Trump's populist message connected with so many voters, but it should also help illustrate why so many react with such strong feelings against Trump.[41] That is, this is not an attempt to castigate Trump voters as emotional while holding up Trump's critics as rational. Instead, it is a call to recognize how thoroughly emotion and identity have seeped into political life. A lack of cross-cutting identities only strengthens this trend.[42] This helps explain the effectiveness of Trump's demagoguery as not some spell that Trump alone has cast, but as a marker of the political conditions of contemporary life. The success of right-wing populists elsewhere also underscores that this is not just an isolated American phenomenon. How much of this deepening of political identity is related to a changing media culture is hard to pinpoint, and we do not attempt to assign causality. Nevertheless, the question of what the norms of *citizenry* should be bears directly on expectations of what *journalism* should be.

The need to reevaluate and reassess democratic norms of citizenship extends to thinking about journalism. If journalists mediate between political agents and the public, and if we treat news accounts as more than neutral information transfer, then we need a better conception of democratic norms if we are to for-mulate an idea of what the news ought to accomplish. Building off the critiques already levied, democratic norms need to account for sociality, identity, and emotionality without denigrating these attributes as inferior to the rational indi-vidual model. Emphasizing sociality recognizes the positionality of citizens and the diversity of social positions and standpoints. This is an epistemic issue: we are embedded within multiple group dynamics, and our knowledge of the world relates to our identities and our social positions. Identity indicates deeply felt political attachments, which emerge through our emotional reactions to our environment and help us build our personalized moral framework. We should be sure that people are not normatively castigated as irrational but recognized as responding to everyday life and social circumstances. This approach is plu-ralist in its appreciation of diversity. Furthermore, such a set of norms is made stronger by drawing on an epistemological approach that recognizes that facts are never isolated, free-floating things but rather are socially produced and embedded in complex systems.[43] This recognition does not prevent factual claims from being scrutinized, but instead casts suspicion on any view of facts as existing apart from the systems that produce and circulate them.

Finally, we need to be aware of what we expect from journalism, and how we often expect too much.[44] Increasingly, the degree to which democratic service should be the underlying purpose of journalism has been questioned for what it overlooks.[45] For one thing, this view tends to emphasize a narrow range of so-called hard news stories while omitting the fuller breadth and context of what news can offer. Instead, we promote a broad view of the corpus of news, with its multiple registers and functions that come together to provide a shared picture of what the world looks like to many different groups. We also need to recognize how the overwhelming majority of journalism remains for-profit, and the need to generate profits in excess of what it costs to produce news con-tinues to be a priority (and in many cases the *top* priority) for the owners and shareholders of news organizations. All of this requires confronting the nor-mative frameworks that justify journalism's authority if we are to evaluate how journalism can address the question of its relevance.

Which Path to Relevance?

Rethinking norms may be useful, but we also need to make clear what these differences mean for actual news production. In this section, we consider two ways forward that are meant to address journalism's relevance to its audiences by examining differing views of what legitimate news norms and practices might look like. This is not meant to overlook nuances between these positions, but rather to place them next to each other to make clear their differences. These positions emerge from the internal and external discourses about the role of journalism in a democracy that carry across this book, and they function as two approaches for understanding what news should be. They connect to public efforts by members of the journalistic community (and some from outside of news) to figure out what to do with journalism or, even more fundamentally, to clarify what journalism ought to be. Even if, for some, that answer is to continue to hold fast to existing norms and practices, this becomes a choice that gets articulated and defended as the world around journalism changes. It matters, then, to consider both the status quo and alternatives to it.

The Standard Model

The first way forward is what we call the standard model of journalism— a recommitment to objectivity-based news that accentuates journalistic professionalism. It doubles down on the social position of journalists as central-yet-distant: journalists as emplaced within the structures of power but without any direct control over the mechanisms of power. This route is predicated on the notion that trust between journalists and their audiences is built on facticity above all. Against a sea of partisan politics; social media sources overrun by fabricators, conspiracy theorists, and the ill-informed; and an audience prone to confirmation bias—against them all, journalists tout their value as trusted sources. Fact-checking becomes the utmost expression of accountability. In a sense, journalism has always defined itself against the institutional forms that it is *not*—for example, government propaganda, paid speech, partisan rhetoric—but now, increasingly, it defines itself against less-institutionalized forms arising through digital platforms via assertions of its informational credibility. Supporters of this approach locate the path for journalists in opposition to these other forms, appealing to a fact-starved public confused or overwhelmed by the flood of mediated discourse that defines the present media culture.

This fact-forward vision of journalism emphasizes procedure over personality. In doing so, it resurrects a belief in facticity and the rational citizen model. News is a form of information—trusted information laundered through journalistic practices for clarity and accuracy and lauded for having minimal interpretation. Objectivity remains a guiding principle, even if it is a watered-down variety that acknowledges the barriers to the ideal. Erasing the position of the reporter is still seen as what to aim for, however imperfect this may be. Trust accrues around institutional ways of knowing at the cost of developing a more substantial sense of shared community.

Perhaps the strongest argument for a continuation (even accentuation) of the standard model lies in data showing that a majority of Americans say they want "objective" news.[46] Some 60% of US adults prefer to get news from news sources that have no apparent point of view, compared to 30% who favor sources that share their point of view and 10% who say they want outlets that challenge their point of view. The message, it seems at first glance, is a resounding call for staying the course with the standard model—even revisiting and reinforcing a bygone era when a just-the-facts orientation was most pronounced in US journalism. As the Reuters Institute for the Study of Journalism notes in its 2020 report on these numbers, despite the many pressures toward partisanship in the current information environment— including the economic imperative for news organizations to differentiate themselves in a world of commoditized news online—there remains a "silent majority" of consumers primarily interested in news that maintains a traditional, neutral register.[47] However, a closer look at the survey data shows a slightly different picture when we break down preferences by people's most frequent source of news. Americans who regularly watch cable television news are almost as likely to prefer news sources that share their point of view (42%) as have no point of view (51%); there is a similar, though less pronounced, set of attitudes among people who regularly turn to social media for news (35% vs. 56%).[48] While these findings are not entirely surprising— cable news in the United States has made partisan fare its stock-in-trade, and social media and their algorithms are designed to serve up high-engagement hot takes—they nevertheless point to a trend that doesn't bode well for the standard model's continued relevance. As newspapers, the flagship form of objectivity in American journalism, continue their slow demise, hemorrhaging readership and influence, attention will increasingly shift to news spaces that, by nature, are more oriented to deliver news with a point of view.

In the meantime, however, many journalists and media watchers have determined that the standard model is the safest route. It is familiar and earnest, founded on good intentions and appealing to the higher ideals of democracy. It sounds good in theory (even if its record is mixed), and we do not question the sincerity of its proponents. But we have our doubts about its practicality and, frankly, its viability today. It ignores how much politics has become about identity, and the degree to which press-bashing has become built into right-wing political identities through generations of claims about media bias, capped off by the populist critique of journalists as hopeless elites. Even while the standard model has a laudable emphasis on facticity above all else, we are pessimistic that large swaths of the public will return to support this approach to journalism given political trends (toward polarization) as well as shifts in the media culture (toward fragmentation). In short, there are many obstacles to this model's return to dominance. And if attitudes toward journalism are indeed embedded as part of people's increasingly strident political and social identities, then changing public attitudes about news will require, to some degree, getting people to rethink their self-conception—who they are, what they represent, what they value. That's a lot to ask.

Even more fundamentally, the good intentions of this model are complicated by the practical weaknesses of objectivity—even in its more active forms—as a position for observing and representing the world. Candis Callison and Mary Lynn Young apply feminist epistemology to journalism to challenge journalism's view-from-nowhere perspective as deeply entrenched in the power structures of society.[49] Knowledge production is never neutral, detached, or agent-less. Rather, it emerges from embodied individuals arrayed across institutions that materially and symbolically support certain knowledge forms. The suppression of such positions blinds us to how journalism favors particular voices while omitting others.

Perhaps we can best get to the issues underlying this model of journalism by asking two simple questions: Whom does this model of journalism work for? And whom does it work against? In a sense, the standard model seems like it *can* work for everyone, which is both the attractiveness and the danger of this model. Neutrality, in particular, is a norm that is intended to work for all as an antonym of bias. But decades of journalism research have shown that this model disproportionality supports elites and the already powerful while excluding others.[50] It is prone to both-siderism. It tends to equate objectivity with non-adjudication of opposing (usually elite) viewpoints, while hampering the ability of journalists to respond when false equivalencies arise in such contests. Those who are not in positions of power find it difficult to gain a voice in the news as a subject and not just an object. And this model does little to dispel the critiques of its critics because its official position is that it does not take a position.

Journalist Wesley Lowery illustrates this point well in his critique of journalistic objectivity as a racialized vantage point:

> Since American journalism's pivot many decades ago from an openly partisan press to a model of professed objectivity, the mainstream has allowed what it considers objective truth to be decided almost exclusively by white reporters and their mostly white bosses. And those selective truths have been calibrated to avoid offending the sensibilities of white readers. On opinion pages, the contours of acceptable public debate have largely been determined through the gaze of white editors.[51]

Lowery argues that objectivity has been built on avoiding offending the white majority audience at the expense of exposing the systemic racism that affects non-white communities. It is a reminder that all viewpoints are selective in whose perception is supported and whose is ignored or denigrated as unworthy.

If objectivity in journalism is not sustainable, what is the alternative? This question hovers above all critiques of journalistic objectivity, or its decomposition into elements like neutrality and balance. The straw-man answer is pure opinion, where all news mimics the style of journalism now sequestered in editorial sections, exercised by critics, or epitomized by the talking heads of cable news. Journalism then devolves into one-sided echo chambers driven by self-interest and a need for reinforcing one's views. In the face of all news sounding this way, returning to objectivity, however flawed, seems preferable. However, a more complex alternative emerges from an amalgamation of principles both familiar and unfamiliar to journalistic orthodoxy. We need an approach that confronts the reasons we defend journalism from wanton press-bashing and yet critiques journalism for its failings. Such an approach confronts the contractions that underlie contemporary journalism as simultaneously a potent and important symbol-producing system and an institution experiencing questions about its continued relevance in the present media culture.

The Moral Voice in Journalism

With this goal in mind, we promote a second way forward that we call the moral voice in journalism. This approach has two parts to it. The first stems from a recognition that all factual knowledge representations are socially constructed and rendered from the perspective of their creators. This does not mean that facts have been vanquished by postmodern relativism and we should give up on producing an authoritative account of the world. Rather, it recognizes the inherent partiality of witnessing and reporting, and asks us to take into account that news is produced by people, with all the limitations that entails. Epistemologically, this perspective builds on the notion of "active objectivity," which accentuates how the positionality of a reporter alters what news knowledge looks like.[52] This is more aligned with the diverse experiences of a diverse populace and begins to address the systemic inequalities of who has access to producing news accounts and who does not.

The second part of the moral voice in journalism addresses the capacity of journalists to make judgments. Instead of dismissing the procedures of professionalized journalism, it begins by questioning the ways that objectivity and professionalism norms stifle a broader moral voice. The starting point comes with accepting journalists not as detached or distant observers but as situated, embodied actors whose morality is grounded in broad public morality rather than a limited professional one. Returning to the discussion from Chapter 5, morality is about judgments of what is right or wrong, particularly with regard to violations of social or political norms. The moral voice in journalism is about occupying a supraprofessional position to be able to speak and render pronouncements from beyond the journalistic identity. After all, calling out oppressive systems or policies or declaring a politician's statement to be a lie or racist is not inherently subjective. Rather, when ample evidence supports such assertions as factual, doing so is exactly what journalists purport to do: tell the truth. The moral voice, then, by avoiding the quicksand of false equivalence, is about freeing up journalists to portray things *as they really are* to the best of their knowledge and experience.

In this vision of the moral voice in journalism, the voice of individual journalists would be stronger in contrast to a diminished belief in facts speaking for themselves. News texts are not neutral conduits but are representations produced through the knowledge logic of professional news, created by journalists who are both trained for the work they do and exist as subjects in the larger world. Authenticity—often elided in the discussion of journalism—emerges as a way of considering how the positionality of the reporter matters in the account being reported. For example, in responding to BBC News reprimanding one of its hosts for expressing personal fury at racist comments by Trump, Nieman Lab's Joshua Benton argued that the identity of journalists should not be ignored:

> I don't think journalism is going to thrive if it keeps telling people that they have to leave core parts of their identity at the door. If black journalists can't say racism is bad, if gay journalists can't say discrimination against gay people is bad, if women journalists aren't allowed to say sexism is bad, you're asking people to put their own humanity up for debate—to put themselves in the "sphere of legitimate controversy."[53]

In proposing that journalists' identities become part of the journalistic equation, he is suggesting that the professional moral code of journalism needs to expand. Linking journalists more closely to their reporting is not about amplifying the personality of the journalist, but rather about recognizing that all representations emanate from particular perspectives. Again, this is not the same as partisanship that filters facts through a coherent political position, but rather one that asks about the responsibilities of communicators and the value of authenticity.

In many ways this model of journalistic moral voice may not look or feel that different from contemporary journalism. The moral voice in journalism is still an autonomous voice. Journalists normatively should conduct their work free from being encumbered by other powerful actors. In this sense, the moral voice in journalism is still more centrist than revolutionary, but it is pluralist in spirit rather than assuming a cultural uniformity. In being more flexible and adaptable to the media culture and political environment that encases journalism, the moral voice allows for a reexamination of journalistic autonomy for ways in which it serves the public and ways in which it alienates journalists *from* its public. As Stephanie Craft notes in her critique of profession-centric ethics, "Autonomy—from the market and the state—is integral to journalism's ability to serve the public. Autonomy from the *public*, however, is not."[54]

Instead, journalists need to be reinserted back into the public that they represent through their work. They are recognized as community stakeholders, not scientists watching a petri dish or referees monitoring a game. Likewise, the news audience should not be turned into a monolith with a singular view, but instead should be seen as diverse interpretive agents who will understand news based in no small part on their social positions.[55] In this sense, the moral voice in journalism is built around journalists not as supplying the only authoritative voice, but in providing an authentic voice that forges a stronger connection not only between journalist and audience, but also between policymakers, stakeholders, and citizens. Such connections should be oriented around mutually beneficial reciprocity,[56] allowing journalists and their communities alike to more effectively identify and act on local problems toward potential solutions.[57] Indeed, there is growing evidence that the strongest journalism reform effort at the moment—the ongoing push to embrace "engaged journalism" that treats the public as a potential partner in news-making—has at its very core an emphasis on rebuilding public trust in the news by first building personal relationships in communities.[58] Building such relationships through engagement is neither easy nor a ready fix for journalism's many problems,[59] but a turn toward more relational forms of journalism at least signals that journalists recognize that the detachedness of the standard model is out of touch with the values and expectations of our current media culture.[60]

The types of engagement we are proposing are already happening in different ways. For example, Logan Molyneux shows how female journalists use social media as spaces of personalization in which they communicate about themselves beyond their role as journalists.[61] Rather than chiding this approach for being unprofessional, we can instead see that it allows these female journalists to further embed themselves into our shared social fabric. A recent experiment indicated that when journalists disclose more of their personal selves on social media, it leads people to be more likely to follow the news these journalists produce.[62] Through this social media use, journalists communicate their shared allegiances with audiences. While this may not seem overly radical, it can be controversial. For example, in the wake of nationwide protests following the police killing of George Floyd in 2020, editors at the *Pittsburgh Post-Gazette* faced accusations of removing two journalists from covering the story because of their race. One Black reporter was accused of bias because of her tweets.[63] Meanwhile, white journalists report on white people routinely without accusations of bias. These are barriers to the moral voice, but working through these conflicts is important for forging a journalistic epistemology that respects and values the social position of journalists.

The differences between the standard model of detachment and the moral voice is captured in a study of journalists' orientations to their audiences. Megan Zahay and her colleagues interviewed forty-two journalists, about half of them designated "engagement oriented" and the others "traditionally oriented." Based on a rhetorical analysis of what these journalists *said* (via the interviews) as well as what they *did* (via hundreds of pages of website materials and social media conversation threads), the researchers developed a picture of two camps of journalists—both deeply concerned about the crisis of public trust in journalism, but each with divergent ideas about what should be done about it. For traditionally oriented journalists (acting on what we would call the standard model), trust is achieved by transmitting facts and helping people perform their democratic duties, without any particular public participation involved in that process. Fixing the trust problem, in this view, means accentuating objectivity, transparency, and accuracy. By contrast, rather than focusing on institutionalized norms as the defining elements of journalism, "engagement-oriented journalists view [journalism] as a set of relationships, prone to complexity and messiness"— and they are quite comfortable with that uncertainty, recognizing that it's to be expected as journalists experiment and move forward. From this perspective, public trust in news flows out of efforts that emphasize mutual understanding and empathy with communities, even ones that are slow, gradual, and longer-term in nature. In the words of a cofounder of an engagement organization who was interviewed, "It's ineffective to double down on 'Trust me, I'm a journalist.' . . . If you're not in relationship with someone, if you haven't proved your value to them . . . then you don't have trust."[64]

Building trust through the incremental work of building relationships with the public points to a key element of the moral voice of journalism: it is real *work*, particularly of a kind that journalists may not be used to, and one they likely have not been taught in journalism school or newsroom training. Far more than journalists simply inserting more of their personal selves into the news text, the moral voice requires that journalists more carefully investigate and understand—even relationship by relationship— the values, needs, and cultural contexts of the communities they serve, to a degree previously unexplored. Journalists, already overworked and overburdened, can hardly be expected to spend all of their time on listening tours. That's simply unrealistic. But if journalists are to provide greater representation for people's voices and lived experiences—particularly in marginalized communities—then they will need to adapt to what has been called "the labor of building trust," or an entirely new set of work practices that situate trust-building and relationship management as key activities of what it means to actually *do* journalism.[65]

Some will critique this perspective as veiled partisanship because no universal moral belief system exists. A shared sense of morality may seem possible in the abstract, but once notions of right and wrong are connected to practice, values get caught up in the swirl of partisan politics. Perhaps what is needed in response is to revisit basic moral principles that are socially beneficial, such as proscriptions against antisocial actions and exclusionary rhetoric, as we learned from Stephen Ward's call for the democratically engaged journalist.[66] Others will see the introduction of subjectivity as further fracturing the media environment through the suggestion that news content will splinter into a multitude of differing reports on any one incident. An allegiance to reporting procedure alleviates this concern to some degree, but it also might be useful to have some divergent views—not least because that would counteract the homogenizing effects of pack journalism that values uniformity over nuance and difference. Another critique is that by not upending journalism more completely, the vision we put forth still privileges an elite worldview. However, a recognition that individual journalistic voices matter more than a professionalized mono-voice only supports the need for more diverse newsrooms—on matters of race and ethnicity, yes, but also on questions of class, religion, politics, veteran status, and so on.[67] In promoting more diverse newsrooms, we're not suggesting that one's personal identity matters over and above every other qualification or criteria for hire, or that individuals are reducible to a social categorization. Rather, we argue that a more heterogeneous newsroom matters because it engages a wider set of experiences that can serve as a corrective for the closed vision of any single account.

Returning to the questions applied to the standard journalistic model, we can ask: Whom does this work for? Whom does it work against? The argument here is that the moral voice in journalism works for the larger public by giving journalists more leeway to issue judgments, that it provides more perspectives on any single issue, and that it recognizes that the world appears differently to different people. It works against elites who are accustomed to manipulating the standard procedures of journalists by having whatever they say normalized through the news. Indeed, a moral orientation would work against the likes of Trump, whose words and behavior, while asymmetrically outlandish compared to his political opponents, are often downplayed, ignored, or soft-pedaled by journalists attempting to achieve a "both sides" kind of balance in pursuit of the standard model of journalism that is so deeply ingrained.

Toward a New Relevance for Journalism

In proposing a moral voice in journalism, we want to be clear about our expectations. Two of the three authors of this book are former journalists and know well how the necessary routinization that allows newsrooms to manage the flood of events also tends to stifle any attempt, however well-intentioned or high-minded, to fundamentally rethink what the news will look like.[68] We cannot provide ready-made molds into which journalists can simply pour in their reporting. We recognize that morality is a fraught topic, and prone to disagreements in judgment. But our contention remains that journalism has little choice but to revisit and reconceptualize its place in the political and media culture. Its relevance and its very survival requires a mix of resilience and adaptation as well as introspection and reconciliation.

Journalism has never been perfect, and it is a mistake to hearken back to some golden period. We reject, too, a whiggish history of the impending future perfection of news. Journalism will never be perfect. But it cannot be so easily classified by cynical elites as an enemy of the people. It also cannot be so defenseless that it cannot fight for itself or that journalists cannot make obvious moral claims about what is right and wrong. Journalism also cannot invent better conditions for itself—it is subject to the whims of a shifting media culture of which it is a shrinking part, and influenced by political conditions for which it is only somewhat responsible. There is no secret formula, no way to reverse declines in trust, to ensure economic stability, to stem the tide of caustic political discourse. But there are ways of making progress, of adapting to the media culture, of finding ways to be professionally assertive while also grounded in a communal morality, of avoiding past mistakes.

The Trump era was one of extremes. For journalists, this meant long-simmering trends came to a boil and put journalists in a position of having to reckon publicly with their continued relevance amid political, technological, and cultural trends. But it is important to maintain perspective. The accumulation of external and internal factors that led to questions about journalism's relevance have been decades in the making. It will take decades to repair. But our hope is that if journalists can advocate for norms and values more rooted in community and a sense of moral voice, they can create conditions to foster a healthier communicative environment. In such a scenario, a "moral voice" is not about making political statements (e.g., about hot-button issues such as abortion or gun control), but rather about an unflinching evaluation of whether a fact is a lie, whether a statement is racist, or whether a policy is inherently flawed because of systemic oppression.

But journalists alone cannot fix what's wrong. Just as they are not entirely complicit for their decline in relevance, they are not entirely capable of fixing things either. In the larger media culture, there are different spaces in which norms can be created. Journalists control one space (and not even a cohesive one at that), but when not everyone is in this space, what happens? What we need is a larger intervention that recognizes the many democratic guardrails that have vanished and are probably not coming back, at least not in the same form as in the past. To work toward a robust democratic society and a media culture capable of supporting it requires extending responsibility to everyone.

As President Joe Biden said in his inaugural address only two weeks after the attack on the US Capitol in January 2021: "There is truth and there are lies, lies told for power and for profit. And each of us has a duty and a responsibility as citizens, as Americans, and especially as leaders, leaders who have pledged to honor our Constitution and protect our nation, to defend the truth and defeat the lies."[69] The emphasis here is on the necessity of trust-building and pro-democracy tools to foster shared community connections around public affairs information. The task must be a shared one, Biden reminded us, which means it cannot be limited to news producers alone. It must also include news seekers, technology companies, journalism schools and universities, the K–12 education system, parents, and especially our politicians. The next generation depends on a proactive approach, and there is no time to lose if we want to move past Trump's legacy of corrosive divisiveness, habitual lying, racist statements, and anti-democratic rhetoric. This is about charting a much better path for the future.

Notes

Introduction

1. Al Jazeera, "Trump's Speech That 'Incited' Capitol Violence."
2. Yahoo! News, "'Let's Have Trial by Combat' over Election—Giuliani."
3. Tompkins, "What Words Should We Use to Describe What Happened in the Capitol?"
4. Hsu and Robertson, "Covering Pro-Trump Mobs, the News Media Became a Target."
5. Although critique of Trump was far from universal. A majority of the Republicans in the House of Representatives and a handful of Republicans in the Senate still persisted, hours after the Capitol attack, in attempting to overturn the results of the presidential election. And only ten Republicans joined Democratic congressional representatives to vote for Trump's subsequent impeachment. This continued support underscores our argument that we need to look beyond just Trump to understand the current political moment.
6. Adapted from Couldry, *Media Rituals*.
7. Deuze, *Media Life*.
8. These three aspects are similar to how Laura Ahva discusses the aspects of practice theory. Ahva, "Practice Theory for Journalism Studies."
9. Williams, *The Long Revolution*.
10. See Nadler and Bauer, *News on the Right*.
11. For more on this argument see, Waisbord, "Truth Is What Happens to News."
12. A similar argument is made in Wasserman, "Relevance, Resistance, Resilience."
13. Hallin, "The Passing of the 'High Modernism' of American Journalism."
14. Carlson, "The Information Politics of Journalism in a Post-truth Age."
15. This model extends outward to situate news audiences either as attentive citizens or as public waiting to be mobilized in particular moments. See Zaller, "A New Standard of News Quality"; Schudson, *The Good Citizen*.
16. Esser and Strömbäck, *Mediatization of Politics*.
17. Schudson, *Why Journalism Still Matters*.
18. Ansolabehere and Iyengar, "Of Horseshoes and Horse Races."
19. Berkowitz, "Reporters and Their Sources."
20. Phillips, "The Oxygen of Amplification."
21. Robinson, *Networked News, Racial Divides*.
22. Fawcett, "Why Peace Journalism Isn't News."
23. Boynton and Richardson, "Agenda Setting in the Twenty-First Century."
24. Yglesias, "The Case for Fox News Studies"; Peck, *Fox Populism*.
25. Prior, *Post-broadcast Democracy*.
26. Nielsen, "The Business of News"; Pickard, *Democracy without Journalism?*

27. Deuze and Witschge, *Beyond Journalism*; Lewis, "The Tension between Professional Control and Open Participation"; Napoli, *Social Media and the Public Interest.*
28. Ekdale et al., "Newswork within a Culture of Job Insecurity"; Örnebring et al., "The Space of Journalistic Work"; Cohen, "Entrepreneurial Journalism and the Precarious State of Media Work."
29. Abernathy, *The Expanding News Desert.*
30. Hamilton, *Democracy's Detectives.*
31. Hayes and Lawless, "The Decline of Local News and Its Effects."
32. Williams and Delli Carpini, *After Broadcast News.*
33. Broersma and Peters, "Rethinking Journalism."
34. Schudson, *Why Journalism Still Matters.*
35. See details and discussion in Nielsen, "Valuing Journalism in a World of Near-Infinite Content"; Nielsen, "How Much Time Do People Spend with News across Media?"
36. Of course, news practices themselves are quite varied in their multiple forms, depending on the medium of production, the type of media organization, the news genre involved, and so forth.
37. Park, "News as a Form of Knowledge."
38. Ekström, "Epistemologies of TV Journalism."
39. Tuchman, *Making News.*
40. Gieryn, *Cultural Boundaries of Science.*
41. On institutionalism and journalism, see Reese, *The Crisis of the Institutional Press.*
42. Deuze, "What Is Journalism?"
43. Lewis, "Journalism."
44. Reese, "The Threat to the Journalistic Institution"; Deuze and Witschge, "Beyond Journalism."
45. Carlson and Usher, "News Startups as Agents of Innovation."
46. For discussion of the social boundaries of journalism, see Carlson and Lewis, *Boundaries of Journalism.*
47. Lewis, "Journalism." See also Lewis, "The Tension between Professional Control and Open Participation"; and Schudson, "Why Journalism Still Matters."
48. Cf. Deuze, "What is Journalism?"
49. Mendes, "Digital Demagogue."
50. See Chapter 5.
51. Holloway, "5 Things Trump Said He Invented, But Didn't."
52. For a detailed journalistic account, see Stelter, *Hoax.*
53. Peck, *Fox Populism.*
54. Müller, *What Is Populism?*
55. Shafer, "Trump Is Making Journalism Great Again."
56. Buettner et al., "Long-Concealed Records Show Trump's Chronic Losses and Years of Tax Avoidance."
57. Mellinger, *Chasing Newsroom Diversity*; Bennett, *News.*
58. Quandt, "Dark Participation"; Figenschou and Ihlebæk, "Challenging Journalistic Authority."
59. Nielsen and Ganter, "Dealing with Digital Intermediaries."

60. Carey, "A Plea for the University Tradition."
61. Ibid.
62. Portrayals of Washington and New York political journalists as insular and elitist institutions can be found in the critiques of the left-leaning organization Fairness and Accuracy In Reporting (FAIR) and the right-leaning organization Media Research Center (MRC).
63. Carey, "A Plea for the University Tradition"; see also Craft, "Distinguishing Features."
64. Shoemaker and Reese, *Mediating the Message in the 21st Century.*
65. Fishman, *Manufacturing the News.*
66. Hall et al., *Policing the Crisis.*
67. Lewis et al., "Online Harassment and Its Implications for the Journalist-Audience Relationship"; Waisbord, "Mob Censorship."
68. Beiser, "More Journalists Killed on the Job as Reprisal Murders Nearly Double"; Brambila and Hughes, "Violence against Journalists"; Löfgren Nilsson and Örnebring, "Journalism under Threat."
69. Ward, *Ethical Journalism in a Populist Age.*
70. Smith, "Inside the Revolts Erupting in America's Big Newsrooms."
71. Bump, "Donald Trump Will Be President Thanks to 80,000 People in Three States." However, if forty-four thousand people in three states (Arizona, Georgia, and Wisconsin) had voted differently in 2020, an Electoral College tie would have led to a Trump victory and this book would need a sequel. See Montanaro, "President-Elect Joe Biden Hits 80 Million Votes in Year of Record Turnout."

Chapter 1

1. Katz, "Who Will Be President?"
2. Woodward, *Fear.*
3. Esquire Editors, "The Untold Stories of Election Day 2016."
4. Brownstein, "How the Rustbelt Paved Trump's Road to Victory."
5. Pew Research Center, "Newspaper Fact Sheet."
6. Grieco, "U.S. Newspapers Have Shed Half of Their Newsroom Employees since 2008."
7. Cuts have not abated; a Pew Research Center study found that 36% of newspapers had cut staff in the following year. See Grieco et al., "About a Third of Large U.S. Newspapers Have Suffered Layoffs since 2017."
8. See Abernathy, "The Expanding News Desert."
9. Hagey et al., "In News Industry, a Stark Divide between Haves and Have-Nots."
10. For discussion of these dynamics, see, for example, Toff and Nielsen. " 'I Just Google It' "; Thorson and Wells, "Curated Flows."
11. Deuze, "What Journalism Is (Not)."
12. Edgerly and Vraga, "Deciding What's News."
13. Napoli and Mahone, "Local Newspapers Are Suffering."
14. Callison and Young, *Reckoning.*

15. Pew Research Center, "For Local News, Americans Embrace Digital but Still Want Strong Community Connection." The online news figure included both digital news sites and social media as a means for getting the news.
16. Thurman et al., "Algorithms, Automation, and News."
17. Bergström and Jervelycke Belfrage, "News in Social Media."
18. Coddington, *Aggregating the News*.
19. Although our phones often become our televisions.
20. Sheller, "News Now."
21. Molyneux, "Mobile News Consumption."
22. Peters and Schrøder, "Beyond the Here and Now of News Audiences." For an overview, see Costera Meijer, "Journalism, Audiences and News Experience."
23. Boczkowski et al., " 'News Comes across When I'm in a Moment of Leisure' "; Fletcher and Nielsen, "Are People Incidentally Exposed to News on Social Media?"; Kümpel, "The Issue Takes It All?"
24. Nelson and Lewis, "Only 'Sheep' Trust Journalists?"; Toff and Nielsen, " 'I Just Google it.' "
25. Prior, *Post-broadcast Democracy*.
26. Gil de Zúñiga et al., "Effects of the News-Finds-Me Perception in Communication."
27. Toff and Palmer, "Explaining the Gender Gap in News Avoidance."
28. Edgerly et al., "New Media, New Relationship to Participation?"
29. Robinson, *Networked News, Racial Divides*.
30. Prior, *Post-broadcast Democracy*; Williams and Delli Carpini, *After Broadcast News*.
31. Stroud, "Polarization and Partisan Selective Exposure."
32. Dubois and Blank, "The Echo Chamber Is Overstated."
33. Prior, "Media and Political Polarization."
34. Levendusky, *How Partisan Media Polarize America*; Arceneaux and Johnson, *Changing Minds or Changing Channels?*
35. Young, *Irony and Outrage*.
36. Picone et al., "Small Acts of Engagement."
37. Moyo, "Citizen Journalism and the Parallel Market of Information in Zimbabwe's 2008 Election."
38. Pew Research Center, "State of the News Report."
39. See Hamilton, *All the News That's Fit to Sell*.
40. Pew Research Center, "Newspaper Fact Sheet." This amounted to $48.7 billion from advertising and $10.5 billion from circulation.
41. Edmonds, "Classified Ad Revenue Down 70 Percent in 10 Years."
42. Hagey et al., "In News Industry, a Stark Divide between Haves and Have-Nots."
43. Peiser, "The New York Times Co. Reports $709 Million in Digital Revenue for 2018."
44. Pew Research Center, "Cable News Fact Sheet."
45. Grieco, "One-in-Five U.S. Newsroom Employees Live in New York, Los Angeles or D.C."
46. PEN America, "Executive Summary for Losing the News."
47. Schulman, "Newspaper Publishing in the US: 51111."
48. Pen America, "Executive Summary for Losing the News."

49. Newman, "Executive Summary and Key Findings of the 2019 Report."
50. Pew Research Center, "For Local News, Americans Embrace Digital," Section 4.
51. Carlson, "What Do We Do When Journalism Stops Working?"
52. Brenan, "Americans' Trust in Mass Media Edges Down to 41%."
53. Ladd, *Why Americans Hate the Media and How It Matters.*
54. Schudson, *The Rise of the Right to Know.*
55. Cappella and Jamieson, *Spiral of Cynicism.*
56. See Carlson, *Journalistic Authority,* 111–116. There is a related notion in the way interviewees described their perceptions about news in Nelson and Lewis, "Only 'Sheep' Trust Journalists?"
57. Gottfried et al., "Partisans Remain Sharply Divided in Their Attitudes about the News Media."
58. Brenan, "Americans Remain Distrustful of Mass Media."
59. Brenan, "Americans' Trust in Mass Media." This is compared to 26% who thought their local news was too liberal.
60. Hemmer, *Messengers of the Right.*
61. Jamieson and Cappella, *Echo Chamber.*
62. Perloff, "A Three-Decade Retrospective on the Hostile Media Effect."
63. Waisbord, "Mob Censorship."
64. Reyes, "Journalists Blinded, Injured, Arrested Covering George Floyd Protests Nationwide."
65. BBC News, "Walmart Pulls 'Lynch Journalists' T-Shirt from Sale."
66. Ingber, "The U.S. Now Ranks as a 'Problematic' Place for Journalists."
67. Brambila et al., "Violence against Journalists."
68. Löfgren Nilsson and Örnebring, "Journalism under Threat."
69. Lewis et al., "Online Harassment and Its Implications for the Journalist-Audience Relationship."
70. Westcott, " 'The Threats Follow Us Home.' "
71. International Women's Media Foundation, "Attacks and Harassment."
72. Finneman et al., " 'I Always Watched Eyewitness News Just to See Your Beautiful Smile' "; Pain and Chen, "This Reporter Is So Ugly"; Vickery and Everbach, *Mediating Misogyny.*
73. Miller and Lewis, "Journalists, Harassment, and Emotional Labor."
74. Waisbord, "Mob Censorship."
75. Lewis et al., "Online Harassment and Its Implications."
76. Cramer, *The Politics of Resentment.*
77. Peck, *Fox Populism,* 37.
78. Hart, *Trump and Us.*
79. Steiner and Waisbord, *News of Baltimore.*
80. Robinson and Bartzen Culver, "When White Reporters Cover Race."
81. Robinson, *Networked News, Racial Divides.*
82. Couldry, *Media Rituals,* 41.
83. Arana, "17% of U.S. Newsroom Staff Is Not White."
84. Usher, *News for the Rich, White, and Blue.*

85. Alemán, "Locating Whiteness in Journalism Pedagogy."
86. White, "Where Are All the Minority Journalists?"
87. Ibid.
88. Donald J. Trump (@realDonaldTrump), "As I have stated strongly before," Twitter, October 7, 2019, 11:38 a.m., https://www.thetrumparchive.com/.
89. A Google search of "Trump boasts" brings up a litany of other examples.
90. Turner, "Trump on Twitter."
91. Fahrenthold, "A Time Magazine with Trump on the Cover Hangs in His Golf Clubs."
92. Weber, *The Theory of Social and Economic Organization*, 358.
93. Ibid., 370.
94. Wahl-Jorgensen, *Emotions, Media and Politics*.
95. Neumann, "The Rule of the Demagogue."
96. Bedingfield, "Tillman's Rebellion."
97. Kazin, *The Populist Persuasion*, 1; see also Berlet and Lyons, *Right-Wing Populism in America*.
98. Kazin, *The Populist Persuasion*, 4.
99. Fishwick, "Father Coughlin Time."
100. Modras, "Father Coughlin and Anti-Semitism."
101. Carlson, "The Rhetoric of the Know-Nothing Party."
102. Mudde, "The Populist Zeitgeist," 543.
103. See also Ward, *Ethical Journalism in a Populist Age* for an in-depth, philosophical discussion about populism and journalism.
104. For more regarding distrust, see Rosanvallon, *Counter-democracy*.
105. Hofstadter, "The Paranoid Style in American Politics."
106. Merica, "Trump Says Both Sides to Blame amid Charlottesville Backlash."
107. Iyengar et al., "The Origins and Consequences of Affective Polarization in the United States."
108. Mason, *Uncivil Agreement*.
109. Cramer, *The Politics of Resentment*; see also Hart, *Trump and Us*.
110. Sides et al., *Identity Crisis*, 71.
111. Ibid., 175.
112. Mason, *Uncivil Agreement*, 63.
113. Iyengar et al., "The Origins and Consequences of Affective Polarization," 143.
114. Kyle and Glutchin, "Populists in Power around the World."
115. Ibid.
116. Betz, *Radical Right-Wing Populism in Western Europe*, 4.
117. This is coupled by a tendency for the news media to hew to the center in its reporting.
118. Mouffe, "The 'End of Politics' and the Challenge of Right-Wing Populism."
119. Mazzoleni, "Populism and the Media"; White, *The Branding of Right-Wing Activism*; Weyland, "Latin America's Authoritarian Drift."
120. Stone et al., "A Guide to Statistics on Historical Trends in Income Inequality."
121. Inglehart and Norris, "Trump and the Populist Authoritarian Parties."
122. Ibid., 452.
123. Couch and McDermott, "Donald Trump Campaign Offered Actors $50."

124. Time Staff, "Here's Donald Trump's Presidential Announcement Speech."
125. Johnson, "Trump Calls for 'Total and Complete Shutdown of Muslims Entering the United States.'"
126. Hirschfeld Davis, "Trump to Cap Refugees Allowed into U.S. at 30,000."
127. Baker, "Trump Declares a National Emergency."
128. See White House, "The Inaugural Address."
129. The term is a reminder of the America First Party, which was a pro-fascist, anti-Semitic, antiwar political movement popular before the start of World War II. See Thomas, "America First."
130. Cramer, *The Politics of Resentment.*
131. Quinones, *Dreamland.*
132. Cross, "'Stop Overlooking Us!'"
133. Tyson and Maniam, "Behind Trump's Victory."
134. Rakich and Mehta, "Trump Is Only Popular in Rural Areas."
135. Kopf, "The Rural-Urban Divide Is Still the Big Story of American Politics."
136. Leonhardt, "The Rich Really Do Pay Lower Taxes Than You."

Chapter 2

1. CNN, "CNN/ORC International Poll, May 29–31, 2015."
2. Crouse, *The Boys on the Bus.*
3. Indeed, an infatuation with Trump's outrageousness masked the underlying populist message that many of his supporters found resonant.
4. Patterson, "Pre-Primary News Coverage of the 2016 Presidential Race."
5. Folkenflik, "Donald Trump Has Escalated His Rhetoric."
6. Grynbaum, "Television Networks Struggle to Provide Equal Airtime in the Era of Trump."
7. Zamith, "Quantified Audiences in News Production."
8. Patterson, "News Coverage of the 2016 Presidential Primaries."
9. Ibid.
10. Tyndall, "Donald Trump, King of All Earned Media."
11. Ibid.
12. Confessore and Yourish, "$2 Billion Worth of Free Media for Donald Trump."
13. Corasaniti and Haberman, "Donald Trump Suggests."
14. Tyndall Report, "Tyndall Year in Review."
15. Patterson, "News Coverage of the 2016 Election."
16. Ibid.
17. Farhi, "Trump Gets Way More TV News Time Than Clinton."
18. Patterson, "News Coverage of the 2016 Election."
19. Real Clear Politics, "Election 2016 Favorability Ratings." Clinton finished the election only slightly better, with an RCP average favorability of 41.8% and an unfavorability average of 54.4%.

20. This included the Trump campaign's use of Facebook to place advertisements targeting niche groups of voters in crucial swing states in ways that escaped broader scrutiny.

21. Politico Staff, "Full Text."

22. Jamieson and Cappella, *Echo Chamber*.

23. Boorstin, *The Image*.

24. Strömbäck and Van Aelst, "Why Political Parties Adapt to the Media."

25. Saunders, "Who Are All These Trump Supporters?"

26. CBS News, "What Do Trump Supporters See in Their Candidate?"

27. Ibid.

28. Ibid.

29. Pilkington, "Inside a Donald Trump Rally."

30. Wahl-Jorgensen, *Emotions, Media and Politics*. This also explains why Trump was so eager to hold in-person rallies during the 2020 election, despite coronavirus restrictions on crowds.

31. Altschull, *Agents of Power*.

32. Ironically, this tendency toward the sensational benefited Trump, as discussed earlier in this chapter.

33. Tur, *Unbelievable*, 81–82.

34. Ibid., 5.

35. Media Matters for America, "Everyone Should Watch This."

36. Graves, "Trump Says the Media Doesn't Show His Crowds at Rallies."

37. Wemple, "Donald Trump Again Singles Out Camera Operator for Mass Derision."

38. Factbase, "Speech: Donald Trump Holds a Political Rally in Battle Creek, Michigan."

39. Factbase, "Speech: Donald Trump Holds a Political Rally in El Paso, Texas."

40. Meeks, "Defining the Enemy."

41. Donald J. Trump (@realDonaldTrump), "I am not just running against Crooked Hillary Clinton," Twitter, August 6, 2016, 9:53 p.m. Trump's tweets were acquired from the Trump Twitter Archive at https://www.thetrumparchive.com/.

42. Donald J. Trump (@realDonaldTrump), "The press is so totally biased," Twitter, June 15, 2016, 9:44 a.m.

43. Retweets were excluded from the sample.

44. The number of tweets does not equal the number of appearances, as Trump would often tweet more than once to promote an upcoming interview.

45. Donald J. Trump (@realDonaldTrump), "I will be doing a major sit down interview," Twitter, October 25, 2015, 6:28 a.m.

46. Donald J. Trump (@realDonaldTrump), "I will be interviewed by Anderson Cooper," Twitter, February 4, 2016, 5:28 p.m.

47. Donald J. Trump (@realDonaldTrump), "@CNN has to do better reporting," Twitter, November 28, 2015, 11:03 p.m.

48. Donald J. Trump (@realDonaldTrump), "Watching @CNN and consider @secupp," Twitter, December 22, 2015, 5:39 p.m.

49. Donald J. Trump (@realDonaldTrump), "Thank you @davidaxelrod for your nice words this morning," December 16, 2015, 8:40 a.m.

50. Donald J. Trump (@realDonaldTrump), "Fantastic job on @CNN tonight," Twitter, January 11, 2016, 10:34 p.m.

51. Donald J. Trump (@realDonaldTrump), "My wife, Melania, will be interviewed tonight at 8:00pm by Anderson Cooper on @CNN," Twitter, October 17, 2016, 6:27 p.m. This was Trump's final tweet tagging CNN before the election.

52. Donald J. Trump (@realDonaldTrump), "I am watching @CNN very little lately because they are so biased against me," Twitter, June 5, 2016, 5:56 p.m.

53. Donald J. Trump (@realDonaldTrump), "I am watching @FoxNews and how fairly they are treating me and my words," Twitter, June 13, 2016, 11:08 a.m.

54. Donald J. Trump (@realDonaldTrump), "@FoxNews is much better," Twitter, July 17, 2016, 9:04 a.m.

55. Donald J. Trump (@realDonaldTrump), "@CNN is unwatchable," Twitter, September 9, 2016, 10:37 a.m.

56. Donald J. Trump (@realDonaldTrump), "Wow, just saw the really bad @CNN ratings," Twitter, October 1, 2016, 5:25 p.m.

57. Donald J. Trump (@realDonaldTrump), "Wow, @CNN got caught fixing their 'focus group' in order to make Crooked Hillary look better," Twitter, October 10, 2016, 3:31 p.m.

58. Donald J. Trump (@realDonaldTrump), "Congratulations to @FoxNews for being number one in inauguration ratings," Twitter, January 24, 2017, 9:16 p.m.

59. Trump Twitter Archive. "Archive - CNN."

60. Wells et al., "Trump, Twitter, and News Media Responsiveness."

61. Ibid., 659.

62. For additional discussion, see Boydstun and Lawrence, "When Celebrity and Political Journalism Collide"; Turner, "Trump on Twitter"; Wells et al., "Modeling the Formation of Attentive Publics in Social Media."

63. For some context about how Americans use Twitter, see Hughes and Wojcik, "10 Facts about Americans and Twitter."

64. Lewis and Molyneux, "A Decade of Research on Social Media and Journalism," 11.

65. Media Matters Staff, "The Guide to Donald Trump's War on the Press."

66. Rucker, "Trump Says Fox's Megyn Kelly."

67. Kelly would leave Fox News in January 2017, shortly before Trump's inauguration.

68. Schleifer, "Univision Anchor Ejected from Trump News Conference."

69. Haberman, "Donald Trump Says His Mocking of New York Times Reporter Was Misread."

70. de Moraes, "Donald Trump Calls ABC Reporter 'a Sleaze.'"

71. Carlson, "The Perpetual Failure of Journalism."

72. Patterson, "News Coverage of the 2016 Presidential Primaries"; Brettschneider, "Horse Race Coverage."

73. D'Angelo and Esser, "Metacoverage and Mediatization in US Presidential Elections."

74. Goodman and Moynihan, "How the Media Iced Out Bernie Sanders."

75. Pressman, *On Press.*

76. Watts and Rothschild, "Don't Blame the Election on Fake News."

77. Patterson, "News Coverage of the 2016 General Election."

78. Ibid.
79. Pew Research Center, "3. Voters' Evaluations of the Campaign."
80. Swift, "Americans' Trust in Mass Media Sinks to New Low."
81. Gottfried et al., "Trusting the News in the Trump Era."
82. This was discussed in Chapter 1.
83. Sides et al., *Identity Crisis*, 55.

Chapter 3

1. Donald J. Trump (@realDonaldTrump), Twitter, June 13, 2017, 5:35 a.m.
2. Donald J. Trump (@realDonaldTrump), Twitter, June 13, 2017, 7:48 a.m.
3. Gans, *Deciding What's News*, 145.
4. Benen, "We're All Victims."
5. For a broader discussion of "the conservative cult of victimhood," see Frum, "The Conservative Cult of Victimhood."
6. Quoted in ibid.
7. Foran, "Taking a Stand."
8. His Republican rivals Ted Cruz and Marco Rubio received 40% and 30% of the votes. Collins, "Cruz Wins CPAC Straw Poll."
9. Carlson et al., "Digital Press Criticism."
10. Factbase, "Speech: Donald Trump at CPAC."
11. This statement is particularly ironic given Trump's past of serving as an unnamed source on his own behalf. See Swan, "Trump Was the King of Anonymous Sources."
12. "How Popular Is Donald Trump?" FiveThirtyEight, the day of the election, his ratings stood at 52.6% disapprove, 44.6% approve.
13. Remnick, "Trump and the Enemies of the People."
14. Journalists' efforts at speaking on behalf of the public are explored in Chapter 4.
15. Carlson et al., "Digital Press Criticism."
16. Donald J. Trump (@realDonaldTrump), Twitter, August 5, 2018, 7:38 a.m.
17. Donald J. Trump (@realDonaldTrump), Twitter, February 17, 2019, 7:56 a.m.
18. Donald J. Trump (@realDonaldTrump), Twitter, August 30, 2018, 7:11 a.m.
19. Donald J. Trump (@realDonaldTrump), Twitter, May 5, 2020, 12:55 p.m.
20. Donald J. Trump (@realDonaldTrump), Twitter, August 3, 2020, 7:49 a.m.
21. Factbase, "Speech: Donald Trump Holds a Political Rally in Wheeling, West Virginia."
22. Rev, "Donald Trump Rally Speech Transcript Tampa, Florida, October 29."
23. Donald J. Trump (@realDonaldTrump), Twitter, August 16, 2018. 8:50 a.m.
24. Donald J. Trump (@realDonaldTrump), Twitter, January 9, 2019, 10:43 p.m.
25. Donald J. Trump (@realDonaldTrump), Twitter, October 7, 2020, 11:25 a.m. He retweeted this message later that day.
26. Barr, "Palin Trashes 'Lamestream Media.'"
27. Donald Trump (@realDonaldTrump), Twitter, August 10, 2019, 8:07 a.m.
28. Donald Trump (@realDonaldTrump), Twitter, September 2, 2019, 8:22 a.m.

29. Donald Trump (@realDonaldTrump), Twitter, November 7, 2019, 10:41 a.m..
30. Collins and Abdallah, "Trump Abruptly Ends '60 Minutes' Interview."
31. Donald J. Trump (@realDonaldTrump), Twitter, October 22, 2020, 8:05 a.m.
32. A transcript of the interview can be found in Stahl, "The 60 Minutes Interview That President Trump Cut Short."
33. Aronson et al., "Reducing the Effects of Stereotype," 113–125.
34. Lopez, "Donald Trump's Long History of Racism."
35. Kakamura, "Trump's Insults toward Black Reporters."
36. Donald J. Trump (@realDonaldTrump), Twitter, December 11, 2017, 9:17 a.m.
37. Donald J. Trump (@realDonaldTrump), Twitter, May 23, 2019, 11:19 p.m.
38. Donald J. Trump (@realDonaldTrump), Twitter, August 3, 2018, 11:37 p.m.
39. Caron, "Trump Mocks LeBron James's Intelligence."
40. Donald J. Trump (@realDonaldTrump), Twitter, July 31, 2019, 11:31 a.m.
41. Donald J. Trump (@realDonaldTrump), Twitter, April 30, 2020, 12:23 a.m.
42. Farhi, " 'What a Stupid Question.' "
43. NABJ, "NABJ Appalled by Trump's Disrespect of Black Female Journalists."
44. Darcy, "Trump Abruptly Ends Press Conference."
45. Robertson, "Trump Turns Attack on MSNBC Journalist into Rally Fodder."
46. Burns, "Police Targeted Journalists Covering the George Floyd Protests."
47. Clayman and Heritage, "Questioning Presidents."
48. Factbase, "Press Conference: Donald Trump in New York, New York.
49. Factbase, "Press Conference: Donald Trump in New York."
50. Factbase, "Press Conference: Donald Trump Meets with Reporters after Election Day 2018."
51. Harwell, "White House Shares Doctored Video to Support Punishment of Journalist Jim Acosta."
52. Factbase, "Press Gaggle."
53. Enjtei et al., "Full Transcript of Trump's Oval Office Interview with the Daily Caller."
54. Berman, "To Trump Supporters, CNN's Jim Acosta Is an Enemy and a Selfie Trophy."
55. Factbase, "Remarks."
56. Ibid.
57. Trump had insisted that undocumented immigrants were major causes of crime and overloaded the prison population, but existing research consistently has disproven this claim. See Gore, "Trump's Misdirection on 'Criminal Aliens.' "
58. Donald J. Trump (@realDonaldTrump), Twitter, August 5, 2020, 10:05 a.m.
59. Factbase, "Interview: Sean Hannity Interviews Donald Trump via Telephone."
60. Factbase, "Interview: Laura Ingraham Interviews Donald Trump on Fox's The Ingraham Angle."
61. Nadler and Bauer, News on the Right.
62. For background and discussion, see, for example, Bauer, "Journalism History and Conservative Erasure"; Brock, The Republican Noise Machine; Hemmer, Messengers of the Right; Nadler and Bauer, News on the Right; Peck, Fox Populism.
63. Nadler and Bauer, News on the Right, 5.
64. Allan, News Culture.

65. Nadler and Bauer, *News on the Right*, 6.
66. Bauer, "Journalism History and Conservative Erasure."
67. For a closer examination of Fox News and its particularly important role in media and politics during the past two decades, see Peck, *Fox Populism*; Peck, "'Listen to Your Gut.'"
68. Nadler and Bauer, *News on the Right*, 8.
69. Ibid.
70. Schradie, *The Revolution That Wasn't*.
71. For a detailed network analysis of the US right-wing media infrastructure and its role in contemporary politics, see Benkler et al., *Network Propaganda*.
72. Nadler and Bauer, *News on the Right*.
73. Roose, "What If Facebook Is the Real 'Silent Majority'?"
74. Nadler and Bauer, *News on the Right*, 5.
75. Polskin, "How Conservative Media Has Grown under Trump."
76. For illustration of related dynamics, see Benkler et al., *Network Propaganda*.
77. Stelter, *Hoax*.
78. Stelter, "Reliable Sources."
79. Stelter, "Trump Is Self-Isolating at His Safe Space."
80. Peters and Grynbaum, "As Trump Recovers, He Retreats to a Conservative Media Safe Space."
81. Ibid.
82. For some examples and analysis of this phenomenon, see Wells et al., "Trump, Twitter, and News Media Responsiveness"; Lewandowsky et al., "Using the President's Tweets to Understand Political Diversion in the Age of Social Media."
83. Rattner, "Trump's Election Lies Were among His Most Popular Tweets."
84. Stelter and Darcy, "Trump Election Dead-Enders Have a Home on Fox News and Right-Wing Radio."
85. Barr and Ellison, "Conservative Media Has Stayed Devoted to Trump's Bogus Claims of Victory."
86. Snyder, "The American Abyss."
87. Sasse, "QAnon Is Destroying the GOP from Within."
88. Stelter, "Five Alarm Fire."
89. Berry and Frenkel, "Be There."
90. Al Jazeera, "Trump's Speech That 'Incited' Capitol Violence."
91. Boot, "Trump Couldn't Have Incited Sedition without the Help of Fox News."
92. Stelter, "Capitol Insurrection Denialism Is Already Here."
93. Ibid.
94. Ibid.
95. For more about the role of Fox News in cultivating a "listen to your gut" populist aesthetic in opposition to elite expertise and legacy journalism, see Peck, "'Listen to Your Gut.'"
96. Illing, "Trump's War on Fox News and the Future of Right-Wing Media."
97. Sullivan, "The Pro-Trump Media World Peddled the Lies That Fueled the Capitol Mob."

98. The Hill, "Poll."
99. Quinnipiac University Poll, "U.S. Voters Still Say 2-1 Trump Committed Crime."
100. Gans, *Deciding What's News*, 81.
101. This is a familiar finding in journalism research at least since Gieber and Johnson, "The City Hall 'Beat.'"
102. That Trump won the Electoral College but lost the popular vote in the 2016 election speaks to the thin margins by which this strategy succeeded.
103. Ericson, "How Journalists Visualize Fact."
104. Fischer, "1 Big Thing."

Chapter 4

1. Vore, "U-T Builds Site."
2. Beard, "Freedom."
3. Repucci et al., "Media Freedom." It's notable, for example, that press freedom is considered to be on the decline throughout much of the world.
4. Grieco, "Newsroom Employees."
5. Lewis, "The Tension between Professional Control and Open Participation."
6. For example, see Nadler and Bauer, *News on the Right*.
7. Brenan, "Trust in Mass Media."
8. Donnelly, "24 Hours." See also Fu, "Reporters Covering the Capitol Attack Were Used to Harassment and Heckling."
9. We return to this idea in the Conclusion.
10. Adebanwi, *Nation as Grand Narrative*; Halverson et al., *Islamist Extremism*, 14; Stephens and McCallum, *Retelling Stories*.
11. Scholarship shows how journalists have been pivotal in crafting "grand narratives" through their work for their designated communities. Herbert Gans, for example, called them "values" and identified eight, ranging from responsible capitalism to small-town pastoralism. While these values are important to note, our focus in this chapter is less about the metanarratives that journalism helps to produce and reproduce than the metadiscourse that props up journalism.
12. Wyatt-Nichol, "American Dream."
13. Halverson et al., *Islamist Extremism*, 12.
14. Ibid., 13.
15. Cook, *Governing with the News*, 70.
16. MacIntyre, *After Virtue*.
17. Giddens, *Central Problems in Social Theory*.
18. Lyotard, *The Postmodern Condition*.
19. Trust in institutions varies by country, but the trend has largely been negative. See Ortiz-Ospina and Roser, "Trust."
20. Bertens, *The Idea of the Postmodern*. Lyotard also argued so in his seminal works on postmodernism.

21. They made these normative ideals and baked them into the Constitution, and yet in practice, the founders routinely criticized the press—especially the coverage of themselves—and found ways to try to limit journalists' power here and there.
22. See any history of the press, such as Schudson, *The Power of News*.
23. Carey, "The Problem of Journalism History."
24. Schudson, *Discovering the News*.
25. For example, the Society of Professional Journalists began in 1909 as part of DePauw University.
26. Hamilton, *All the News That's Fit to Sell*.
27. Though the report didn't articulate the complaints quite in this way, this was essentially the outcome. See Commission on Freedom of the Press, *A Free and Responsible Press*.
28. Ibid., 18.
29. Cater, *The Fourth Branch of Government*.
30. Feldstein, "Wallowing in Watergate"; Schudson, *Watergate in American Memory*.
31. Schudson, *Watergate in American Memory*, 553.
32. Ehrlich and Saltzman, *Heroes and Scoundrels*.
33. Ibid., 32.
34. Carlson, "Embodying Deep Throat."
35. Hackett, "Decline of a Paradigm"; Bennett et al., "Repairing the News"; Reese, "The News Paradigm."
36. Berkowitz, "Doing Double Duty," 125.
37. Ibid., 125; Ettema and Whitney, "Professional Mass Communicators"; Soloski, "News Reporting and Professionalism."
38. Carlson, "Gone, but Not Forgotten."
39. Zelizer, *Covering the Body*.
40. Ibid., 3.
41. Robinson, "Jockey for Authority," 802.
42. Joe Saltzman has created a database called the Image of the Journalist in Popular Culture out of the University of Southern California with more than eighty-five thousand depictions of the press in the entertainment industries.
43. Brennen, "Peasantry of the Press"; Campbell, *Getting It Wrong*; Carey, "The Problem of Journalism History"; Feldstein, "Wallowing in Watergate"; McKerns, "The Limits of Progressive Journalism History"; Nerone, "The Problem of Teaching Journalism History."
44. See, for example, Bekken, "Newsboys"; Ehrlich and Saltzman, *Heroes and Scoundrels*.
45. Bekken, "Newsboys"; Ehrlich and Saltzman, *Heroes and Scoundrels*.
46. Zelizer, "Journalists as Interpretive Communities."
47. See a full discussion of these grand virtues versus individual freedoms in Hart, *Trump and Us*.
48. Ingram, "Lost Trust in the Media."
49. See, for example, Martens et al., "The Digital Transformation of News Media."
50. "Boston Globe Seeks Coordinated Editorial."
51. Barre Montpelier Times Argus Editorial Board, "We Are the Enemy."

52. Interior Journal Editorial Board, "First Amendment under Attack."
53. Billings Gazette Editorial Board, "Support Freedom of Press."
54. Crowe, "President Trump"; Eagle Editorial Board, "News and the Media That Report It."
55. McClatchy Opinion Staff, "President Trump."
56. Philadelphia Tribune Editorial Board, "Trump's Alarming Attack."
57. Albuquerque Journal Editorial Board, "A Check on Power."
58. Jefferson Chronicle Editorial Board, "We Have Met the Enemy."
59. Monroe County Post Editorial Board, "No 'Enemy' Here."
60. Garcia, "What Our Investigative Journalists Expose."
61. Pueblo Chieftain Editorial Board, "Your Enemy?"
62. Rapid City Journal Editorial Board, "Journalists Are Hardly 'the Enemy of the People.'"
63. Hillsboro Tribune Editorial Board, "The News Isn't 'Fake.'"
64. Morning Call Editorial Board, "Why Newspapers Are Not the 'Enemy of the People.'"
65. Anchorage Daily News Editorial Board, "Why Attacks on Free Speech and the Free Press Are So Dangerous."
66. Albuquerque Journal Editorial Board, "A Check on Power."
67. This comes from Epstein, *News from Nowhere*.
68. Hess and Waller, *Local Journalism in a Digital World*.
69. See, for example, Newport This Week Editorial Board, "Enemy of the People"; Jones, "A Free Press and Its Enemies"; Daily Press Editorial Board, "We, the Press, Will Not Be Bullied."
70. Spokesman-Review Editorial Board, "The Spokesman-Review Isn't 'the Enemy of the People.'"
71. See, for example, Denton Record-Chronicle Editorial Board, "We Are Not Fake News"; Magic Valley Editorial Board, "A Free Press Is Not the Enemy"; Shawnee News-Star Editorial Board, "Freedom of the Press Makes America Great."
72. Goldberg, "The Los Angeles Times Is Not Participating."
73. Diaz, "Why the San Francisco Chronicle Isn't Joining."
74. Donald Trump (@realDonaldTrump), "There is nothing that I would want more for our Country than true FREEDOM OF THE PRESS," Twitter, August 16, 2018, 9:10 a.m.
75. This term comes from a distinction that Democracy Fund wrote about in a blog post in 2017 between "affective" kinds of trust and "cognitive" kinds of trust: "Cognitive trust has been described as 'trusting from the head.' It includes factors such as dependability, predictability, and reputation. Affective trust, on the other hand, involves having mutual care and concern or emotional bonds. This has been described as 'trusting from the heart.' Most trusting relationships have both cognitive and affective aspects that often reinforce one another." Gopal and Mazzola, "Understanding Trust to Strengthen Democracy."
76. Massing, "Journalism in the Age of Trump."
77. Donnelly, "24 Hours."

Chapter 5

1. Swaine, "Trump Inauguration Crowd Photos."
2. See Washington Post, "In Four Years, President Trump Made 30,573 False or Misleading Claims." The fact-checking team went on to collate these lies in a 2020 book: Kessler et al., *Donald Trump and His Assault on the Truth*.
3. For a history of Trump's racist discourse, see Lopez, "Donald Trump's Long History of Racism."
4. Donald Trump (@realDonaldTrump), ". . . and viciously telling the people of the United States, the greatest and most powerful Nation on earth, how our government is to be run," Twitter, July 14, 2019, 7:27 a.m.
5. Stracqualursi and Westwood, "Trump Thanked 'Great People.' "
6. Felton, "Black Police Officers Describe the Racist Attacks They Faced as They Protected the Capitol."
7. Wells et al., "Proud Boys."
8. Blake, "What Trump Said Before His Supporters Stormed the Capitol."
9. Ettema and Glasser, *Custodians of Conscience*, 3.
10. Ward, *Ethical Journalism in a Populist Age*. Ward (pp. 127–130) lays out a whole framework of action for journalists on how to detect threats to democracy in a populist leader—specifically to counter demagogues like Trump.
11. Gert and Gert, "The Definition of Morality."
12. Carson, *Lying and Deception*.
13. For example, see the condemnation of journalistic tactics in Malcolm, *The Journalist and the Murderer*.
14. We do not need to reiterate all the scholarship about objectivity. Key works include Mindich, *Just the Facts*; Kovach and Rosenstiel, *The Elements of Journalism*; Maras, *Objectivity in Journalism*, to name a few.
15. Tuchman, "Objectivity as Strategic Ritual."
16. Schudson, "The Objectivity Norm in American Journalism."
17. Rosen, "The View from Nowhere."
18. Gans, *Deciding What's News*, 182–213.
19. Ibid., 57.
20. See Ettema and Glasser, *Custodians of Conscience*, 10, on investigative journalism and transforming moral claims into empirical claims.
21. Ettema and Glasser, "Narrative Form and Moral Force," 10.
22. Darnton, "Writing News and Telling Stories."
23. Ettema and Glasser, *Custodians of Conscience*, 9.
24. Ibid., 11.
25. For an overview, see Berkowitz, "Reporters and Their Sources."
26. Bayley, *Joe McCarthy and the Press*.
27. Keith and Thornton, "Where the Truth Lies"; but also Alterman, *When Presidents Lie*; Getler, "Wanted"; McDermott, *Risk-Taking in International Politics*; Pfiffner, "Presidential Lies."
28. Bernstein, "The Road to Watergate and Beyond," 60.

29. Robinson, *Networked News, Racial Divides*; Bonilla-Silva, *Racism without Racists*. But also see Squires, *Dispatches from the Color Line*; Hartmann and Husband, *Racism and the Mass Media*; van Dijk, *News as Discourse, Racism and the Press*.

30. Steiner and Waisbord, *News of Baltimore*, 13.

31. In this chapter, we use the term "lie" as the descriptor of choice, although we also use "falsehood" interchangeably. While some may argue that accusing someone of lying necessitates proving intention, the sheer number of untrue statements made by Trump in the face of widely available contradictory evidence establishes a pattern that obviates wrangling over what Trump believes in any particular instance.

32. PolitiFact, "Donald Trump."

33. Farley, "Trump's Misguided Tweet"; Rieder, "Trump's Baseless Attacks"; Robertson and McDonald, "Trump's False Claim"; Robertson, "Trump's False Military Equipment Claim."

34. Greenberg, *Republic of Spin*. We recommend Kessler et al., *Donald Trump and His Assault on the Truth*. While it is of course the case that all presidents have lied to the press and the public for some reason—from John F. Kennedy's and Clinton's personal affairs to Nixon's atrocious falsehoods during Watergate to Lyndon B. Johnson's terrible lies about the US involvement in Vietnam. As the *Washington Post* fact checkers document in *Donald Trump and His Assault on the Truth*, Trump is in a pernicious class all by himself.

35. Qiu, "Fact-Checking Trump's Claim."

36. Leonhardt and David, "Trump's Lies."

37. Rauch, "Fact-Checking the President in Real Time."

38. Keith and Thornton, "Where the Truth Lies."

39. Ingram, "When Should Journalists Use the 'L' Word?"

40. Thompson, "Trump's Lies Are a Virus."

41. Vernon, "Lie?"

42. Bauder, "News Media Hesitate to Use 'Lie' for Trump's Misstatements."

43. Wattles, "How to Know When Trump Is Lying."

44. Farhi, "Lies?"

45. Roser et al., "Coronavirus Pandemic."

46. Jarecki, "Trump's Covid-19 Inaction Killed Americans."

47. Bump and Parker, "13 Hours of Trump."

48. Paz, "All the President's Lies about the Coronavirus."

49. Colarossi, "11 Times Trump Has Lashed Out at Reporters."

50. Alcindor responded by tweeting: "I'm not the first human being, woman, black person or journalist to be told that while doing a job." Yamiche Alcindor (@Yamiche), "President Trump today at the White House said to me: 'Be nice. Don't be threatening,'" Twitter, March 29, 2020, 6:55 p.m., https://twitter.com/Yamiche/status/1244413018026491905.

51. Blow, "Stop Airing Trump's Briefings!"

52. Rosen, "Switching Our Coverage of Donald Trump."

53. Yglesias, "Cancel the Trump Show."

54. Nuzzi, "Trump's Coronavirus Briefings."

55. It's important to note, however, that fact-checking is not universally revered. The Pew Research Center found that 70% of Republicans believe fact-checkers to be biased. See Walker and Gottfried, "Republicans Far More Likely Than Democrats to Say Fact-Checkers Tend to Favor One Side."

56. Graham et al., "Oral History of Trump's Bigotry."

57. Konrad, "Denial of Racism and the Trump Presidency," 16.

58. Squires, *Post-racial Mystique*.

59. Stevens, "Half of Voters Believe President Trump Is Racist."

60. Lemire, "Trump Stokes Racial Rancor to Motivate Voters."

61. Gantt Shafer, "Donald Trump's 'Political Incorrectness,'" 1.

62. Stelter, "'Moral Dimension' of Covering Trump."

63. Wemple, "'Racially Charged.'"

64. For the original Reuters article, see Cornwell and Cowan, "House Condemns Trump."

65. By contrast, in the *Washington Post*, Erik Wemple urged, "Let the sun shine on these deliberations!" See Wemple, "Racially Charged."

66. King, "Jason Kessler on His 'Unite the Right' Rally."

67. Attiah, "NPR Teaches Listeners."

68. López, "Jason Kessler's False Equivalence Frame."

69. Vernon, "How Journalists Cover White Nationalism."

70. Jensen, "How to Cover Racist Viewpoints."

71. Noel King (@NoelKing), "I'm a biracial woman. Our Executive Producer is a Black woman," Twitter, August 10, 2018, 10:54 a.m., https://twitter.com/NoelKing/status/1027946345078968320

72. Keith, "Strategy of Division to Win Reelection."

73. Pompeo, "Not-So-Bitter Rivalry."

74. Allsop, "Protecting the Institution."

75. New York Times Editorial Board, "A Times Headline about Trump Stoked Anger."

76. Darcy, "Inside the New York Times."

77. Allsop, "Dean Baquet, Marty Baron, and Protecting the Institution."

78. Feinberg, "The New York Times Unites vs. Twitter."

79. WashPostPR, "Washington Post Executive Editor Martin Baron."

80. Powell, "The Danger of 'Misinformation, Disinformation, Delusions, and Deceit.'"

81. Smith, "Marty Baron Made the Post Great Again."

82. Schudson, *Discovering the News*.

83. For a summary, see Maras, *Objectivity in Journalism*.

84. Haas, "Mainstream News Media Self-Criticism"; Fengler, "Holding the News Media Accountable."

85. Vernon, "The Unavoidable Brian Stelter."

86. Stelter, "Stelter Defines 'Creeping Authoritarianism.'"

87. Cohen, "Trump 2020 Attorney Spars."

88. Stelter, *Hoax*.

89. Flood, "CNN's Brian Stelter Widely Ridiculed," "CNN's Brian Stelter Lampooned," "CNN's 'Reliable Sources'"; Flood and Wulfsohn, "CNN's Brian Stelter's Apparent Hesitance."

90. Donald Trump (@realDonaldTrump), "@brianstelter is just a poor man's lapdog for AT&T," Twitter, May 10, 2020, 12:51 p.m.
91. See Chapter 3.
92. Stelter, "Media Must Stand up for Morality and Decency."
93. Stelter, *Reliable Sources.*
94. Sullivan agreed to teach a course at Duke called News as a Moral Battleground. See Adair, "Washington Post Media Columnist Margaret Sullivan."
95. Sullivan, "Tiptoeing around Trump's Racism."
96. Sullivan, "Journalists Can't Repeat Their Watergate-Hero Act."
97. James Poniewozik (@poniewozik), "A real problem is that politics in Trump's era has taken on a moral dimension that news outlets either aren't equipped to cover," Twitter, July 14, 2019, 7:36 p.m., https://twitter.com/poniewozik/status/1150564692886261760.
98. Zurawik, "Furor over Trump's Baltimore Tweets Continues."
99. Kristof, "Impeachment Is a Call for Moral Clarity."
100. In all, we conducted 109 surveys, four focus groups, and in-depth interviews with forty journalists at all sizes of news outlets. All were promised anonymity, were asked questions about their role, especially as it was changing, and received Amazon gift cards for their time. As with the trade-press accountings we examined, this material was analyzed using critical discourse analysis, looking for how conceptualizations about journalists' roles intersected with their understandings of truth.
101. Please note that these interviews and surveys tended to be with more rank-and-file reporters at the smaller and mid-sized publications. We received much different responses from the engagement specialists we also talked to as part of this data collection. But such people also viewed themselves as being on the cutting edge of journalism; at the time of this writing in 2021, they were not the majority of mainstream journalists.
102. Singer, "Out of Bounds."
103. Longform Podcast, "#398."
104. Wemple, "CNN, MSNBC Refused to Carry Full Trump Coronavirus Briefing."
105. Grynbaum and Hsu, "Major Networks Cut Away from Trump's Baseless Fraud Claims."
106. Carey, *Communication as Culture.*
107. Putnam, *Bowling Alone*; see also Davis and Fields, "In Places with Fraying Social Fabric."
108. Billman, "Donald Trump Wants to Eviscerate the Public's Trust in Journalism."

Conclusion

1. Lepore, "Does Journalism Have a Future?"
2. Examples include Jones, *Losing the News*; Ryfe, *Can Journalism Survive?*; McChesney and Pickard, *Will the Last Reporter Please Turn Out the Lights*; Anderson et al., *Post-industrial Journalism.*

3. Homeland Security, "National Terrorism Advisory System."
4. Of note, while Donald Trump's approval rating plunged nationally and even among Republicans in the immediate aftermath of the assault on the Capitol, by the time Joe Biden's administration had taken power in late January 2021, Trump's popularity had begun to rebound, with eight in ten Republicans having a positive view of the former president. See Durkee, "Trump's Popularity with GOP Bounces Back after Capitol Attack."
5. Eldridge, *Online Journalism from the Periphery.*
6. Lewis and Westlund, "Actors, Actants, Audiences, and Activities in Cross-Media News Work."
7. Mason, *Uncivil Agreement.*
8. Brenan, "Americans Remain Distrustful of Mass Media"; Edelman, "Edelman Trust Barometer 2021."
9. Andén-Papadopoulos, "Citizen Camera-Witnessing"; Richardson, *Bearing Witness While Black.*
10. Bennett and Segerberg, "The Logic of Connective Action."
11. Quandt, "Dark Participation."
12. Tandoc et al., "Defining 'Fake News'."
13. Del Vicario et al., "The Spreading of Misinformation Online."
14. Phillips, *This Is Why We Can't Have Nice Things.*
15. Benjamin, *Race after Technology.*
16. Löfgren Nilsson and Örnebring, "Journalism under Threat"; Miller and Lewis, "Journalists, Harassment, and Emotional Labor."
17. Mendes et al., "# MeToo and the Promise and Pitfalls of Challenging Rape Culture through Digital Feminist Activism."
18. Burgess and Matamoros-Fernández, "Mapping Sociocultural Controversies across Digital Media Platforms."
19. See Hindman, *The Internet Trap*; Wu, *The Attention Merchants.*
20. Kalogeropoulos et al., "News Brand Attribution in Distributed Environments."
21. Hermida, "Twittering the News"; Molyneux, "Mobile News Consumption."
22. Pettman, *Infinite Distraction.*
23. For some discussion of news and its value proposition for audiences, see Lewis, "The Objects and Objectives of Journalism Research during the Coronavirus Pandemic and Beyond."
24. Cf. Lewis, "'This Is What the News Won't Show You'"; See also Cunningham, and Craig, "Being 'Really Real' on YouTube."
25. Duffy and Hund, "Gendered Visibility on Social Media."
26. Aslama and Pantti, "Talking Alone."
27. Hart, *Trump and Us.*
28. For a review of this literature, see Nikunen, "Media, Emotions and Affect."
29. Wahl-Jorgensen, *Emotions, Media and Politics.*
30. Social media companies find themselves grappling with what role they need to play in determining who gets to identify what is true or not. In 2020, Twitter and Reddit, for example, both started taking actions against Trump-inspired hate speech, and

Facebook has debated what its own commitments are in curbing misinformation and disinformation in light of its desire to avoid policing content. In 2021, Trump was indefinitely banned from Twitter and other social media platforms.

31. Schudson, "The Objectivity Norm in American Journalism."
32. Korsgaard, *The Sources of Normativity*, 8.
33. Fine, "Enacting Norms," 140.
34. Zelizer, "Journalists as Interpretive Communities."
35. Schudson, *The Food Citizen*.
36. Ibid., 171.
37. Achen and Bartels, *Democracy for Realists*, 213–214.
38. Delli Carpini and Keeter, *What Americans Know about Politics and Why It Matters*.
39. Cramer and Toff, "The Fact of Experience."
40. Marcus, "Emotions in Politics."
41. Wahl-Jorgensen, *Emotions, Media and Politics*; Wagner and Boczkowski, "Angry, Frustrated, and Overwhelmed."
42. Mason, *Uncivil Agreement*.
43. This idea is well explored in Callison and Young, *Reckoning*.
44. Nielsen, "The One Thing Journalism Just Might Do for Democracy"; See also Ytre-Arne and Moe, "Approximately Informed, Occasionally Monitorial?"
45. Josephi, "How Much Democracy Does Journalism Need?"; Zelizer, "On the Shelf Life of Democracy in Journalism Scholarship."
46. Newman et al., "Digital News Report 2020." These numbers are roughly in line with ratios from other major countries, though there are exceptions, such as Germany (where eight in ten prefer neutral news) and Brazil (where, by contrast, nearly as many people want news sources that share their view as compared to the number of people who want news sources lacking a particular view).
47. Ibid.
48. Ibid.
49. Callison and Young, *Reckoning*.
50. See the critiques reviewed in Chapter 1.
51. Lowery, "A Reckoning over Objectivity, Led by Black Journalists."
52. Robinson and Bartzen Culver, "When White Reporters Cover Race"; See also Durham, "On the Relevance of Standpoint Epistemology to the Practice of Journalism"; and Maras, *Objectivity in Journalism*.
53. Benton, "Is a Journalist Calling Out the Impact of Racism 'Bias'?" Benton is invoking Daniel Hallin's sphere model, from Hallin, *The Uncensored War*.
54. Craft, "Distinguishing Features," 296.
55. This is a central finding in early cultural studies research on news audiences. In particular, see the seminal study by David Morley on class-inspired readings: Morley, *The Nationwide Audience*.
56. Lewis et al., "Reciprocal Journalism."
57. Wenzel et al., "Engaging Stigmatized Communities through Solutions Journalism."
58. Robinson, *How Journalists Engage*.
59. Nelson, *Imagined Audiences*.

60. Boczkowski and Lewis, "The Center of the Universe No More"; Lewis, "Lack of Trust in the News Media, Institutional Weakness, and Relational Journalism as a Potential Way Forward"; Min, "What the Twenty-First Century Engaged Journalism Can Learn from the Twentieth Century Public Journalism."
61. Molyneux, "A Personalized Self-Image."
62. Lee, " 'Friending' Journalists on Social Media."
63. Deto, "*Pittsburgh Post-Gazette* Removes a Black Reporter from George Floyd Protest Coverage."
64. Zahay et al., "The Labor of Building Trust."
65. Ibid.
66. Ward, *Ethical Journalism in a Populist* Age.
67. See Usher, *News for the Rich, White, and Blue.*
68. See, for example, Wenzel, "Sourcing Diversity, Shifting Culture."
69. Blake and Scott, "Joe Biden's Inauguration Speech Transcript."

Bibliography

Abernathy, Penelope M. *The Expanding News Desert*. Chapel Hill: University of North Carolina Press, 2018.

Abernathy, Penelope M. "The Expanding News Desert." University of North Carolina Hussman School of Journalism and Media. Last modified June 15, 2020. https://www.usnewsdeserts.com.

Achen, Christopher H., and Larry M. Bartels. *Democracy for Realists: Why Elections Do Not Produce Responsive Government*. Princeton, NJ: Princeton University Press, 2017.

Adair, Bill. "Washington Post Media Columnist Margaret Sullivan to Teach Journalism Ethics Course." DeWitt Wallace Center for Media & Democracy, May 28, 2020. https://dewitt.sanford.duke.edu/margaret-sullivan-to-teach-journalism-at-duke/.

Adebanwi, Wale. *Nation as Grand Narrative: The Nigerian Press and the Politics of Meaning*. Rochester: University of Rochester Press, 2016.

Ahva, Laura. "Practice Theory for Journalism Studies: Operationalizing the Concept of Practice for the Study of Participation." *Journalism Studies* 18, no. 12 (2017): 1523–1541.

Albuquerque Journal Editorial Board. "A Check on Power—Journalism, Free Speech Helped Make America Great in the First Place." *Albuquerque Journal*, August 15, 2018. https://www.abqjournal.com/1209372/a-check-on-power-journalism-free-speech-helped-make-america-great-in-the-first-place.html.

Alemán, Sonya M. "Locating Whiteness in Journalism Pedagogy." *Critical Studies in Media Communication* 31, no. 1 (2014): 72–88.

Al Jazeera. "Trump's Speech That 'Incited' Capitol Violence." January 11, 2021. https://www.aljazeera.com/news/2021/1/11/full-transcript-donald-trump-january-6-incendiary-speech.

Allan, Stuart. *News Culture*. Maidenhead: Open University Press, 2010.

Allsop, Jon. "Dean Baquet, Marty Baron, and Protecting the Institution." *Columbia Journalism Review*, June 29, 2020. https://www.cjr.org/the_media_today/dean_baquet_marty_baron.php.

Alterman, Eric. *When Presidents Lie: A History of Official Deception and Its Consequences*. New York: Penguin Books, 2004.

Altschull, J. Herbert. *Agents of Power: The Role of the News Media in Human Affairs*. New York: Longman, 1984.

Anchorage Daily News Editorial Board. "Why Attacks on Free Speech and the Free Press Are So Dangerous." *Anchorage Daily News*, August 15, 2018. https://www.adn.com/opinions/editorials/2018/08/15/why-attacks-on-free-speech-and-the-free-press-are-so-dangerous/.

Andén-Papadopoulos, Kari. "Citizen Camera-Witnessing: Embodied Political Dissent in the Age of 'Mediated Mass Self-Communication.'" *New Media & Society* 16, no. 5 (2014): 753–769.

Anderson, C. W., Emily Bell, and Clay Shirky. *Post-Industrial Journalism*. Tow Center for Digital Journalism. Columbia University, 2014. https://towcenter.columbia.edu/news/post-industrial-journalism-adapting-present.

Ansolabehere, Stephen, and Shanto Iyengar. "Of Horseshoes and Horse Races: Experimental Studies of the Impact of Poll Results on Electoral Behavior." *Political Communication* 11, no. 4 (1994): 413–430.

Arana, Gabriel. "17% of U.S. Newsroom Staff Is Not White." *Columbia Journalism Review*, November 5, 2018. https://www.cjr.org/special_report/race-ethnicity-newsrooms-data.php.

Arceneaux, Kevin, and Martin Johnson. *Changing Minds or Changing Channels? Partisan News in an Age of Choice*. Chicago: University of Chicago Press, 2013.

Aronson, Joshua, Carrie B. Fried, and Catherine Good. "Reducing the Effects of Stereotype Threat on African American College Students by Shaping Theories of Intelligence." *Journal of Experimental Social Psychology* 38, no. 2 (2002): 113–125.

Aslama, Minna, and Mervi Pantti. "Talking Alone: Reality TV, Emotions and Authenticity." *European Journal of Cultural Studies* 9, no. 2 (2006): 167–184.

Attiah, Karen. "NPR Teaches Listeners about the Proper Care and Feeding of White Nationalists." *Washington Post*, August 11, 2018. https://www.washingtonpost.com/blogs/post-partisan/wp/2018/08/11/npr-teaches-listeners-on-the-proper-care-and-feeding-of-white-nationalists/.

Baker, Peter. "Trump Declares a National Emergency, and Provokes a Constitutional Clash." *New York Times*, February 15, 2019. https://www.nytimes.com/2019/02/15/us/politics/national-emergency-trump.html.

Barr, Andy. "Palin Trashes 'Lamestream Media.'" *Politico*, November 18, 2009. https://www.politico.com/story/2009/11/palin-trashes-lamestream-media-029693.

Barr, Jeremy, and Sarah Ellison. "Conservative Media Has Stayed Devoted to Trump's Bogus Claims of Victory—but Cracks Are Starting to Show." *Washington Post*, November 20, 2020. https://www.washingtonpost.com/lifestyle/trump-conservative-media-fox-election-fraud-claims/2020/11/20/c6febaf0-29d2-11eb-b847-66c66ace1afb_story.html.

Barre Montpelier Times Argus Editorial Board. "Yes, We Are the Enemy." *Barre Montpelier Times Argus*, August 16, 2018. https://www.timesargus.com/opinion/editorials/yes-we-are-the-enemy/article_9bbe3a93-2cb3-54d5-a3ab-2fc5add152ed.html.

Barry, Dan, and Sheera Frenkel. "'Be There. Will Be Wild!': Trump All but Circled the Date." *New York Times*, January 8, 2021. https://www.nytimes.com/2021/01/06/us/politics/capitol-mob-trump-supporters.html.

Bauder, David. "News Media Hesitate to Use 'Lie' for Trump's Misstatements." *Associated Press*, August 29, 2018. https://apnews.com/88675d3fdd674c7c9ec70f170f6e4a1a.

Bauer, A. J. "Journalism History and Conservative Erasure." *American Journalism* 35, no. 1 (2018): 2–26.

Bayley, Edwin R. *Joe McCarthy and the Press*. Madison: University of Wisconsin Press, 2005.

BBC News. "Walmart Pulls 'Lynch Journalists' T-Shirt from Sale." December 1, 2017. https://www.bbc.com/news/world-us-canada-42195042.

Beard, David. "Freedom: 411 Papers Editorialize to Preserve America's Free Press." *Poynter*, August 16, 2018. https://www.poynter.org/newsletters/2018/freedom-411-papers-editorialize-to-preserve-america%C2%92s-free-press/.

Bedingfield, Sid. "Tillman's Rebellion, South Carolina." In *Journalism and Jim Crow: The Making of White Supremacy in the New South*, edited by Kathy Roberts Forde and Sid Bedingfield. Urbana: University of Illinois Press, forthcoming.

Beiser, Elana. "More Journalists Killed on the Job as Reprisal Murders Nearly Double." Committee to Protect Journalists, December 19, 2018. https://cpj.org/reports/2018/12/journalists-killed-murdered-afghan-saudi-us.php.

Bekken, Jon. "Newsboys: The Exploitation of 'Little Merchants' by the Newspaper Industry." In *Newsworkers: Toward a History of the Rank and File*, edited by Hanno Hardt and Bonnie Brennen, 190–226. Minneapolis: University of Minnesota Press, 1995.

Benen, Steve. "'We're All Victims': Trump Pushes Persecution Complex to Supporters." MSNBC, December 7, 2020. https://www.msnbc.com/rachel-maddow-show/we-re-all-victims-trump-pushes-persecution-complex-supporters-n1250206.

Benjamin, Ruha. *Race after Technology: Abolitionist Tools for the New Jim Code*. Cambridge: Polity Press, 2019.

Benkler, Yochai, Robert Faris, and Hal Roberts. *Network Propaganda: Manipulation, Disinformation, and Radicalization in American Politics*. Oxford: Oxford University Press, 2018.

Bennett, W. Lance. *News: The Politics of Illusion*. Chicago: University of Chicago Press, 2016.

Bennett, Lance W., Lynne A. Gressett, and William Haltom. "Repairing the News: A Case Study of the News Paradigm." *Journal of Communication* 35, no. 2 (1985): 50–68.

Bennett, W. Lance, and Alexandra Segerberg. "The Logic of Connective Action: Digital Media and the Personalization of Contentious Politics." *Information, Communication & Society* 15, no. 5 (2012): 739–768.

Benton, Joshua. "Is a Journalist Calling Out the Impact of Racism 'Bias'?" *Nieman Lab*, September 27, 2019. https://www.niemanlab.org/2019/09/is-a-journalist-calling-out-the-impact-of-racism-bias/.

Bergström, Annika, and Maria Jervelycke Belfrage. "News in Social Media: Incidental Consumption and the Role of Opinion Leaders." *Digital Journalism* 6, no. 5 (2018): 583–598.

Berkowitz, Dan. "Doing Double Duty: Paradigm Repair and the Princess Diana What-a-Story." *Journalism* 1, no. 2 (2000): 125–143.

Berkowitz, Daniel A. "Reporters and Their Sources." In *The Handbook of Journalism Studies*, edited by Karin Wahl-Jorgensen and Thomas Hanitzsch, 122–135. New York: Routledge, 2009.

Berlet, Chip, and Matthew N. Lyons. *Right-Wing Populism in America: Too Close for Comfort*. New York: Guilford Press, 2000.

Berman, Nina. "To Trump Supporters, CNN's Jim Acosta Is an Enemy and a Selfie Trophy." *Columbia Journalism Review*, November 8, 2018. https://www.cjr.org/politics/cnn-jim-acosta-trump-rallies.php.

Bernstein, Barton J. "The Road to Watergate and Beyond: The Growth and Abuse of Executive Authority since 1940." *Law and Contemporary Problems* 40, no. 2 (1976): 58–86.

Bertens, Johannes Willem. *The Idea of the Postmodern: A History*. New York: Routledge, 1995.

Betz, Hans-Georg. *Radical Right-Wing Populism in Western Europe*. New York: St. Martin's Press, 1994.

Billings Gazette Editorial Board. "Gazette Opinion: Support Freedom of Press in Montana." *Billings Gazette*, August 19, 2018. https://billingsgazette.com/opinion/editorial/gazette-opinion-support-freedom-of-press-in-montana/article_f5320cbe-6657–55ce-9b8b-281da34dd7e5.html.

Billman, Jeffrey C. "Donald Trump Wants to Eviscerate the Public's Trust in Journalism. If He Succeeds, Our Democracy Is at Risk." *Indy Week*, August 16, 2018. https://indyweek.com/news/soapboxer/donald-trump-wants-eviscerate-public-s-trust-journalism.-succeeds-democracy-risk./.

Blake, Aaron. "What Trump Said before His Supporters Stormed the Capitol." *Washington Post*, January 11, 2021. https://www.washingtonpost.com/politics/interactive/2021/annotated-trump-speech-jan-6-capitol/.

Blake, Aaron, and Eugene Scott. "Joe Biden's Inauguration Speech Transcript, Annotated." *Washington Post*, January 20, 2021. https://www.washingtonpost.com/politics/interactive/2021/01/20/biden-inauguration-speech/.

Blow, Charles M. "Stop Airing Trump's Briefings!" *New York Times*, April 19, 2020. https://www.nytimes.com/2020/04/19/opinion/trump-coronavirus-briefings.html.

Boczkowski, Pablo J., and Seth C. Lewis. "The Center of the Universe No More: From the Self-Centered Stance of the Past to the Relational Mindset of the Future." In *Trump and the Media*, edited by Pablo J. Boczkowski and Zizi Papacharissi, 177–185. Cambridge, MA: MIT Press, 2018.

Boczkowski, Pablo J., Eugenia Mitchelstein, and Mora Matassi. "'News Comes across When I'm in a Moment of Leisure': Understanding the Practices of Incidental News Consumption on Social Media." *New Media & Society* 20, no. 10 (2018): 3523–3539.

Bonilla-Silva, Eduardo. *Racism without Racists: Color-Blind Racism and the Persistence of Racial Inequality in America*. 4th ed. Lanham, MD: Rowman & Littlefield, 2014.

Boorstin, Daniel J. *The Image: A Guide to Pseudo-Events in America*. New York: Vintage, 1962.

Boot, Max. "Opinion: Trump Couldn't Have Incited Sedition without the Help of Fox News." *The Washington Post*, January 18, 2021. https://www.washingtonpost.com/opinions/2021/01/18/trump-couldnt-have-incited-sedition-without-help-fox-news/.

Boydstun, Amber E., and Regina G. Lawrence. "When Celebrity and Political Journalism Collide: Reporting Standards, Entertainment, and the Conundrum of Covering Donald Trump's 2016 Campaign." *Perspectives on Politics* 18, no. 1 (2020): 128–143.

Boynton, G. R., and Glenn W. Richardson Jr. "Agenda Setting in the Twenty-First Century." *New Media & Society* 18, no. 9 (2016): 1916–1934.

Brambila, Julieta Alejandra, and Sallie Hughes. "Violence against Journalists." In *The International Encyclopedia of Journalism Studies*, edited by Tim P. Vos, Folker Hanusch, Dimitra Dimitrakopoulou, Margaretha Geertsema-Sligh, and Annika Sehl, 1614–1621. New York: John Wiley and Sons, 2019.

Brenan, Megan. "Americans Remain Distrustful of Mass Media." Gallup, September 30, 2020. https://news.gallup.com/poll/321116/americans-remain-distrustful-mass-media.aspx.

Brenan, Megan. "Americans' Trust in Mass Media Edges Down to 41%." Gallup, September 26, 2019. https://news.gallup.com/poll/267047/americans-trust-mass-media-edges-down.aspx.

Brennen, Bonnie. "Peasantry of the Press: A History of American News-Workers from Novels 1919–1938." PhD diss., University of Iowa, 1993.

Brettschneider, Frank. "Horse Race Coverage." In *The International Encyclopedia of Communication*, edited by Wolfgang Donsbach. New York: John Wiley and Sons, 2008. https://onlinelibrary.wiley.com/doi/10.1002/9781405186407.wbiech022

Brock, David. *The Republican Noise Machine: Right-Wing Media and How It Corrupts Democracy*. New York: Crown Publishers, 2004.

Broersma, Marcel, and Chris Peters. "Rethinking Journalism: The Structural Transformation of Public Good." In *Rethinking Journalism: Trust and Participation in a Transformed News Landscape*, edited by Chris Peters and Marcel J. Broersma, 13–24. New York: Routledge, 2013.

Brownstein, Ronald. "How the Rustbelt Paved Trump's Road to Victory." *The Atlantic*, November 10, 2016. https://www.theatlantic.com/politics/archive/2016/11/trumps-road-to-victory/507203/.

Buettner, Russ, Susanne Craig, and Mike McIntire. "Long-Concealed Records Show Trump's Chronic Losses and Years of Tax Avoidance." *New York Times*, September 27, 2020. https://www.nytimes.com/interactive/2020/09/27/us/donald-trump-taxes.html.

Bump, Philip. "Donald Trump Will Be President Thanks to 80,000 People in Three States." *Washington Post*, December 1, 2016. https://www.washingtonpost.com/news/the-fix/wp/2016/12/01/donald-trump-will-be-president-thanks-to-80000-people-in-three-states/.

Bump, Philip, and Ashley Parker. "13 Hours of Trump: The President Fills Briefings with Attacks and Boasts, but Little Empathy." *Washington Post*, April 26, 2020. https://www.washingtonpost.com/politics/13-hours-of-trump-the-president-fills-briefings-with-attacks-and-boasts-but-little-empathy/2020/04/25/7eec5ab0–8590–11ea-a3eb-e9fc93160703_story.html.

Burgess, Jean, and Ariadna Matamoros-Fernández. "Mapping Sociocultural Controversies across Digital Media Platforms: One Week of #gamergate on Twitter, YouTube, and Tumblr." *Communication Research and Practice* 2, no. 1 (2016): 79–96.

Burns, Katelyn. "Police Targeted Journalists Covering the George Floyd Protests." *Vox*, May 31, 2020. https://www.vox.com/identities/2020/5/31/21276013/police-targeted-journalists-covering-george-floyd-protests.

California News Publishers Association. "Boston Globe Seeks Coordinated Editorial to Stand Up to Attack on Journalism." August 10, 2018. https://cnpa.com/boston-globe-seeks-coordinated-editorial-to-stand-up-to-attack-on-journalism/.

Callison, Candis, and Mary Lynn Young. *Reckoning: Journalism's Limits and Possibilities*. New York: Oxford University Press, 2020.

Campbell, W. Joseph. *Getting It Wrong: Ten of the Greatest Misreported Stories in American Journalism*. Berkeley: University of California Press, 2010.

Cappella, Joseph N., and Kathleen Hall Jamieson. *Spiral of Cynicism: The Press and the Public Good*. New York: Oxford University Press, 1997.

Carey, James W. *Communication as Culture: Essays on Media and Society*. Boston: Unwin Hyman, 1989.

Carey, James W. "A Plea for the University Tradition." *Journalism Quarterly* 55, no. 4 (1978): 846–855.

Carey, James W. "The Problem of Journalism History." *Journalism History* 1, no. 1 (1974): 3–27.

Carlson, A. Cheree. "The Rhetoric of the Know-Nothing Party: Nativism as a Response to the Rhetorical Situation." *Southern Communication Journal* 54, no. 4 (1989): 364–383.

Carlson, Matt. "Embodying Deep Throat: Mark Felt and the Collective Memory of Watergate." *Critical Studies in Media Communication* 27, no. 3 (2010): 235–250.

Carlson, Matt. "Gone, but Not Forgotten: Memories of Journalistic Deviance as Metajournalistic Discourse." *Journalism Studies* 15, no. 1 (2014): 33–47.

Carlson, Matt. "The Information Politics of Journalism in a Post-Truth Age." *Journalism Studies* 19, no. 13 (2018): 1879–1888.

Carlson, Matt. *Journalistic Authority.* New York: Columbia University Press, 2017.

Carlson, Matt. "The Perpetual Failure of Journalism." *Journalism* 20, no. 1 (2019): 95–97.

Carlson, Matt. "What Do We Do When Journalism Stops Working?" *Political Communication* 37, no. 4 (2020): 582–584.

Carlson, Matt, and Seth C. Lewis, eds. *Boundaries of Journalism: Professionalism, Practices and Participation.* New York: Routledge, 2015.

Carlson, Matt, Sue Robinson, and Seth C. Lewis. "Digital Press Criticism: The Symbolic Dimensions of Donald Trump's Assault on U.S. Journalists as the 'Enemy of the People.'" *Digital Journalism*, November 5, 2020. https://doi.org/10.1080/21670811.2020.1836981.

Carlson, Matt, and Nikki Usher. "News Startups as Agents of Innovation: For-Profit Digital News Startup Manifestos as Metajournalistic Discourse." *Digital Journalism* 4, no. 5 (2016): 563–581.

Caron, Christina. "Trump Mocks LeBron James's Intelligence and Calls Don Lemon 'Dumbest Man' on TV." *New York Times*, August 4, 2018. https://www.nytimes.com/2018/08/04/sports/donald-trump-lebron-james-twitter.html.

Carson, Thomas L. *Lying and Deception: Theory and Practice.* Oxford: Oxford University Press, 2010.

Cater, Douglass. *The Fourth Branch of Government.* Boston: Houghton Mifflin, 1959.

CBS News. "What Do Trump Supporters See in Their Candidate?" September 11, 2016. https://www.cbsnews.com/news/what-do-trump-supporters-see-in-their-candidate.

Clayman, Steven E., and John Heritage. "Questioning Presidents: Journalistic Deference and Adversarialness in the Press Conferences of U.S. Presidents Eisenhower and Reagan." *Journal of Communication* 52, no. 4 (2002): 749–775.

Coddington, Mark. *Aggregating the News: Secondhand Knowledge and the Erosion of Journalistic Authority.* New York: Columbia University Press, 2019.

Cohen, David. "Trump 2020 Attorney Spars with CNN Host over Presidential Poll." *Politico*, June 14, 2020. https://www.politico.com/news/2020/06/14/jenna-ellis-white-house-brian-stelter-317693.

Cohen, Nicole S. "Entrepreneurial Journalism and the Precarious State of Media Work." *South Atlantic Quarterly* 114, no. 3 (2015): 513–533.

Colarossi, Natalie. "11 Times Trump Has Lashed Out at Reporters and Called Them 'Nasty' during His Coronavirus Press Briefings." *Business Insider*, May 13, 2020. https://www.businessinsider.com/trump-lashes-out-at-reporters-during-coronavirus-press-briefings-2020-4.

Collins, Eliza. "Cruz Wins CPAC Straw Poll." *Politico*, March 5, 2016. https://www.politico.com/blogs/2016-gop-primary-live-updates-and-results/2016/03/ted-cruz-wins-cpac-straw-poll-220301.

Collins, Kaitlan, and Khalil Abdallah. "Trump Abruptly Ends '60 Minutes' Interview before Planned Taping of Joint Appearance with Pence." *CNN*, October 22, 2020. https://www.cnn.com/2020/10/20/politics/trump-interview-60-minutes/index.html.

Commission on Freedom of the Press. *A Free and Responsible Press: A General Report on Mass Communication*. Chicago: University of Chicago Press, 1947.

Confessore, Nicholas, and Karen Yourish. "$2 Billion Worth of Free Media for Donald Trump." *New York Times*, March 15, 2016. https://www.nytimes.com/2016/03/16/upshot/measuring-donald-trumps-mammoth-advantage-in-free-media.html.

Cook, Timothy E. *Governing with the News: The News Media as a Political Institution*. Chicago: University of Chicago Press, 1998.

Corasaniti, Nick, and Maggie Haberman. "Donald Trump Suggests 'Second Amendment People' Could Act against Hillary Clinton." *New York Times*, August 9, 2016. https://www.nytimes.com/2016/08/10/us/politics/donald-trump-hillary-clinton.html.

Cornwell, Susan, and Richard Cowan. "House Condemns Trump over 'Racist Comments' Tweeted at Congresswomen." *Reuters*, July 16, 2019. https://www.reuters.com/article/us-usa-trump-democrats-republicans/house-condemns-trump-over-racist-comments-tweeted-at-congresswomen-idUSKCN1UB1QO.

Costera Meijer, Irene. "Journalism, Audiences and News Experience." In *Handbook of Journalism Studies*, 2nd ed., edited by Karin Wahl-Jorgensen and Thomas Hanitzsch, 730–761. New York: Routledge, 2019.

Couch, Aaron, and Emmet McDermott. "Donald Trump Campaign Offered Actors $50 to Cheer for Him at Presidential Announcement." *Hollywood Reporter*, June 17, 2015. https://www.hollywoodreporter.com/news/donald-trump-campaign-offered-actors-803161.

Couldry, Nick. *Media Rituals: A Critical Approach*. New York: Routledge, 2003.

CNN. "CNN/ORC International Poll, May 29–31, 2015." June 2, 2015. http://i2.cdn.turner.com/cnn/2015/images/06/01/2016.poll.pdf.

Cramer, Katherine J. *The Politics of Resentment: Rural Consciousness in Wisconsin and the Rise of Scott Walker*. Chicago: University of Chicago Press, 2016.

Cramer, Katherine J., and Benjamin Toff. "The Fact of Experience: Rethinking Political Knowledge and Civic Competence." *Perspectives on Politics* 15, no. 3 (2017): 754–770.

Craft, Stephanie. "Distinguishing Features: Reconsidering the Link between Journalism's Professional Status and Ethics." *Journalism & Communication Monographs* 19, no. 4 (2017): 260–301.

Cross, Al. "'Stop Overlooking Us!': Missed Intersections of Trump, Media, and Rural America." In *The Trump Presidency, Journalism, and Democracy*, edited by Robert E. Gutsche Jr., 231–256. New York: Routledge, 2018.

Crouse, Timothy. *The Boys on the Bus*. New York: Ballantine Books, 1973.

Crowe, J. D. "President Trump: Frenemy of the People?" *Alabama Local News*, August 17, 2018. https://www.al.com/news/2018/08/president_trump_frenemy_of_the.html.

Cunningham, Stuart, and David Craig. "Being 'Really Real' on YouTube: Authenticity, Community and Brand Culture in Social Media Entertainment." *Media International Australia* 164, no. 1 (2017): 71–81.

Daily Press Editorial Board. "We, the Press, Will Not Be Bullied." *Daily Press*, August 18, 2018. https://www.dailypress.com/opinion/dp-edt-press-freedom-0819-story.html.

D'Angelo, Paul, and Frank Esser. "Metacoverage and Mediatization in US Presidential Elections: A Theoretical Model and Qualitative Case Study." *Journalism Practice* 8, no. 3 (2014): 295–310.

Darcy, Oliver. "Inside the New York Times as It Debates Its Coverage of Trump and Racism." *CNN*, August 14, 2019. https://www.cnn.com/2019/08/14/media/new-york-times-criticism/index.html.

Darcy, Oliver. "President Trump Abruptly Ends Press Conference after Contentious Exchange with Reporters." *CNN*, May 12, 2020. https://edition.cnn.com/2020/05/11/media/trump-press-briefing-weijia-jian-kaitlan-collins/index.html.

Darnton, Robert. "Writing News and Telling Stories." *Daedalus* 104, no. 2 (1975): 175–194.

Davis, Bob, and Gary Fields. "In Places with Fraying Social Fabric, a Political Backlash Rises." *Wall Street Journal*, September 20, 2016. https://www.wsj.com/articles/in-places-with-fraying-social-fabric-a-political-backlash-rises-1473952729.

Delli Carpini, Michael X., and Scott Keeter. *What Americans Know about Politics and Why It Matters*. New Haven, CT: Yale University Press, 1996.

Del Vicario, Michela, Alessandro Bessi, Fabiana Zollo, Fabio Petroni, Antonio Scala, Guido Caldarelli, H. Eugene Stanley, and Walter Quattrociocchi. "The Spreading of Misinformation Online." *Proceedings of the National Academy of Sciences* 113, no. 3 (2016): 554–559.

de Moraes, Lisa. "Donald Trump Calls ABC Reporter 'a Sleaze' during News Conference about Veterans Fundraiser." *Deadline*, May 31, 2016. https://deadline.com/2016/05/donald-trump-attacks-abc-tom-llamas-veteran-fundraiser-press-conference-1201764697/.

Denton Record-Chronicle Editorial Board. "Our View: We Are Not Fake News—We Are Your News." *Denton Record-Chronicle*, August 16, 2018. https://dentonrc.com/news/our-view-we-are-not-fake-news-we-are-your-news/article_caf55de5-7222-5131-b2ce-a42ae688ada3.html.

Deto, Ryan. "Pittsburgh Post-Gazette Removes a Black Reporter from George Floyd Protest Coverage." *Pittsburgh CityPaper*, June 4, 2020. https://www.pghcitypaper.com/pittsburgh/pittsburgh-post-gazette-removes-a-black-reporter-from-george-floyd-protest-coverage-says-union/Content?oid=17403485.

Deuze, Mark. *Media Life*. Cambridge: Polity Press, 2012.

Deuze, Mark. "What Is Journalism? Professional Identity and Ideology of Journalists Reconsidered." *Journalism* 6, no. 4 (2005): 442–464.

Deuze, Mark. "What Journalism Is (Not)." *Social Media + Society* 5, no. 3 (2019). https://doi.org/10.1177/2056305119857202.

Deuze, Mark, and Tamara Witschge. *Beyond Journalism*. Medford, MA: Polity, 2020.

Deuze, Mark, and Tamara Witschge. "Beyond Journalism: Theorizing the Transformation of Journalism." *Journalism* 19, no. 2 (2018): 165–181.

Diaz, John. "Why the San Francisco Chronicle Isn't Joining the Editorial Crowd on Trump." *San Francisco Chronicle*, August 17, 2018. https://www.sfchronicle.com/opinion/diaz/article/Why-the-San-Francisco-Chronicle-isn-t-joining-13159007.php.

Dijk, Teun A. van. *News as Discourse*. Hillsdale, NJ: Lawrence Erlbaum Associates, 1988.

Dijk, Teun A. van. *Racism and the Press*. New York: Routledge, 1991.

Donnelly, Jim. "24 Hours: Assault on the Capitol." ABC News, January 22, 2021. https://abc.com/news/insider/watch-24-hours-assault-on-the-capitol-abc-news-special-streaming-exclusively-on-hulu.

Dubois, Elizabeth, and Grant Blank. "The Echo Chamber Is Overstated: The Moderating Effect of Political Interest and Diverse Media." *Information, Communication & Society* 21, no. 5 (2018): 729–745.

Duffy, Brooke Erin, and Emily Hund. "Gendered Visibility on Social Media: Navigating Instagram's Authenticity Bind." *International Journal of Communication* (2019). https://ijoc.org/index.php/ijoc/article/view/11729.

Durham, Meenakshi Gigi. "On the Relevance of Standpoint Epistemology to the Practice of Journalism: The Case for 'Strong Objectivity.'" *Communication Theory* 8, no. 2 (1998): 117–140.

Durkee, Alison. "Trump's Popularity with GOP Bounces Back after Capitol Attack, Poll Finds." *Forbes*, January 27, 2021. https://www.forbes.com/sites/alisondurkee/2021/01/27/trump-popularity-with-gop-bounces-back-after-capitol-attack-poll-finds/?sh=3a2611ee1806.

Eagle Editorial Board. "News and the Media That Report It Are Not 'Fake' and It Is Dangerous for Trump to Say So." *The Eagle*, August 15, 2018. https://www.theeagle.com/opinion/editorials/news-and-the-media-that-report-it-are-not-fake/article_26ac591c-9ed8-57a7-9945-1c2b419b5a03.html.

Edelman. "Edelman Trust Barometer 2021." Accessed February 3, 2021. https://www.edelman.com/trust/2021-trust-barometer.

Edgerly, Stephanie, and Emily K. Vraga. "Deciding What's News: News-ness as an Audience Concept for the Hybrid Media Environment." *Journalism & Mass Communication Quarterly* 97, no. 2 (2020): 416–434.

Edgerly, Stephanie, Emily K. Vraga, Leticia Bode, Kjerstin Thorson, and Esther Thorson. "New Media, New Relationship to Participation? A Closer Look at Youth News Repertoires and Political Participation." *Journalism & Mass Communication Quarterly* 95, no. 1 (2018): 192–212.

Edmonds, Rick. "Classified Ad Revenue Down 70 Percent in 10 Years, with One Bright Spot." *Poynter*, February 1, 2010. https://www.poynter.org/reporting-editing/2010/classified-ad-revenue-down-70-percent-in-10-years-with-one-bright-spot.

Ehrlich, Matthew C., and Joe Saltzman. *Heroes and Scoundrels: The Image of the Journalist in Popular Culture*. Urbana: University of Illinois Press, 2015.

Ekdale, Brian, Melissa Tully, Shawn Harmsen, and Jane B. Singer. "Newswork within a Culture of Job Insecurity." *Journalism Practice* 9, no. 3 (2015): 383–398.

Ekström, Mats. "Epistemologies of TV Journalism: A Theoretical Framework." *Journalism* 3, no. 3 (2002): 259–282.

Eldridge, Scott A., II. *Online Journalism from the Periphery: Interloper Media and the Journalistic Field*. London: Routledge, 2017.

Enjtei, Saagar, Benny Johnson, and Amber Athey. "Full Transcript of Trump's Oval Office Interview with the Daily Caller." *Daily Caller*, November 14, 2018. https://dailycaller.com/2018/11/14/transcript-trump-daily-caller-interview.

Epstein, Jay. *News from Nowhere: Television and the News*. New York: Random House, 1973.

Ericson, Richard. "How Journalists Visualize Fact." *Annals of the American Academy of Political and Social Science* 560 (1998): 83–95.

Esquire Editors. "The Untold Stories of Election Day 2016." *Esquire*, November 6, 2017. https://www.esquire.com/news-politics/a13266971/election-2016-behind-the-scenes/.

Esser, Frank, and Jesper Strömbäck, eds. *Mediatization of Politics: Understanding the Transformation of Western Democracies*. London: Palgrave Macmillan, 2014.

Ettema, James S., and Theodore L. Glasser. *Custodians of Conscience: Investigative Journalism and Public Virtue*. New York: Columbia University Press, 1998.

Ettema, James S., and Theodore L. Glasser. "Narrative Form and Moral Force: The Realization of Innocence and Guilt through Investigative Journalism." *Journal of Communication* 38, no. 3 (1988): 8–26.

Ettema, James S., and D. Charles Whitney. "Professional Mass Communicators." In *Handbook of Communication Science*, edited by Charles R. Berger and Steven H. Chaffee, 747–780. Newbury Park, CA: Sage, 1987.

Factbase. "Interview: Laura Ingraham Interviews Donald Trump on Fox's The Ingraham Angle—October 29, 2018." October 29, 2018. https://factba.se/transcript/donald-trump-interview-laura-ingraham-fox-news-october-29-2018.

Factbase. "Interview: Sean Hannity Interviews Donald Trump via Telephone—July 25, 2019." July 25, 2019. https://factba.se/transcript/donald-trump-interview-sean-hannity-fox-telephone-july-25-2019.

Factbase. "Press Conference: Donald Trump in New York—January 11, 2017." January 11, 2017. https://factba.se/transcript/donald-trump-press-conference-new-york-ny-january-11-2017.

Factbase. "Press Conference: Donald Trump in New York, New York—March 31, 2016." March 31, 2016. https://factba.se/transcript/donald-trump-speech-new-york-ny-may-31-2016.

Factbase. "Press Conference: Donald Trump Meets with Reporters after Election Day 2018—November 7, 2018." November 7, 2018. https://factba.se/transcript/donald-trump-press-conference-midterm-elections-november-7-2018.

Factbase. "Press Gaggle: Donald Trump Speaks to the Press before Marine One Departure—November 9, 2018." November 9, 2018. https://factba.se/transcript/donald-trump-press-gaggle-marine-one-departure-november-9-2018.

Factbase. "Remarks: Donald Trump Announces Border National Emergency at the White House—February 15, 2019." February 15, 2019. https://factba.se/transcript/donald-trump-remarks-border-wall-emergency-february-15-2019.

Factbase. "Speech: Donald Trump at CPA—Oxon Hill, MD—February 24, 2017." February 24, 2017. https://factba.se/transcript/donald-trump-speech-cpac-oxon-hill-md-february-24-2017.

Factbase. "Speech: Donald Trump Holds a Political Rally in Battle Creek, Michigan—December 18, 2019." December 18, 2019. https://factba.se/transcript/donald-trump-speech-kag-rally-battle-creek-mi-december-18-2019.

Factbase. "Speech: Donald Trump Holds a Political Rally in El Paso, Texas—February 11, 2019." February 11, 2019. https://factba.se/transcript/donald-trump-speech-maga-rally-el-paso-february-11-2019. Factbase. "Speech: Donald Trump Holds a Political Rally in Wheeling, West Virginia—September 29, 2018." September 29, 2018. https://factba.se/transcript/donald-trump-speech-maga-rally-wheeling-wv-september-29-2018.

Fahrenthold, David A. "A Time Magazine with Trump on the Cover Hangs in His Golf Clubs. It's Fake." *Washington Post*, June 27, 2017. https://www.washingtonpost.com/politics/a-time-magazine-with-trump-on-the-cover-hangs-in-his-golf-clubs-its-fake/2017/06/27/0adf96de-5850-11e7-ba90-f5875b7d1876_story.html.

Farhi, Paul. "Lies? The News Media Is Starting to Describe Trump's 'Falsehoods' That Way." *Washington Post*, June 5, 2019. https://www.washingtonpost.com/lifestyle/style/lies-the-news-media-is-starting-to-describe-trumps-falsehoods-that-way/2019/06/05/413cc2a0-8626-11e9-a491-25df61c78dc4_story.html.

Farhi, Paul. "Trump Gets Way More TV News Time Than Clinton. So What?" *Washington Post*, September 21, 2016. https://www.washingtonpost.com/lifestyle/style/trump-gets-way-more-tv-news-time-than-clinton-so-what/2016/09/21/719d1bac-7ea9-11e6-8d0c-fb6c00c90481_story.html.

Farhi, Paul. "'What a Stupid Question': Trump Demeans Three Black Female Reporters in Three Days." *Washington Post*, November 9, 2018. https://www.washingtonpost.com/lifestyle/style/what-a-stupid-question-trump-demeans-three-black-female-reporters-in-two-days/2018/11/09/272113d0-e441-11e8-b759-3d88a5ce9e19_story.html.

Farley, Robert. "Trump's Misguided Tweet Seeking Wallace Apology for Noose 'Hoax.'" FactCheck.org, July 6, 2020. https://www.factcheck.org/2020/07/trumps-misguided-tweet-seeking-wallace-apology-for-noose-hoax/.

Fawcett, Liz. "Why Peace Journalism Isn't News." *Journalism Studies* 3, no. 2 (2002): 213–223.

Feinberg, Ashley. "The New York Times Unites vs. Twitter." *Slate*, August 15, 2019. https://slate.com/news-and-politics/2019/08/new-york-times-meeting-transcript.html.

Feldstein, Mark. "Wallowing in Watergate: Historiography, Methodology, and Mythology in Journalism's Celebrated Moment." *American Journalism* 31, no. 4 (2014): 550–570.

Felton, Emmanuel. "Black Police Officers Describe the Racist Attacks They Faced as They Protected the Capitol." *Buzzfeed News*, January 9, 2021. https://www.buzzfeednews.com/article/emmanuelfelton/black-capitol-police-racism-mob.

Fengler, Susanne. "Holding the News Media Accountable: A Study of Media Reporters and Media Critics in the United States." *Journalism & Mass Communication Quarterly* 80, no. 4 (2003): 818–832.

Figenschou, Tine Ustad, and Karoline Andrea Ihlebæk. "Challenging Journalistic Authority: Media Criticism in Far-Right Alternative Media." *Journalism Studies* 20, no. 9 (2019): 1221–1237.

Fine, Gary Alan. "Enacting Norms: Mushrooming and the Culture of Expectation and Explanation." In *Social Norms*, edited by Michael Hechter and Karl-Dieter Opp, 139–164. New York: Russell Sage Foundation, 2001.

Finneman, Teri, Ryan J. Thomas, and Joy Jenkins. "'I Always Watched Eyewitness News Just to See Your Beautiful Smile': Ethical Implications of U.S. Women TV Anchors' Personal Branding on Social Media." *Journal of Media Ethics* 34, no. 3 (2019): 146–159.

Fischer, Sara. "1 Big Thing: Journalism Enters Dangerous New Era." *Axios*, January 19, 2021. https://www.axios.com/newsletters/axios-media-trends-13b9540a-ea69–4942-95cc-3c80d6682783.html.

Fishman, Mark. *Manufacturing the News.* Austin: University of Texas Press, 1980.

Fishwick, Marshall W. "Father Coughlin Time: The Radio and Redemption." *Journal of Popular Culture* 22, no. 2 (1988): 33–47.

FiveThirtyEight. "How Popular Is Donald Trump?" Accessed November 3, 2020. https://projects.fivethirtyeight.com/trump-approval-ratings.

Fletcher, Richard, and Rasmus Kleis Nielsen. "Are People Incidentally Exposed to News on Social Media? A Comparative Analysis." *New Media & Society* 20, no. 7 (2018): 2450–2468.

Flood, Brian. "CNN's Brian Stelter Lampooned on Social Media over Documentary Announcement." Fox News, January 15, 2020. https://www.foxnews.com/media/cnn-brian-stelter-hbo-documentary.

Flood, Brian. "CNN's Brian Stelter Widely Ridiculed after Blaming Tech Issues for Bizarre Anti-Trump Segment." Fox News, August 27, 2019. https://www.foxnews.com/media/cnn-brian-stelter-rough-week-trump.

Flood, Brian. "CNN's 'Reliable Sources' with Brian Stelter Hits Rock Bottom in Key Demo." Fox News, December 30, 2019. https://www.foxnews.com/media/cnns-reliable-sources-with-brian-stelter-hits-rock-bottom-in-key-demo.

Flood, Brian, and Joseph A. Wulfsohn. "CNN's Brian Stelter's Apparent Hesitance to Cover Tara Reade's Biden Accusations Raises Eyebrows." Fox News, April 27, 2020. https://www.foxnews.com/media/cnn-brian-stelter-tara-reade-joe-biden.

Folkenflik, David. "Donald Trump Has Escalated His Rhetoric. So Has the Press Covering Him." NPR, December 11, 2015. https://www.npr.org/2015/12/11/459369520/donald-trump-has-escalated-his-rhetoric-so-has-the-press-covering-him.

Foran, Clare. "Taking a Stand—Sort Of—against Trump at CPAC." The Atlantic, March 4, 2016. https://www.theatlantic.com/politics/archive/2016/03/donald-trump-cpac/472251.

Frum, David. "The Conservative Cult of Victimhood." The Atlantic, January 11, 2021. https://www.theatlantic.com/ideas/archive/2021/01/conservatism-reaches-dead-end/617629/.

Gans, Herbert J. Deciding What's News: A Study of CBS Evening News, NBC Nightly News, "Newsweek," and "Time." New York: Vintage Books, 1980.

Gantt Shafer, Jessica. "Donald Trump's 'Political Incorrectness': Neoliberalism as Frontstage Racism on Social Media." Social Media + Society 3, no. 3 (2017). https://doi.org/10.1177/2056305117733226.

Garcia, Manny. "What Our Investigative Journalists Expose Isn't Fake News." Lancaster Eagle Gazette, August 16, 2018. https://www.lancastereaglegazette.com/story/opinion/columnists/2018/08/16/what-our-investigative-journalists-expose-isnt-fake-news-column/1000454002/.

Gert, Bernard, and Joshua Gert. "The Definition of Morality." In Stanford Encyclopedia of Philosophy, edited by Edward N. Zalta, February 8, 2016. https://plato.stanford.edu/archives/fall2017/entries/morality-definition/.

Getler, Michael. "Wanted: More Woodwards (and Bernsteins)." Washington Post, May 2, 2004. https://www.washingtonpost.com/archive/opinions/2004/05/02/wanted-more-woodwards-and-bernsteins/3a04576e-4ce1-4dbd-8bc7-936f29df2b5c/.

Giddens, Anthony. Central Problems in Social Theory: Action, Structure, and Contradiction in Social Analysis. Berkeley: University of California Press, 1979.

Gieber, Walter, and Walter Johnson. "The City Hall 'Beat': A Study of Reporter and Source Roles." Journalism Quarterly 38, no. 3 (1961): 289–297.

Gieryn, Thomas. Cultural Boundaries of Science: Credibility on the Line. Chicago: University of Chicago Press, 1999.

Gil de Zúñiga, Homero, Brian Weeks, and Alberto Ardèvol-Abreu. "Effects of the News-Finds-Me Perception in Communication: Social Media Use Implications for News Seeking and Learning about Politics." Journal of Computer-Mediated Communication 22, no. 3 (2017): 105–123.

Goldberg, Nicholas. "The Los Angeles Times Is Not Participating in Today's Nationwide Editorial Page Protest against Trump's Attacks on the Press. Here's Why." Los Angeles Times, August 16, 2018. https://www.latimes.com/opinion/la-ol-enter-the-fray-the-los-angeles-times-is-not-1534376775-htmlstory.html.

Goodman, Amy, and Denis Moynihan. "How the Media Iced Out Bernie Sanders & Helped Donald Trump Win." Common Dreams, December 3, 2016. https://www.commondreams.org/views/2016/12/03/how-media-iced-out-bernie-sanders-helped-donald-trump-win.

Gopal, Srik, and Francesca Mazzola. "Understanding Trust to Strengthen Democracy." Democracy Fund, August 21, 2017. https://democracyfund.org/idea/understanding-trust-to-strengthen-democracy/.

Gore, D'Angelo. "Trump's Misdirection on 'Criminal Aliens.'" FactCheck.org, February 26, 2019. https://www.factcheck.org/2019/02/trumps-misdirection-on-criminal-aliens.

Gottfried, Jeffrey, Galen Stocking, and Elizabeth Greico. "Partisans Remain Sharply Divided in Their Attitudes about the News Media." Pew Research Center, September 25, 2018. https://www.journalism.org/2018/09/25/partisans-remain-sharply-divided-in-their-attitudes-about-the-news-media.

Gottfried, Jeffrey, Galen Stocking, Elizabeth Greico, Mason Walker, Maya Khuzam, and Amy Mitchell. "Trusting the News Media in the Trump Era." Pew Research Center, December 12, 2019. https://www.journalism.org/2019/12/12/trusting-the-news-media-in-the-trump-era.

Graham, David A., Adrienne Green, Cullen Murphy, and Parker Richards. "An Oral History of Trump's Bigotry." *The Atlantic*, June 2019. https://www.theatlantic.com/magazine/archive/2019/06/trump-racism-comments/588067.

Graves, Allison. "Trump Says the Media Doesn't Show His Crowds at Rallies. He's Wrong." PolitiFact, November 3, 2016. https://www.politifact.com/truth-o-meter/statements/2016/nov/03/donald-trump/trump-says-media-doesnt-show-his-crowds-rallies-he.

Greenberg, David. *Republic of Spin: An Inside History of the American Presidency*. New York: W. W. Norton, 2016. https://www.overdrive.com/search?q=B8574C1A-D648-411C-B0C4-350595529859.

Greico, Elizabeth. "One-in-Five U.S. Newsroom Employees Live in New York, Los Angeles or D.C." Pew Research Center, October 24, 2019. https://www.pewresearch.org/fact-tank/2019/10/24/one-in-five-u-s-newsroom-employees-live-in-new-york-los-angeles-or-d-c.

Greico, Elizabeth. "U.S. Newspapers Have Shed Half of Their Newsroom Employees since 2008." Pew Research Center, April 20, 2020. https://www.pewresearch.org/fact-tank/2020/04/20/u-s-newsroom-employment-has-dropped-by-a-quarter-since-2008/.

Greico, Elizabeth, Nami Sumida, and Sophia Fedeli. "About a Third of Large U.S. Newspapers Have Suffered Layoffs since 2017." Pew Research Center, July 23, 2018. https://www.pewresearch.org/fact-tank/2018/07/23/about-a-third-of-large-u-s-newspapers-have-suffered-layoffs-since-2017.

Grynbaum, Michael M. "Television Networks Struggle to Provide Equal Airtime in the Era of Trump." *New York Times*, May 30, 2016. https://www.nytimes.com/2016/05/31/business/media/television-networks-struggle-to-provide-equal-airtime-in-the-era-of-trump.html.

Grynbaum, Michael M., and Tiffany Hsu. "Major Networks Cut Away from Trump's Baseless Fraud Claims." *New York Times*, November 10, 2020. https://www.nytimes.com/2020/11/05/business/media/trump-tv.html.

Haas, Tanni. "Mainstream News Media Self-Criticism: A Proposal for Future Research." *Critical Studies in Media Communication* 23, no. 4 (2006): 350–355.

Haberman, Maggie. "Donald Trump Says His Mocking of New York Times Reporter Was Misread." *New York Times*, November 26, 2015. https://www.nytimes.com/2015/11/27/us/politics/donald-trump-says-his-mocking-of-new-york-times-reporter-was-misread.html.

Hackett, Robert A. "Decline of a Paradigm? Bias and Objectivity in News Media Studies." *Critical Studies in Mass Communication* 1, no. 3 (1984): 229–259.

Hagey, Keach, Lukas Alpert, and Yaryna Serkez. "In News Industry, a Stark Divide between Haves and Have-Nots." *Wall Street Journal*, May 4, 2019. https://www.wsj.com/graphics/local-newspapers-stark-divide.

Hall, Stuart, Chas Critcher, Tony Jefferson, John Clarke, and Brian Roberts. *Policing the Crisis: Mugging, the State, and Law and Order.* London: Palgrave, 1978.

Hallin, Daniel C. *The Uncensored War: The Media and Vietnam.* Berkeley: University of California Press, 1986.

Hallin, Daniel C. "The Passing of the 'High Modernism' of American Journalism." *Journal of Communication* 42, no. 3 (1992): 14–25.

Halverson, Jeffry R., H. Lloyd Goodall, and Steven R. Corman. *Master Narratives of Islamist Extremism.* New York: Palgrave Macmillan, 2011.

Hamilton, James T. *All the News That's Fit to Sell: How the Market Transforms Information into News.* Princeton, NJ: Princeton University Press, 2004.

Hamilton, James T. *Democracy's Detectives: The Economics of Investigative Journalism.* Cambridge, MA: Harvard University Press, 2016.

Hart, Roderick P. *Trump and Us: What He Says and Why People Listen.* New York: Cambridge University Press, 2020.

Hartmann, Paul G., and Charles Husband. *Racism and the Mass Media: A Study of the Role of the Mass Media in the Formation of White Beliefs and Attitudes in Britain.* Totowa, NJ: Rowman & Littlefield, 1974.

Harwell, Drew. "White House Shares Doctored Video to Support Punishment of Journalist Jim Acosta." *Washington Post*, November 8, 2018. https://www.washingtonpost.com/technology/2018/11/08/white-house-shares-doctored-video-support-punishment-journalist-jim-acosta.

Hayes, Danny, and Jennifer L. Lawless. "The Decline of Local News and Its Effects: New Evidence from Longitudinal Data." *Journal of Politics* 80, no. 1 (2018): 332–336.

Hemmer, Nicole. *Messengers of the Right: Conservative Media and the Transformation of American Politics.* Philadelphia: University of Pennsylvania Press, 2016.

Hermida, Alfred. "Twittering the News: The Emergence of Ambient Journalism." *Journalism Practice* 4, no. 3 (2010): 297–308.

Hess, Kristy, and Lisa Waller. *Local Journalism in a Digital World.* London: Palgrave, 2017.

Hillsboro Tribune Editorial Board. "The News Isn't 'Fake' Just Because You See Things Differently." *Hillsboro Tribune*, August 15, 2018. https://pamplinmedia.com/hillsboro-tribune-home.

Hindman, Matthew. *The Internet Trap: How the Digital Economy Builds Monopolies and Undermines Democracy.* Princeton, NJ: Princeton University Press, 2018.

Hirschfeld Davis, Julie. "Trump to Cap Refugees Allowed into U.S. at 30,000, a Record Low." *New York Times*, September 17, 2018. https://www.nytimes.com/2018/09/17/us/politics/trump-refugees-historic-cuts.html.

Hofstadter, Richard. "The Paranoid Style in American Politics." *Harper's Magazine*, November 1964. https://harpers.org/archive/1964/11/the-paranoid-style-in-american-politics.

Holloway, Kali. "5 Things Trump Said He Invented, But Didn't." *Salon*, October 13, 2017. https://www.salon.com/2017/10/13/5-things-trump-said-he-invented-but-didnt_partner/

Homeland Security. "National Terrorism Advisory System." Accessed January 27, 2021. https://www.dhs.gov/ntas/advisory/national-terrorism-advisory-system-bulletin-january-27-2021.

Hsu, Tiffany, and Katie Robertson. "Covering Pro-Trump Mobs, the News Media Became a Target." *Nieman Lab*, January 7, 2021. https://www.niemanlab.org/reading/covering-pro-trump-mobs-the-news-media-became-a-target/.

Hughes, Adam, and Stefan Wojcik. "10 Facts about Americans and Twitter." Pew Research Center, August 2, 2019. https://www.pewresearch.org/fact-tank/2019/08/02/10-facts-about-americans-and-twitter/.

Illing, Sean. "Trump's War on Fox News and the Future of Right-Wing Media." *Vox*, November 13, 2020. https://www.vox.com/policy-and-politics/21557244/2020-election-fox-news-newsmax-oan-brian-stelter.

Image of the Journalist in Popular Culture. Accessed March 24, 2019. http://www.ijpc.org/.

Ingber, Sasha. "The U.S. Now Ranks as a 'Problematic' Place for Journalists." *NPR*, April 18, 2019. https://www.npr.org/2019/04/18/714625907/the-u-s-now-ranks-as-a-problematic-place-for-journalists.

Inglehart, Ronald, and Pippa Norris. "Trump and the Populist Authoritarian Parties: The Silent Revolution in Reverse." *Perspectives on Politics* 15, no. 2 (2017): 443–454.

Ingram, Mathew. "Most Americans Say They Have Lost Trust in the Media." *Columbia Journalism Review*, September 12, 2018. https://www.cjr.org/the_media_today/trust-in-media-down.php.

Ingram, Mathew. "When Should Journalists Use the 'L' Word?" *Fortune*, January 26, 2017. https://fortune.com/2017/01/26/donald-trump-facts-lies/.

Interior Journal Editorial Board. "First Amendment under Attack: America's Free Press Is a Friend to Democracy, Not Its Enemy." *Interior Journal*, August 16, 2018. https://www.theinteriorjournal.com/2018/08/16/first-amendment-under-attack-americas-free-press-is-a-friend-to-democracy-not-its-enemy/.

International Women's Media Foundation. "Attacks and Harassment: The Impact on Female Journalists and Their Reporting." https://www.iwmf.org/attacks-and-harassment.

Iyengar, Shanto, Yphtach Lelkes, Matthew Levendusky, Neil Malhotra, and Sean J. Westwood. "The Origins and Consequences of Affective Polarization in the United States." *Annual Review of Political Science* 22 (2018): 129–146.

Jamieson, Kathleen Hall, and Joseph N. Cappella. *Echo Chamber: Rush Limbaugh and the Conservative Media Establishment*. Oxford: Oxford University Press, 2008.

Jarecki, Eugene. "Trump's Covid-19 Inaction Killed Americans. Here's a Counter That Shows How Many." *Washington Post*, May 6, 2020. https://www.washingtonpost.com/outlook/2020/05/06/trump-covid-death-counter/.

Jefferson Chronicle Editorial Board. "We Have Met the Enemy, and It Is Not Us." *Jefferson Chronicle*, August 15, 2018. http://www.thejeffersonchronicle.com/met-enemy-not-us/.

Jensen, Elizabeth. "Kessler Interview Puts Spotlight on How to Cover Racist Viewpoints." *NPR*, August 13, 2018. https://www.npr.org/sections/publiceditor/2018/08/13/638153970/kessler-interview-puts-spotlight-on-how-to-cover-racist-viewpoints.

Johnson, Jenna. "Trump Calls for 'Total and Complete Shutdown of Muslims Entering the United States.'" *Washington Post*, December 17, 2015. https://www.washingtonpost.com/news/post-politics/wp/2015/12/07/donald-trump-calls-for-total-and-complete-shutdown-of-muslims-entering-the-united-states.

Jones, Alex S. *Losing the News: The Future of the News That Feeds Democracy*. New York: Oxford University Press.

Jones, Dennis. "A Free Press and Its Enemies." *Rawlins Times*, August 22, 2018. https://www.rawlinstimes.com/opinion/guest_column/a-free-press-and-its-enemies/article_aa2e94af-4384-5c29-bbf8-22ce8424a035.html.

Josephi, Beate. "How Much Democracy Does Journalism Need?" *Journalism* 14, no. 4 (2013): 474–489.

Kakamura, David. "Trump's Insults toward Black Reporters, Candidates Echo 'Historic Playbooks' Used against African Americans, Critics Say." *Washington Post*, November 9, 2018. https://www.washingtonpost.com/politics/trumps-insults-toward-black-reporters-candidates-echo-historic-playbooks-used-against-african-americans/2018/11/09/74653438-e440-11e8-b759-3d88a5ce9e19_story.html.

Kalogeropoulos, Antonis, Richard Fletcher, and Rasmus Kleis Nielsen. 2019. "News Brand Attribution in Distributed Environments: Do People Know Where They Get Their News?" *New Media & Society* 21 (3): 583–601.

Katz, Josh. "Who Will be President?" *New York Times*, November 8, 2016. https://www.nytimes.com/interactive/2016/upshot/presidential-polls-forecast.html.

Kazin, Michael. *The Populist Persuasion: An American History*. Ithaca, NY: Cornell University Press, 1998.

Keith, Susan, and Leslie-Jean Thornton. "Where the Truth Lies: Grappling with Falsehood and Objectivity in the Trump Era." *Electronic Journal of Communication* 28, nos. 1–2 (2018). http://www.cios.org/www/ejc/v28n12toc.htm.

Keith, Tamara. "Trump Appears to Be Betting on a Strategy of Division to Win Reelection." *NPR*, July 7, 2020. https://www.npr.org/2020/07/07/888102320/trump-appears-to-be-betting-on-a-strategy-of-division-to-win-reelection.

Kessler, Glenn, Salvador Rizzo, and Meg Kelly. *Donald Trump and His Assault on the Truth: The President's Falsehoods, Misleading Claims and Flat-Out Lies*. New York: Scribner, 2020.

King, Noel. "Jason Kessler On His 'Unite the Right' Rally Move to D.C." *Morning Edition*, August 10, 2018. https://www.npr.org/2018/08/10/637390626/a-year-after-charlottesville-unite-the-right-rally-will-be-held-in-d-c.

Konrad, Alison M. "Denial of Racism and the Trump Presidency." *Equality, Diversity and Inclusion* 37, no. 1 (2018): 14–30.

Kopf, Dan. "The Rural-Urban Divide Is Still the Big Story of American Politics." *Quartz*, November 6, 2020. https://qz.com/1927392/the-rural-urban-divide-continues-to-be-the-story-of-us-politics/.

Korsgaard, Christine. *The Sources of Normativity*. Cambridge: Cambridge University Press, 1996.

Kovach, Bill, and Tom Rosenstiel. *The Elements of Journalism: What Newspeople Should Know and the Public Should Expect*. New York: Three Rivers Press, 2001.

Kristof, Nicholas. "Impeachment Is a Call for 'Moral Clarity.'" *New York Times*, January 13, 2021. https://www.nytimes.com/2021/01/13/opinion/trump-impeachment-morality.html.

Kümpel, Anna Sophie. "The Issue Takes It All? Incidental News Exposure and News Engagement on Facebook." *Digital Journalism* 7, no. 2 (2019): 165–186.

Kyle, Jordan, and Limor Glutchin. "Populists in Power around the World." Tony Blair Institute for Global Change, November 7, 2018. https://institute.global/insight/renewing-centre/populists-power-around-world.

Ladd, Jonathan M. *Why Americans Hate the Media and How It Matters*. Princeton, NJ: Princeton University Press, 2011.

Lee, Jayeon. "'Friending' Journalists on Social Media: Effects on Perceived Objectivity and Intention to Consume News." *Journalism Studies* 21, no. 15 (2020): 2096–2112.

Lemire, Jonathan. "In Risky Bid, Trump Stokes Racial Rancor to Motivate Voters." Associated Press, July 7, 2020. https://apnews.com/10f096038019ee7a0d798c6d51ecd3b4.

Leonhardt, David. "The Rich Really Do Pay Lower Taxes Than You." *New York Times*, October 6, 2019. https://www.nytimes.com/interactive/2019/10/06/opinion/income-tax-rate-wealthy.html.

Leonhardt, David, and Stuart A. David. "Trump's Lies." *New York Times*, December 14, 2017. https://www.nytimes.com/interactive/2017/06/23/opinion/trumps-lies.html.

Lepore, Jill. "Does Journalism Have a Future?" *New Yorker*, January 28, 2019. https://www.newyorker.com/magazine/2019/01/28/does-journalism-have-a-future.

Levendusky, Matthew. *How Partisan Media Polarize America*. Chicago: University of Chicago Press, 2013.

Lewandowsky, Stephan, Michael Jetter, and Ullrich K. H. Ecker. "Using the President's Tweets to Understand Political Diversion in the Age of Social Media." *Nature Communications* 11, no. 1 (2020): article 5764.

Lewis, Rebecca. 2020. "'This Is What the News Won't Show You': YouTube Creators and the Reactionary Politics of Micro-celebrity." *Television & New Media* 21 (2): 201–217.

Lewis, Seth C. "Journalism." In *The International Encyclopedia of Journalism Studies*, edited by Tim P. Vos, Folker Hanusch, Dimitra Dimitrakopoulou, Margaretha Geertsema-Sligh, and Annika Sehl. Hoboken, NJ: Wiley, 2019. https://doi.org/10.1002/9781118841570.iejs0001

Lewis, Seth C. "Lack of Trust in the News Media, Institutional Weakness, and Relational Journalism as a Potential Way Forward." *Journalism* 20, no. 1 (2019): 44–47.

Lewis, Seth C. "The Objects and Objectives of Journalism Research During the Coronavirus Pandemic and Beyond." *Digital Journalism* 8, no. 5 (2020): 681–689.

Lewis, Seth C. "The Tension between Professional Control and Open Participation: Journalism and Its Boundaries." *Information, Communication & Society* 15, no. 6 (2012): 836–866.

Lewis, Seth C., Avery E. Holton, and Mark Coddington. "Reciprocal Journalism: A Concept of Mutual Exchange between Journalists and Audiences." *Journalism Practice* 8, no. 2 (2014): 229–241.

Lewis, Seth C., and Logan Molyneux. "A Decade of Research on Social Media and Journalism: Assumptions, Blind Spots, and a Way Forward." *Media and Communication* 6, no. 4 (2018): 11–23.

Lewis, S. C., and Oscar Westlund. "Actors, Actants, Audiences, and Activities in Cross-Media News Work: A Matrix and a Research Agenda." *Digital Journalism* 3, no. 2 (2015): 19–37.

Lewis, Seth C., Rodrigo Zamith, and Mark Coddington. "Online Harassment and Its Implications for the Journalist-Audience Relationship." *Digital Journalism* 8, no. 8 (2020): 1047–1067.

Löfgren Nilsson, Monica, and Henrik Örnebring. "Journalism under Threat." *Journalism Practice* 10, no. 7 (2016): 880–890.

Longform Podcast. "#398: Dean Baquet." June 2020. https://longform.org/posts/longform-podcast-398-dean-baquet.

Lopez, German. "Donald Trump's Long History of Racism, from the 1970s to 2020." *Vox*, August 13, 2020. https://www.vox.com/2016/7/25/12270880/donald-trump-racist-racism-history.

Lowery, Wesley. "A Reckoning over Objectivity, Led by Black Journalists." *New York Times*, June 23, 2020. https://www.nytimes.com/2020/06/23/opinion/objectivity-black-journalists-coronavirus.html.

Lyotard, Jean-François. *The Postmodern Condition: A Report on Knowledge*. Translated by Geoff Bennington and Brian Massumi. Minneapolis: University of Minnesota Press, 1984.

MacIntyre, Alasdair. *After Virtue: A Study in Moral Theory*. London: Duckworth, 1981.

Magic Valley Editorial Board. "Our View: A Free Press Is Not the Enemy." *Magic Valley*, August 16, 2018. https://magicvalley.com/opinion/editorial/our-view-a-free-press-is-not-the-enemy/article_46e6ac19-625d-5cea-92bf-d829b417acbd.html.

Malcolm, Janet. *The Journalist and the Murderer*. New York: Vintage Books, 1990.

Maras, Steven. *Objectivity in Journalism*. Malden, MA: Polity Press, 2013.

Marcus, George E. "Emotions in Politics." *Annual Review of Political Science* 3, no. 1 (2000): 221–250.

Martens, Bertin, Luis Aguiar, Estrella Gomez-Herrera, and Frank Muller-Langer. "The Digital Transformation of News Media and the Rise of Disinformation and Fake News." European Commission, April 2018. https://ec.europa.eu/jrc/en/publication/eur-scientific-and-technical-research-reports/digital-transformation-news-media-and-rise-disinformation-and-fake-news.

Mason, Lilliana. *Uncivil Agreement: How Politics Became Our Identity*. Chicago: University of Chicago Press, 2018.

Massing, Michael. "Journalism in the Age of Trump: What's Missing and What Matters." *The Nation*, July 19, 2018. https://www.thenation.com/article/journalism-age-trump-whats-missing-matters/.

Mazzoleni, Gianpietro. "Populism and the Media." In *Twenty-First Century Populism: The Spectre of Western European Democracy*, edited by Danielle Albertazzi and Duncan McDonnell, 49–64. London: Palgrave Macmillan, 2008.

McChesney, Robert W., and Victor Pickard, eds. *Will the Last Reporter Please Turn Out the Lights?* New York: New Press, 2011.

McClatchy Opinion Staff. "President Trump, We're Not 'Enemies of the People.' End Your War on Our Free Press." *News & Observer*, August 15, 2018. https://www.newsobserver.com/opinion/article216738730.html.

McDermott, Rose. *Risk-Taking in International Politics: Prospect Theory in American Foreign Policy*. Ann Arbor: University of Michigan Press, 2001.

McKerns, Joseph P. "The Limits of Progressive Journalism History." *Journalism History* 4, no. 3 (1977): 88–92.

Media Matters for America. "Everyone Should Watch This." Facebook, August 3, 2018. https://www.facebook.com/Mediamatters/videos/i-hope-you-get-raped-and-killed-katy-tur-details-trump-supporters-death-threats/10155706037731167.

Media Matters Staff. "The Guide to Donald Trump's War on the Press (So Far)." Media Matters for America, October 11, 2016. https://www.mediamatters.org/donald-trump/guide-donald-trumps-war-press-so-far.

Meeks, Lindsey. "Defining the Enemy: How Donald Trump Frames the News Media." *Journalism & Mass Communication Quarterly* 97, no. 1 (2020): 211–234.

Mellinger, Gwyneth. *Chasing Newsroom Diversity: From Jim Crow to Affirmative Action*. Urbana: University of Illinois Press, 2013.

Mendes, Amy E. "Digital Demagogue: The Critical Candidacy of Donald J. Trump." *Journal of Contemporary Rhetoric* 6, nos. 3–4 (2016): 62–73.

Mendes, Kaitlynn, Jessica Ringrose, and Jessalynn Keller. "#MeToo and the Promise and Pitfalls of Challenging Rape Culture through Digital Feminist Activism." *European Journal of Women's Studies* 25, no. 2 (2018): 236–246.

Merica, Dan. "Trump Says Both Sides to Blame amid Charlottesville Backlash." *CNN*, August 16, 2017. https://www.cnn.com/2017/08/15/politics/trump-charlottesville-delay/index.html.

Miller, Kaitlin C., and Seth C. Lewis. "Journalists, Harassment, and Emotional Labor: The Case of Women in On-Air Roles at US Local Television Stations." *Journalism*, February 3, 2020. https://doi.org/10.1177/1464884919899016.

Min, Seong Jae. "What the Twenty-First Century Engaged Journalism Can Learn from the Twentieth Century Public Journalism." *Journalism Practice* 14, no. 5 (2020): 626–641.

Mindich, David T. Z. *Just the Facts: How "Objectivity" Came to Define American Journalism.* New York: New York University Press, 1998.

Modras, Ronald. "Father Coughlin and Anti-Semitism: Fifty Years Later." *Journal of Church and State* 31, no. 2 (1989): 231–247.

Molyneux, Logan. "Mobile News Consumption: A Habit of Snacking." *Digital Journalism* 6, no. 5 (2017): 634–650.

Molyneux, Logan. "A Personalized Self-Image: Gender and Branding Practices among Journalists." *Social Media + Society* 5, no. 3 (2019). https://doi.org/2056305119872950.

Monroe County Post Editorial Board. "Our View: No 'Enemy' Here; Democracy Depends on a Free Press." *Monroe County Post*, August 16, 2018. https://www.monroecopost.com/news/20180816/our-view-no-enemy-here-democracy-depends-on-free-press.

Montanaro, Domenico. "President-Elect Joe Biden Hits 80 Million Votes in Year of Record Turnout." *NPR*, November 25, 2020. https://www.npr.org/2020/11/25/937248659/president-elect-biden-hits-80-million-votes-in-year-of-record-turnout.

Morley, David G. *The Nationwide Audience.* London: British Film Institute, 1980.

Morning Call Editorial Board. "Morning Call Editorial: Why Newspapers Are Not the 'Enemy of the People.'" *Morning Call*, August 16, 2018. https://www.mcall.com/opinion/mc-opi-editorial-trump-press-media-20180814-story.html.

Mouffe, Chantal. "The 'End of Politics' and the Challenge of Right-Wing Populism." In *Populism and the Mirror of Democracy*, edited by Francisco Panizza, 50–71. London: Verso, 2005.

Moyo, Dumisani. "Citizen Journalism and the Parallel Market of Information in Zimbabwe's 2008 Election." *Journalism Studies* 10, no. 4 (2009): 551–567.

Mudde, Cas. "The Populist Zeitgeist." *Government and Opposition* 39, no. 4 (2004): 541–563.

Müller, Jan-Werner. *What Is Populism?* Philadelphia: University of Pennsylvania Press, 2016.

NABJ. "NABJ Appalled by Trump's Disrespect of Black Female Journalists." November 9, 2018. https://www.nabj.org/news/426366/NABJ-appalled-by-Trumps-disrespect-of-black-female-journalists.htm.

Nadler, Anthony M., and Arnold J. Bauer, eds. *News on the Right: Studying Conservative News Cultures.* New York: Oxford University Press, 2019.

Nagel, Thomas. *The View from Nowhere.* Oxford: Oxford University Press, 1986.

Napoli, Philip M. *Social Media and the Public Interest: Media Regulation in the Disinformation Age.* New York: Columbia University Press, 2019.

Napoli, Philip M., and Jessica Mahone. "Local Newspapers Are Suffering, but They're Still (by Far) the Most Significant Journalism Producers in Their Communities." *Nieman*

Lab, September 9, 2019. https://www.niemanlab.org/2019/09/local-newspapers-are-suffering-but-theyre-still-by-far-the-most-significant-journalism-producers-in-their-communities/.

Nelson, Jacob L. *Imagined Audiences: How Journalists Perceive and Pursue the Public.* New York: Oxford University Press, 2021.

Nelson, Jacob L., and Seth C. Lewis. "Only 'Sheep' Trust Journalists? How Citizens' Self-Perceptions Shape Their Approach to News." *New Media & Society.* Published electronically June 28, 2021. doi: 10.1177/14614448211018160.

Nerone, John. "The Problem of Teaching Journalism History." *Journalism Educator* 45, no. 3 (1990): 16–24.

Neumann, Sigmund. "The Rule of the Demagogue." *American Sociological Review* 3, no. 4 (1938): 487–498.

Newman, Nic. "Executive Summary and Key Findings of the 2019 Report." Reuters Institute for the Study of Journalism, 2019. http://www.digitalnewsreport.org/survey/2019/overview-key-findings-2019.

Newman, Nic, Richard Fletcher, Anne Schulz, Simge Andi, and Rasmus Kleis Nielsen. "Digital News Report 2020." Reuters Institute for the Study of Journalism, University of Oxford. https://reutersinstitute.politics.ox.ac.uk/sites/default/files/2020–06/DNR_2020_FINAL.pdf.

Newport This Week Editorial Board. "Enemy of the People: 'Shush! It Could Get Worse.'" *Newport This Week*, August 16, 2018. https://www.newportthisweek.com/articles/enemy-of-the-people-shush-it-could-get-worse/.

New York Times Editorial Board. "A Times Headline about Trump Stoked Anger. A Top Editor Explains." *New York Times*, August 6, 2019. https://www.nytimes.com/2019/08/06/reader-center/trump-mass-shootings-headline.html.

Nielsen, Rasmus Kleis. "The Business of News." In *The Sage Handbook of Digital Journalism*, edited by Tamara Witschge, C. W. Anderson, David Domingo, and Alfred Hermida, 51–67. Thousand Oaks, CA: Sage, 2016.

Nielsen, Rasmus Kleis. "How Much Time Do People Spend with News across Media?" rasmuskleisnielsen.net, November 30, 2017. https://rasmuskleisnielsen.net/2017/11/30/how-much-time-do-people-spend-with-news-across-media/.

Nielsen, Rasmus Kleis. "The One Thing Journalism Just Might Do for Democracy: Counterfactual Idealism, Liberal Optimism, Democratic Realism." *Journalism Studies* 18, no. 10 (2017): 1251–1262.

Nielsen, Rasmus Kleis. "Valuing Journalism in a World of Near-Infinite Content." Reuters Institute for the Study of Journalism, 2020. https://reutersinstitute.politics.ox.ac.uk/risj-review/valuing-journalism-world-near-infinite-content.

Nielsen, Rasmus Kleis, and Sarah Anne Ganter. "Dealing with Digital Intermediaries: A Case Study of the Relations between Publishers and Platforms." *New Media & Society* 20, no. 4 (2018): 1600–1617.

Nikunen, Kaarina. "Emotions, Affect and the Media." In *Media & Society*, edited by James Curran and David Hesmondhalgh, 400–422. London: Bloomsbury, 2019.

Nuzzi, Olivia. "The American People Should See Trump's Coronavirus Briefings in Their Entirety." *New York Magazine*, April 28, 2020. https://nymag.com/intelligencer/2020/04/trumps-coronavirus-briefings-should-be-seen-in-full.html.

Örnebring, Henrik, Michael Karlsson, Karin Fast, and Johan Lindell. "The Space of Journalistic Work: A Theoretical Model." *Communication Theory* 28, no. 4 (2018): 403–423.

Ortiz-Ospina, Esteban, and Max Roser. "Trust." Our World in Data, 2016. https://ourworldindata.org/trust.

Pain, Paromita, and Victoria Chen. "This Reporter Is So Ugly, How Can She Appear on TV?" *Journalism Practice* 13, no. 2 (2019): 140–158.

Park, Robert E. "News as a Form of Knowledge: A Chapter in the Sociology of Knowledge." *American Journal of Sociology* 45, no. 5 (1940): 669–686.

Patterson, Thomas E. "News Coverage of the 2016 Election: How the Press Failed the Voters." Harvard Kennedy School / Shorenstein Center on Media, Politics and Public Policy, December 7, 2016. https://shorensteincenter.org/news-coverage-2016-general-election.

Patterson, Thomas E. "News Coverage of the 2016 Presidential Primaries: Horse Race Reporting Has Consequences." Harvard Kennedy School / Shorenstein Center on Media, Politics and Public Policy, July 11, 2016. https://shorensteincenter.org/news-coverage-2016-presidential-primaries.

Patterson, Thomas E. "Pre-primary News Coverage of the 2016 Presidential Race: Trump's Rise, Sanders' Emergence, Clinton's Struggle." Harvard Kennedy School / Shorenstein Center on Media, Politics, and Public Policy, June 13, 2016. https://shorensteincenter.org/pre-primary-news-coverage-2016-trump-clinton-sanders.

Paz, Christian. "All the President's Lies about the Coronavirus." *The Atlantic*, August 17, 2020. https://www.theatlantic.com/author/christian-paz/.

Peck, Reece. *Fox Populism: Branding Conservatism as Working Class.* New York: Cambridge University Press, 2019.

Peck, Reece. "'Listen to Your Gut': How Fox News's Populist Style Changed the American Public Sphere and Journalistic Truth in the Process." In *The Routledge Companion to Media Misinformation and Populism,* edited by Silvio Waisbord and Howard Tumber, 160–168. New York: Routledge, 2021.

Peiser, Jaclyn. "The New York Times Co. Reports $709 Million in Digital Revenue for 2018." *New York Times*, February 6, 2019. https://www.nytimes.com/2019/02/06/business/media/new-york-times-earnings-digital-subscriptions.html.

PEN America. "Executive Summary for Losing the News: The Decimation of Local Journalism and the Search for Solutions." PEN America, 2019. Accessed May 16, 2021. https://pen.org/wp-content/uploads/2019/11/Losing-the-News_Executive-Summary.pdf.

Perloff, Richard M. "A Three-Decade Retrospective on the Hostile Media Effect." *Mass Communication & Society* 18, no. 6 (2015): 701–729.

Peters, Chris, and Kim Christian Schrøder. "Beyond the Here and Now of News Audiences: A Process-Based Framework for Investigating News Repertoires." *Journal of Communication* 68, no. 6 (2018): 1079–1103.

Peters, Jeremy W., and Michael M. Grynbaum. "As Trump Recovers, He Retreats to a Conservative Media Safe Space." *New York Times*, October 10, 2020. https://www.nytimes.com/2020/10/10/us/politics/trump-fox-debates.html.

Pettman, Dominic. *Infinite Distraction.* Cambridge: Polity Press, 2016.

Pew Research Center. "3. Voters' Evaluations of the Campaign." November 21, 2016. https://www.pewresearch.org/politics/2016/11/21/voters-evaluations-of-the-campaign/.

Pew Research Center. "Cable News Fact Sheet." June 25, 2019. https://www.journalism.org/fact-sheet/cable-news.

Pew Research Center. "For Local News, Americans Embrace Digital but Still Want Strong Community Connection." March 26, 2019. https://www.journalism.org/2019/03/

26/for-local-news-americans-embrace-digital-but-still-want-strong-community-connection.

Pew Research Center. "Newspaper Fact Sheet." July 9, 2019. https://www.journalism.org/fact-sheet/newspapers.

Pew Research Center. "State of the News Report." March 19, 2004. https://www.pewresearch.org/wp-content/uploads/sites/8/2017/05/State-of-the-News-Media-Report-2004-FINAL.pdf.

Pfiffner, James P. "'The Contemporary Presidency': Presidential Lies." *Presidential Studies Quarterly* 29, no. 4 (1999): 903–917.

Philadelphia Tribune Editorial Board. "Trump's Alarming Attack on the Media." *Philadelphia Tribune*, August 16, 2018. https://www.phillytrib.com/commentary/editorials/trump-s-alarming-attack-on-the-media/article_9f580129–68a8–5471–9ceb-d662cab833ac.html.

Phillips, Whitney. "The Oxygen of Amplification: Better Practices for Reporting on Extremists, Antagonists, and Manipulators Online, Part 2." Data & Society, 2018. https://datasociety.net/wp-content/uploads/2018/05/2-PART-2_Oxygen_of_Amplification_DS.pdf.

Phillips, Whitney. *This Is Why We Can't Have Nice Things: Mapping the Relationship between Online Trolling and Mainstream Culture.* Cambridge, MA: MIT Press, 2015.

Pickard, Victor. *Democracy Without Journalism? Confronting the Misinformation Society.* New York: Oxford University Press, 2019.

Picone, Ike, Jelena Keut, Tereza Pavlockova, and Bojana Romic. "Small Acts of Engagement: Reconnecting Productive Audience Practices with Everyday Agency." *New Media & Society* 21, no. 9 (2019): 2010–2028.

Pilkington, Ed. "Inside a Donald Trump Rally: Good People in a Feedback Loop of Paranoia and Hate." *The Guardian*, October 30, 2016. https://www.theguardian.com/us-news/2016/oct/30/donald-trump-voters-rally-election-crowd.

Politico Staff. "Full Text: Donald Trump 2016 RNC Draft Speech Transcript." *Politico*, July 21, 2016. https://www.politico.com/story/2016/07/full-transcript-donald-trump-nomination-acceptance-speech-at-rnc-225974.

PolitiFact. "Donald Trump." n.d., accessed July 8, 2021. https://www.politifact.com/personalities/donald-trump/.

Polskin, Howard. "How Conservative Media Has Grown under Trump." *Columbia Journalism Review*, August 19, 2019. https://www.cjr.org/analysis/conservative-media-grown.php.

Pompeo, Joe. "The Not-So-Bitter Rivalry of Dean Baquet and Marty Baron." *Politico*, June 19, 2017. https://www.politico.com/magazine/story/2017/06/19/dean-baquet-marty-baron-editors-trump-scoops-215275.

Powell, Alvin. "The Danger of 'Misinformation, Disinformation, Delusions, and Deceit.'" *Howard Gazette*, May 28, 2020. https://news.harvard.edu/gazette/story/2020/05/martin-barons-message-to-class-of-2020-facts-and-truth-matter/.

Pressman, Matthew. *On Press: The Liberal Values That Shaped the News.* Cambridge, MA: Harvard University Press, 2018.

Prior, Markus. "Media and Political Polarization." *Annual Review of Political Science* 16, (2013): 101–127.

Prior, Markus. *Post-broadcast Democracy.* Cambridge: Cambridge University Press, 2007.

Pueblo Chieftain Editorial Board. "Your Enemy? Not Hardly." *Pueblo Chieftain*, August 15, 2018. https://www.chieftain.com/552bbf6e-ac91–5ae1–91a2–646ccfc1c7f0.html.

Putnam, Robert D. *Bowling Alone: The Collapse and Revival of American Community*. New York: Simon & Schuster, 2001.

Qiu, Linda. "Fact-Checking Trump's Claim That Google 'Manipulated' Millions of Votes for Clinton." *New York Times*, August 19, 2019. https://www.nytimes.com/2019/08/19/us/politics/google-votes-election-trump.html.

Quandt, Thorsten. "Dark Participation." *Media and Communication* 6, no. 4 (2018): 36–48.

Quinones, Sam. *Dreamland: The True Tale of America's Opiate Epidemic*. New York: Bloomsbury, 2016.

Rakich, Nathaniel, and Dhrumil Mehta. "Trump Is Only Popular in Rural Areas." *FiveThirtyEight*, December 7, 2018. https://fivethirtyeight.com/features/trump-is-really-popular-in-rural-areas-other-places-not-so-much.

Rapid City Journal Editorial Board. "Journalists Are Hardly 'the Enemy of the People.'" *Rapid City Journal*, August 16, 2018. https://rapidcityjournal.com/news/local/ours-journalists-are-hardly-the-enemy-of-the-people/article_6c56d80e-dd7a-5245-a0f0-11fb76240306.html.

Rattner, Nate. "Trump's Election Lies Were among His Most Famous Tweets." CNBC, January 13, 2021. https://www.cnbc.com/2021/01/13/trump-tweets-legacy-of-lies-misinformation-distrust.html.

Rauch, Jonathan. "Fact-Checking the President in Real Time." *The Atlantic*, June 2019. https://www.theatlantic.com/magazine/archive/2019/06/fact-checking-donald-trump-ai/588028/.

Real Clear Politics. "Election 2016 Favorability Ratings." 2016, accessed June 27, 2021. https://www.realclearpolitics.com/epolls/other/president/clintontrumpfavorability.html

Reese, Stephen D. *The Crisis of the Institutional Press*. Cambridge: Polity Press, 2021.

Reese, Stephen D. "The News Paradigm and the Ideology of Objectivity: A Socialist at the Wall Street Journal." *Critical Studies in Mass Communication* 7, no. 4 (1990): 390–409.

Reese, Stephen D. "The Threat to the Journalistic Institution." *Journalism* 20, no. 1 (2018): 202–205.

Remnick, David. "Trump and the Enemies of the People." *New Yorker*, August 15, 2018. https://www.newyorker.com/news/daily-comment/trump-and-the-enemies-of-the-people.

Repucci, Sarah, Sarah Cook, Zselyke Csaky, and Adrian Shahbaz. "Media Freedom: A Downward Spiral." Freedom House, June 2019. https://freedomhouse.org/report/freedom-and-media/2019/media-freedom-downward-spiral.

Rev. "Donald Trump Rally Speech Transcript Tampa, Florida, October 29." Rev.com, October 29, 2020. https://www.rev.com/blog/transcripts/donald-trump-rally-speech-transcript-tampa-fl-october-29.

Reyes, Lorenzo. "Journalists Blinded, Injured, Arrested Covering George Floyd Protests Nationwide." *USA Today*, May 31, 2020. https://www.usatoday.com/story/news/nation/2020/05/31/journalists-blinded-injured-arrested-covering-george-floyd-protests/5299374002/.

Richardson, Allissa V. *Bearing Witness While Black*. New York: Oxford University Press, 2020.

Rieder, Rem. "Trump's Baseless Attacks on Times, Post Reporting on Russia Probe." FactCheck.org, July 2, 2020. https://www.factcheck.org/2020/07/trumps-baseless-attacks-on-times-post-reporting-on-russia-probe/.

Robertson, Katie. "Trump Turns Attack on MSNBC Journalist into Rally Fodder." *New York Times*, September 23, 2020. https://www.nytimes.com/2020/09/23/business/media/trump-ali-velshi.html.

Robertson, Lori. "Trump's False Military Equipment Claim." FactCheck.org, July 2, 2020. https://www.factcheck.org/2020/07/trumps-false-military-equipment-claim/.

Robertson, Lori, and Jessica McDonald. "Trump's False Claim on Coronavirus Harm." FactCheck.org, July 6, 2020. https://www.factcheck.org/2020/07/trumps-false-claim-on-coronavirus-harm/.

Robinson, Sue. *How Journalists Engage: A Theory of Trust Building for a Multicultural World* (unpublished manuscript).

Robinson, Sue. "'If You Had Been with Us': Mainstream Press and Citizen Journalists Jockey for Authority over the Collective Memory of Hurricane Katrina." *New Media & Society* 11, no. 5 (2009): 795–814.

Robinson, Sue. *Networked News, Racial Divides: How Power and Privilege Shape Public Discourse in Progressive Communities*. Cambridge: Cambridge University Press, 2018.

Robinson, Sue, and Kathleen Bartzen Culver. "When White Reporters Cover Race: News Media, Objectivity and Community (Dis)trust." *Journalism* 20, no. 3 (2019): 375–391.

Roose, Kevin. "What If Facebook Is the Real 'Silent Majority'?" *New York Times*, August 27, 2020. https://www.nytimes.com/2020/08/27/technology/what-if-facebook-is-the-real-silent-majority.html.

Rosanvallon, Pierre. *Counter-democracy: Politics in an Age of Distrust*. Translated by Arthur Goldhammer. New York: Cambridge University Press, 2008.

Rosen, Jay. "Today We Are Switching Our Coverage of Donald Trump to an Emergency Setting." *PressThink*, March 19, 2020. https://pressthink.org/2020/03/today-we-switch-our-coverage-of-donald-trump-to-an-emergency-setting/.

Rosen, Jay. "The View from Nowhere: Questions and Answers." *PressThink*, November 10, 2010. https://pressthink.org/2010/11/the-view-from-nowhere-questions-and-answers/.

Roser, Max, Hannah Ritchie, Esteban Ortiz-Ospina, and Joe Hasell. "Coronavirus Pandemic (COVID-19)." Our World in Data, accessed June 24, 2021. https://ourworldindata.org/coronavirus.

Rucker, Philip. "Trump Says Fox's Megyn Kelly Has 'Blood Coming Out of Her 'Wherever.'" *Washington Post*, August 5, 2015. https://www.washingtonpost.com/news/post-politics/wp/2015/08/07/trump-says-foxs-megyn-kelly-had-blood-coming-out-of-her-wherever.

Ryfe, David M. (2013). *Can Journalism Survive? An Inside Look at American Newsrooms*. Cambridge: Polity Press.

Sasse, Ben. "QAnon Is Destroying the GOP from Within." *The Atlantic*, January 16, 2021. https://www.theatlantic.com/ideas/archive/2021/01/conspiracy-theories-will-doom-republican-party/617707/.

Saunders, George. "Who Are All These Trump Supporters?" *New Yorker*, July 4, 2016. https://www.newyorker.com/magazine/2016/07/11/george-saunders-goes-to-trump-rallie.

Schleifer, Theodore. "Univision Anchor Ejected from Trump News Conference." *CNN Politics*, August 26, 2015. https://www.cnn.com/2015/08/25/politics/donald-trump-megyn-kelly-iowa-rally/index.html.

Schradie, Jen. *The Revolution That Wasn't: How Digital Activism Favors Conservatives*. Cambridge, MA: Harvard University Press, 2019.

Schudson, Michael. *Discovering the News: A Social History of American Newspapers*. New York: Basic Books, 1978.

Schudson, Michael. *The Good Citizen: A History of American Civic Life*. New York: Free Press, 1998.

Schudson, Michael. "The Objectivity Norm in American Journalism." *Journalism* 2, no. 2 (2001): 149–170.

Schudson, Michael. *The Power of News*. Cambridge, MA: Harvard University Press, 1995.

Schudson, Michael. *The Rise of the Right to Know: Politics and the Culture of Transparency, 1945–1975*. Cambridge, MA: Harvard University Press, 2015.

Schudson, Michael. *Watergate in American Memory: How We Remember, Forget, and Reconstruct the Past*. New York: Basic Books, 1993.

Schudson, Michael. *Why Journalism Still Matters*. Cambridge: Polity Press, 2018.

Schulman, Gabriel. "Newspaper Publishing in the US: 51111," *IbisWorld*, April 2021, http://www.ibisworld.com.

Shafer, Jack. "Trump Is Making Journalism Great Again." *Politico*, January 16, 2017. https://www.politico.com/magazine/story/2017/01/trump-is-making-journalism-great-again-214638.

Shawnee News-Star Editorial Board. "Our View: Freedom of the Press Makes America Great." *Shawnee News-Star*, August 16, 2018. https://www.news-star.com/news/20180816/our-view-freedom-of-press-makes-america-great.

Sheller, Mimi. "News Now: Interface, Ambience, Flow, and the Disruptive Spatio-temporalities of Mobile News Media." *Journalism Studies* 16, no. 1 (2014): 12–26.

Shoemaker, Pamela J., and Stephen D. Reese. *Mediating the Message in the 21st Century: A Media Sociology Perspective*. New York: Routledge, 2013.

Sides, John, Michael Tesler, and Lynn Vavreck. *Identity Crisis: The 2016 Presidential Campaign and the Battle for the Meaning of America*. Princeton, NJ: Princeton University Press, 2018.

Singer, Jane. "Out of Bounds." In *Boundaries of Journalism: Professionalism, Practices and Participation*, edited by Matt Carlson and Seth C. Lewis, 21–36. New York: Routledge, 2015.

Smith, Ben. "Inside the Revolts Erupting in America's Big Newsrooms." *New York Times*, June 7, 2020. https://www.nytimes.com/2020/06/07/business/media/new-york-times-washington-post-protests.html.

Smith, Ben. "Marty Baron Made the Post Great Again. Now, the News Is Changing." *New York Times*, June 28, 2020. https://www.nytimes.com/2020/06/28/business/media/martin-baron-washington-post.html.

Snyder, Timothy. "The American Abyss: A Historian of Fascism and Political Atrocity on Trump, the Mob and What Comes Next." *New York Times Magazine*, January 9, 2021. https://www.nytimes.com/2021/01/09/magazine/trump-coup.html.

Soloski, John. "News Reporting and Professionalism: Some Constraints on the Reporting of the News." *Media, Culture & Society* 11, no. 2 (1989): 207–228.

Spokesman-Review Editorial Board. "Editorial: The Spokesman-Review Isn't 'the Enemy of the People.'" *The Spokesman-Review*, August 2018. https://www.spokesman.com/stories/2018/aug/16/editorial-president-trump-were-not-enemies-of-the-/.

Squires, Catherine R. *Dispatches from the Color Line: The Press and Multiracial America*. Albany: State University of New York Press, 2007.

Squires, Catherine R. *The Post-Racial Mystique: Media and Race in the Twenty-First Century*. New York: New York University Press, 2014.

Stahl, Lesley. "The 60 Minutes Interview That President Trump Cut Short." October 26, 2020. https://www.cbsnews.com/news/president-trump-60-minutes-interview-lesley-stahl/.

Steiner, Linda, and Silvio Waisbord, eds. *News of Baltimore: Race, Rage and the City.* New York: Routledge, 2017.

Stelter, Brian. "Capitol Riot Denialism Is Already Here." *CNN*, January 14, 2021. https://edition.cnn.com/2021/01/14/media/capitol-hill-insurrection-denial/index.html.

Stelter, Brian. "Five Alarm Fire: How Right-Wing Media Is Encouraging Trump's Election Denialism." *CNN*, November 10, 2020. https://edition.cnn.com/2020/11/10/media/right-wing-media-election-denialism/index.html.

Stelter, Brian. *Hoax: Donald Trump, Fox News, and the Dangerous Distortion of Truth.* New York: Atria / One Signal Publishers, 2020.

Stelter, Brian. "How News Outlets Are Dealing with the 'Moral Dimension' of Covering Trump and His Racist Tweets." *CNN*, July 15, 2019. https://amp.cnn.com/cnn/2019/07/15/media/trump-twitter-racist-tweetstorm-reliable-sources/index.html.

Stelter, Brian. "Reliable Sources." *CNN*, April 21, 2019.

Stelter, Brian. "Stelter: Mueller Report Shows Why the Media Must Stand Up for Morality and Decency." *CNN*, April 22, 2019. https://www.cnn.com/2019/04/22/media/reliable-sources-04–21-19/index.html.

Stelter, Brian. "Stelter Defines 'Creeping Authoritarianism' in Trump's America." *CNN*, February 16, 2020. https://www.cnn.com/videos/business/2020/02/16/stelter-defines-creeping-authoritarianism-in-trumps-america.cnn.

Stelter, Brian. "Trump Is Self-Isolating at His Safe Space: Fox News." *CNN*, March 30, 2020. https://edition.cnn.com/2020/03/30/media/fox-news-trump/index.html.

Stelter, Brian, and Oliver Darcy. "Trump Election Dead-Enders Have a Home on Fox News and Right-Wing Radio." *CNN*, November 10, 2020. https://edition.cnn.com/2020/11/09/media/right-wing-media-trump-election/index.html.

Stephens, John, and Robyn McCallum. *Retelling Stories, Framing Culture: Traditional Story and Metanarratives in Children's Literature.* New York: Garland, 1998.

Stevens, Matt. "Half of Voters Believe President Trump Is Racist, Poll Shows." *New York Times*, July 30, 2019. https://www.nytimes.com/2019/07/30/us/politics/is-trump-racist.html.

Stone, Chad, Danilo Trisi, Arloc Sherman, and Jennifer Beltrán. "A Guide to Statistics on Historical Trends in Income Inequality." Center on Budget and Policy Priorities. Last modified January 13, 2020. http://www.cbpp.org/files/11–28-11pov.pdf.

Stracqualursi, Veronica, and Sarah Westwood. "Trump Thanked 'Great People' Shown in Twitter Video in Which a Man Chants 'White Power.'" *CNN*, June 29, 2020. https://www.cnn.com/2020/06/28/politics/trump-tweet-supporters-man-chants-white-power/index.html.

Strömbäck, Jesper, and Peter Van Aelst. "Why Political Parties Adapt to the Media: Exploring the Fourth Dimension of Mediatization." *International Communication Gazette* 75, no. 4 (2013): 341–358.

Stroud, Natalie J. "Polarization and Partisan Selective Exposure." *Journal of Communication* 60, no. 3 (2010): 556–576.

Sullivan, Margaret. "Journalists Can't Repeat Their Watergate-Hero Act. The Reasons Should Make Us Grieve." *Washington Post*, June 7, 2019. https://www.washingtonpost.com/lifestyle/style/journalists-cant-repeat-their-watergate-hero-act-the-reasons-should-make-us-grieve/2019/06/07/827e0f02-887f-11e9–98c1-e945ae5db8fb_story.html.

Sullivan, Margaret. "The Pro-Trump Media World Peddled the Lies That Fueled the Capitol Mob. Fox News Led the Way." *Washington Post*, January 7, 2021. https://www.washingtonpost.com/lifestyle/media/fox-news-blame-capitol-mob-media/2021/01/07/f15f668a-50ee-11eb-b96e-0e54447b23a1_story.html.

Sullivan, Margaret. "Tiptoeing around Trump's Racism Is a Betrayal of Journalistic Truth-Telling." *Washington Post*, July 15, 2019. https://www.washingtonpost.com/lifestyle/style/tiptoeing-around-trumps-racism-is-a-betrayal-of-journalistic-truth-telling/2019/07/15/61b5bbea-a705-11e9-9214-246e594de5d5_story.html.

Swaine, Jon. "Trump Inauguration Crowd Photos Were Edited after He Intervened." *The Guardian*, September 6, 2018. https://www.theguardian.com/world/2018/sep/06/donald-trump-inauguration-crowd-size-photos-edited.

Swan, Jonathan. "Trump Was the King of Anonymous Sources." *Axios*, February 24, 2017. https://www.axios.com/trump-was-the-king-of-anonymous-sources-1513300610-f1513d3a-69be-470e-a8f2-4c85bb9fc3c9.html.

Swift, Art. "Americans' Trust in Mass Media Sinks to New Low." Gallup, September 14, 2016. https://news.gallup.com/poll/195542/americans-trust-mass-media-sinks-new-low.aspx.

Tandoc, Edson C., Jr., Zheng Wei Lim, and Richard Ling. "Defining 'Fake News': A Typology of Scholarly Definitions." *Digital Journalism* 6, no. 2 (2018): 137–153.

The Hill. "Poll: One-Third of Americans Say News Media Is the 'Enemy of the People.'" July 2, 2019. https://thehill.com/hilltv/what-americas-thinking/451311-poll-a-third-of-americans-say-news-media-is-the-enemy-of-the-people.

Thomas, Louisa. "America First, for Charles Lindbergh and Donald Trump." *New Yorker*, July 24, 2016. https://www.newyorker.com/news/news-desk/america-first-for-charles-lindbergh-and-donald-trump.

Thompson, Derek. "Trump's Lies Are a Virus, and News Organizations Are the Host." *The Atlantic*, November 19, 2018. https://www.theatlantic.com/ideas/archive/2018/11/should-media-repeat-trumps-lies/576148/.

Thorson, Kjerstin, and Chris Wells. "Curated Flows: A Framework for Mapping Media Exposure in the Digital Age." *Communication Theory* 26, no. 3 (2016): 309–328.

Thurman, Neil, Seth C. Lewis, and Jessica Kunert. "Algorithms, Automation, and News." *Digital Journalism* 7, no. 8 (2019): 980–992.

Time Staff. "Here's Donald Trump's Presidential Announcement Speech." *Time*, June 16, 2015. http://time.com/3923128/donald-trump-announcement-speech.

Toff, Benjamin, and Rasmus Kleis Nielsen. "'I Just Google It': Folk Theories of Distributed Discovery." *Journal of Communication* 68, no. 3 (2016): 636–657.

Toff, Benjamin, and Ruth A. Palmer. "Explaining the Gender Gap in News Avoidance: 'News-Is-for-Men' Perceptions and the Burdens of Caretaking." *Journalism Studies* 20, no. 11 (2019): 1563–1579.

Tompkins, Al. "What Words Should We Use to Describe What Happened in the Capitol?" Poynter, January 8, 2021. https://www.poynter.org/reporting-editing/2021/what-words-should-we-use-to-describe-what-happened-today-in-the-capitol/.

Trump Twitter Archive. "Archive—CNN." http://www.trumptwitterarchive.com/archive/cnn/ttff/1-19-2017_.

Tuchman, Gaye. *Making News: A Study in the Construction of Reality*. New York: Free Press, 1980.

Tuchman, Gaye. "Objectivity as Strategic Ritual: An Examination of Newsmen's Notions of Objectivity." *American Journal of Sociology* 77, no. 4 (1972): 660–679.

Tur, Katy. *Unbelievable: My Front-Row Seat to the Craziest Campaign in American History.* New York: HarperCollins, 2017.

Turner, Fred. "Trump on Twitter: How a Medium Designed for Democracy Became an Authoritarian's Mouthpiece." In *Trump and the Media*, edited by Pablo J. Boczkowski and Zizi Papacharissi, 143–150. Cambridge, MA: MIT Press, 2018.

Tyndall, Andrew. "Donald Trump, King of All Earned Media." Tyndall Report, March 16, 2016. http://tyndallreport.com/comment/20/5775.

Tyndall Report. "Tyndall Year in Review—Top Twenty Stories of 2016." 2016. Accessed May 16, 2021. http://tyndallreport.com/yearinreview2016.

Tyson, Alec, and Shiva Maniam. "Behind Trump's Victory: Divisions by Race, Gender, Education." Pew Research Center, November 9, 2016. https://www.pewresearch.org/fact-tank/2016/11/09/behind-trumps-victory-divisions-by-race-gender-education.

Usher, Nikki. *News for the Rich, White, and Blue: How Place and Power Distort American Journalism.* New York: Columbia University Press, 2021.

Vernon, Pete. "Lie? Falsehood? What to Call the President's Words." *Columbia Journalism Review*, May 29, 2018. https://www.cjr.org/the_media_today/trump-lie-falsehood.php.

Vernon, Pete. "NPR, 'Unite the Right,' and How Journalists Cover White Nationalism." *Columbia Journalism Review*, August 14, 2018. https://www.cjr.org/the_media_today/npr-charlottesville-kessler.php.

Vernon, Pete. "The Unavoidable Brian Stelter: CNN's Media Wonk Doesn't Want to Waste a Moment." *Columbia Journalism Review*, May 4, 2018. https://www.cjr.org/the_profile/brian-stelter-cnn.php.

Vickery, Jacqueline Ryan, and Tracy Everbach, eds. *Mediating Misogyny: Gender, Technology, and Harassment.* New York: Springer, 2018.

Vore, Adrian. "U-T Builds Site to Tell Readers about Its Journalism." *San Diego Union-Tribune*, August 10, 2018. https://www.sandiegouniontribune.com/opinion/readers-rep/sd-me-readersrepnb-0812-story.html.

Wagner, María Celeste, and Pablo J. Boczkowski. "Angry, Frustrated, and Overwhelmed: The Emotional Experience of Consuming News about President Trump." *Journalism* 22 no. 7 (2021): 1577–1593.

Wahl-Jorgensen, Karin. *Emotions, Media and Politics.* Medford, MA: Polity Press, 2019.

Waisbord, Silvio. "Mob Censorship: Online Harassment of US Journalists in Times of Digital Hate and Populism." *Digital Journalism* 8, no. 8 (2020): 1030–1046.

Waisbord, Silvio. "Truth Is What Happens to News: On Journalism, Fake News, and Post-truth." *Journalism Studies* 19, no. 13 (2018): 1866–1878.

Walker, Mason, and Jeffrey Gottfried. "Republicans Far More Likely Than Democrats to Say Fact-Checkers Tend to Favor One Side." Pew Research Center, June 27, 2019. https://www.pewresearch.org/fact-tank/2019/06/27/republicans-far-more-likely-than-democrats-to-say-fact-checkers-tend-to-favor-one-side/.

Ward, Stephen A. *Ethical Journalism in a Populist Age: The Democratically Engaged Journalist.* New York: Rowman & Littlefield, 2019.

Washington Post. "In Four Years, President Trump Made 30,573 False or Misleading Claims." *Washington Post*, January 20, 2021. https://www.washingtonpost.com/graphics/politics/trump-claims-database/.

WashPostPR. "Washington Post Executive Editor Martin Baron Delivers Reuters Memorial Lecture at the University of Oxford." *WashPost PR* Blog, February 19, 2018. https://www.washingtonpost.com/pr/wp/2018/02/19/washington-post-executive-editor-martin-baron-delivers-reuters-memorial-lecture-at-the-university-of-oxford/.

Wasserman, Herman. "Relevance, Resistance, Resilience: Journalism's Challenges in a Global World." *Journalism* 20, no. 1 (2019): 229–232.

Wattles, Jackie. "How to Know When Trump Is Lying." *CNN*, May 27, 2018. https://money.cnn.com/2018/05/27/media/president-trump-lies/index.html.

Watts, Duncan J., and David M. Rothschild. "Don't Blame the Election on Fake News. Blame It On the Media." *Columbia Journalism Review*, December 5, 2017. https://www.cjr.org/analysis/fake-news-media-election-trump.php.

Weber, Max. *The Theory of Social and Economic Organization.* Translated by A. M. Henderson and Talcott Parsons. New York: Free Press, 1947.

Wells, Chris, Dhavan V. Shah, Josephine Lukito, Ayellet Pelled, Jon C. W. Pevehouse, and JungHwan Yang. "Trump, Twitter, and News Media Responsiveness: A Media Systems Approach." *New Media & Society* 22, no. 4 (2020): 659–682.

Wells, Chris, Yini Zhang, Josephine Lukito, and Jon C. W. Pevehouse. "Modeling the Formation of Attentive Publics in Social Media: The Case of Donald Trump." *Mass Communication and Society* 23, no. 2 (2020): 181–205.

Wells, Georgia, Rebecca Ballhaus, and Keach Hagey. "Proud Boys, Seizing Trump's Call to Washington, Helped Lead Capitol Attack." *Wall Street Journal*, January 17, 2021. https://www.wsj.com/articles/proud-boys-seizing-trumps-call-to-washington-helped-lead-capitol-attack-11610911596.

Wemple, Erik. "Donald Trump Again Singles Out Camera Operator for Mass Derision." *Washington Post*, January 11, 2016. https://www.washingtonpost.com/blogs/erik-wemple/wp/2016/01/11/donald-trump-again-singles-out-camera-operator-for-mass-derision.

Wemple, Erik. "Opinion: CNN, MSNBC Refused to Carry Full Trump Coronavirus Briefing. Yay!" *New York Times*, April 1, 2020. https://www.washingtonpost.com/opinions/2020/04/01/cnn-msnbc-refused-carry-full-trump-coronavirus-briefing-yay/.

Wemple, Erik. "'Racially Charged': Reuters Is Struggling with Descriptions of Trump's Racist Tweets." *Washington Post*, July 22, 2019. https://www.washingtonpost.com/opinions/2019/07/22/racially-charged-reuters-is-struggling-with-descriptions-trumps-racist-tweets/.

Wenzel, Andrea. "Sourcing Diversity, Shifting Culture: Building 'Cultural Competence' in Public Media." *Digital Journalism* 9, no. 4 (2021): 461–480.

Wenzel, Andrea, Daniela Gerson, Evelyn Moreno, Minhee Son, and Breanna Morrison Hawkins. 2018. "Engaging Stigmatized Communities through Solutions Journalism: Residents of South Los Angeles Respond." *Journalism* 19 (5): 649–667.

Westcott, Lucy. "'The Threats Follow Us Home': Survey Details Risks for Female Journalists in U.S., Canada." Committee to Protect Journalists, September 4, 2019. https://cpj.org/blog/2019/09/canada-usa-female-journalist-safety-online-harassment-survey.php.

Weyland, Kurt. "Latin America's Authoritarian Drift: The Threat from the Populist Left." *Journal of Democracy* 24, no. 3 (2013): 189, no. 4 (2021): 461-48032.

White, Gillian B. "Where Are All the Minority Journalists?" *The Atlantic*, July 24, 2015. https://www.theatlantic.com/business/archive/2015/07/minorities-in-journalism/399461/.

White, Khadijah Costley. *The Branding of Right-Wing Activism: The News Media and the Tea Party.* Oxford: Oxford University Press, 2018.

White House. "The Inaugural Address." January 20, 2017. https://www.whitehouse.gov/briefings-statements/the-inaugural-address.

Williams, Bruce A., and Michael X. Delli Carpini. *After Broadcast News: Media Regimes, Democracy, and the New Information Environment*. New York: Cambridge University Press, 2011.

Williams, Raymond. *The Long Revolution*. London: Chatto and Windus, 1961.

Woodward, Bob. *Fear: Trump in the White House*. New York: Simon and Schuster, 2018.

Wu, Tim. *The Attention Merchants: The Epic Scramble to Get Inside Our Heads*. New York: Knopf, 2017.

Wyatt-Nichol, Heather. "The Enduring Myth of the American Dream: Mobility, Marginalization, and Hope." *International Journal of Organization Theory & Behavior* 14, no. 2 (2011): 258–279.

Yahoo! News. "'Let's Have Trial by Combat' over Election—Giuliani." Yahoo! News. https://ph.news.yahoo.com/lets-trial-combat-over-election-164935300.html.

Yglesias, Matthew. "Cable News Should Cancel the Trump Show." *Vox*, March 23, 2020. https://www.vox.com/2020/3/23/21190362/trump-daily-coronavirus-briefing-fox-cnn-msnbc.

Yglesias, Matthew. "The Case for Fox News Studies." *Political Communication* 35, no. 4 (2018): 681–683.

Young, Dannagal G. *Irony and Outrage: The Polarized Landscape of Rage, Fear, and Laughter in the United States*. New York: Oxford University Press, 2019.

Ytre-Arne, Brita, and Hallvard Moe. "Approximately Informed, Occasionally Monitorial? Reconsidering Normative Citizen Ideals." *International Journal of Press/Politics* 23, no. 2 (2018): 227–246.

Zahay, Megan L., Kelly Jensen, Yiping Xia, and Sue Robinson. "The Labor of Building Trust: Traditional and Engagement Discourses for Practicing Journalism in a Digital Age." *Journalism & Mass Communication Quarterly*. September 21, 2020. https://doi.org/1077699020954854.

Zamith, Rodrigo. "Quantified Audiences in News Production: A Synthesis and Research Agenda." *Digital Journalism* 6, no. 4 (2018): 418–435.

Zaller, John R. "A New Standard of News Quality: Burglar Alarms for the Monitorial Citizen." *Political Communication* 20, no. 2 (2003): 109–130.

Zelizer, Barbie. *Covering the Body: The Kennedy Assassination, the Media, and the Shaping of Collective Memory*. Chicago: University of Chicago Press, 1992.

Zelizer, Barbie. "Journalists as Interpretive Communities." *Critical Studies in Mass Communication* 10, no. 3 (1993): 219–237.

Zelizer, Barbie. "On the Shelf Life of Democracy in Journalism Scholarship." *Journalism* 14, no. 4 (2013): 459–473.

Zurawik, David. "As Furor over Trump's Baltimore Tweets Continues, CNN Host Asks How the Press Should Cover Them." *Baltimore Sun*, July 29, 2019. https://www.baltimoresun.com/opinion/columnists/zurawik/bs-ed-zontv-cnn-trump-baltimore-20190729-5xje63pnuva6ffa7kuh2jou4ze-story.html.

Index